TOO MUCH COFFEE MAN™

For Dan,
Hope you enjoy
the book
— Shannon

OTHER BOOKS BY SHANNON WHEELER

Too Much Coffee Man's Parade of Tirade

Too Much Coffee Man's Amusing Musings

Too Much Coffee Man's Guide for the Perplexed

Wake Up and Smell the Cartoons

Children with Glue

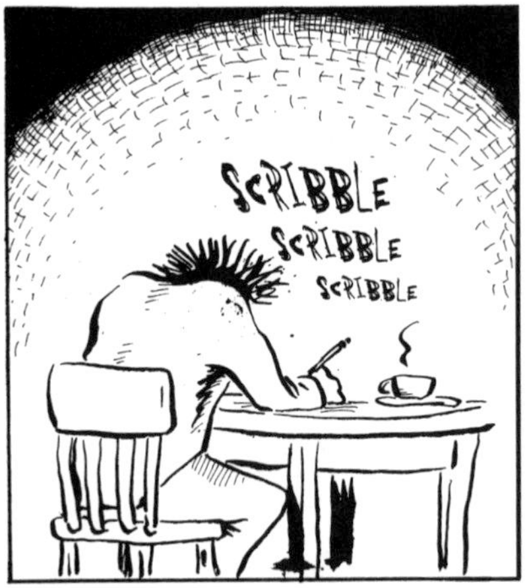
SCRIBBLE
SCRIBBLE
SCRIBBLE

OTHER BOOKS NOT BY SHANNON WHEELER

The Joy of Sex

All the President's Men

Cujo

Are You There God? It's Me, Margaret

Old Yeller

Kaffir Boy

The Cher Scrapbook

HOW TO BE
HAPPY

TOO MUCH COFFEE MAN™

BY SHANNON WHEELER

DARK HORSE BOOKS™

PUBLISHER
Mike Richardson

EDITOR
Shawna Gore

ASSISTANT EDITOR
Rachel Miller

COLLECTION DESIGNER
Debra Bailey

ART DIRECTOR
Lia Ribacchi

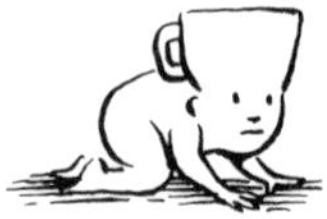

Published by
Dark Horse Books
A division of
Dark Horse Comics, Inc.
10956 SE Main Street
Milwaukie, OR 97222

darkhorse.com

First edition July 2005
ISBN: 1-59307-353-4

1 3 5 7 9 10 8 6 4 2

Printed in United States

TABLE OF CONTENTS

INTRODUCTION
BY TED RALL

I'VE HIT THE DEPTHS OF DESPAIR MORE THAN ONCE, but the moment that stands out took place during the summer of 1984. I know what you're thinking. I'm a political person, a left-leaning sort politically, so my pain must have been related to Ronald Reagan. And you'd be right, albeit for the wrong reasons.

A few years earlier I'd boarded a Greyhound in Dayton, Ohio bound for New York, where a full scholarship awaited me at Columbia University. Three years later, Reagan's financial aid cuts had slashed my finances to shreds. I was up to my ass in student loan debt, working three jobs while attending school full time, too stubborn to drop out. Inevitably, my grades slid. They put me on academic probation. Then they expelled me. I still had my summer dorm room—but then they evicted me. At the same time, a coworker who'd stolen from my boss told her the thief was me. I got fired; he got a raise and a whuppin' when I ran into him on 81st Street. My girlfriend dumped me when I told her about the assault. "I can't sit here and watch you fall apart," she said. "But I won!" I cried.

I suspected that my being broke was bothering her more than her excessive empathy.

To sum up: I was unemployed, expelled, sexless, homeless. With zero prospects and no ideas how to create some, I was as stumped as George W. Bush taking the SAT. I was worth eight bucks, four of which were committed to pizza and Coke for dinner. Bleak would have been an improvement; I was looking from way down low way up high at bleak.

A couple of friends, both of whom had left Columbia under indecorous circumstances the same semester, dropped by my new unofficial dorm room—the university left empty rooms unlocked—with an offering of shoplifted strawberry schnapps. Depressed people sleep a lot. I was napping when they arrived.

For some reason or none whatsoever, I pretended to still be asleep while my two former classmates sat on a bare mattress across the room and talked.

"I'm worried about Ted," said one. "He's never been like this before. Think he'll kill himself?"

The other one paused. "No way. He's too much of a wuss." They chuckled.

Fuck those guys, I thought. I'd show them!

That night I took the elevator to the top, twentieth floor of my dorm. I walked up the stairs to the roof. I went to the side and looked over a short wall at the sidewalk below. That'd do it, all right. I got up on the ledge, got ready to take that last step forward, and carefully considered the sensation of my bones snapping and impaling whatever didn't explode from the impact with the sidewalk as my organs simultaneously shrieked from shutdown pain. Death didn't scare me. Everybody dies. But I cry when I get a shot. I'm a baby when it comes to pain.

It's only a second of agony, I steeled myself. Yeah, but what a second, someone else in there retorted. You can do a second. What, are you insane? That shit's gonna hurt like nobody's business!

Which is worse? Trying to kill yourself to prove that you're brave, or proving that you're not by being unable to go through with it? I still don't know. Whatever, it was a low point.

If I knew Shannon Wheeler only through his work I'd suspect that he hits those rock bottoms more often than the rest of us. For not only does he have little faith in humanity, he gives himself the same treatment in his sly and vicious deconstructions of the human condition. Personal setbacks are child's play to a cartoonist for whom human existence itself is cause for disgust.

"Too Much Coffee Man," Shannon has told me, began as a somewhat cynical exercise in 1990s Gen X consumerism: an edgy strip meant to appear in the sort of publications that are often read in coffee houses by disaffected twentysomethings. But he soon became captivated by his own characters and situations. The loose structure Shannon created to allow ironic detachment proved so seductive that he began to take it seriously. The relationship he created with readers who had never seen anything else quite like it became too important to treat lightly. The soapbox he'd slapped together so disdainfully suddenly represented a unique opportunity, if not to mitigate the innate cruelty and stupidity of humanity, at least to demonstrate to the desperate that they are not alone.

Were he to limit himself to commenting on politicians and current events, Shannon would be one of our most brilliantly perceptive editorial cartoonists. If he only did social commentary cartoons relating the tyrannical angst of the lonely and self-doubting, he would have few peers in the pages of the weekly newspapers perused by mid-'00s Gen Y Starbucks customers. For my money, however, *Too Much Coffee Man* hits its highest, most glorious peaks in its studies of schadenfreude, the phenomenon of feeling joy at the misery of others. (Such is capitalism; you're never a failure as long as someone else is poorer than you.) Whether it's "homeless humor" (the bum scoffing at the suit-wearing bourgie learning that the stock market has wiped out his investments) or "God: the Comedian" (a Santa-jolly bearded deity joyously celebrating the emotional pain and grisly demises of the helpless souls who conjured His ungrateful self in the first place), no American commentator so gleefully and effectively rips off the mask of self-delusion from our denial-high society. Get real, saps—if God exists, he's laughing his ass off at you. Hell, as he writes in another series, could be no worse than what we do to each other (hi, Jean-Paul) or ourselves.

Life sucks and you'd better get used to it. Sounds negative, but nothing could be further from the truth. The sooner you understand that politicians are liars, thieves, and worse, the sooner you stop waiting around for a leader to make everything better. Stop putting your faith in God, friends, family—hell, you may not be such a hot prospect yourself. Truth is hard and absolutely essential.

Twenty-one years ago when I was trying to convince myself to jump off the roof of East Campus, my despair was centered around abstract creations that had let me down because they were bound to do so. My illusions brought me to the brink. Only the truth—that'll hurt!—saved my life.

I don't know whether *TMCM* would have saved my life back then, though I'd like to believe that understanding that we're all sharing the same uncomfortable boat would have helped. On the other hand, Shannon's skill as a draughtsman and craftsman of pithy retorts might have made me give up hope of ever making it as a cartoonist myself. Still: truth is always in short supply, especially in comics, but truth always helps.

So if you're planning to kill yourself, read this book through a few times. If that doesn't work, you can always buy thirty copies, tie them to your feet, and jump into a deep body of water.

That oughtta do it.
Ted Rall
New York, NY
March 24, 2005

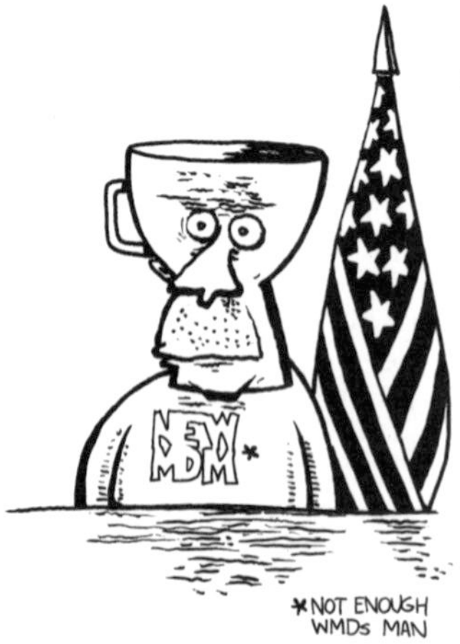
NEW DEAD MDM *
*NOT ENOUGH WMDs MAN

Ted Rall, the syndicated cartoonist and columnist, also edits the Attitude *series featuring cool cartoonists like Shannon Wheeler.*

CHAPTER ONE

HOW TO BE HAPPY

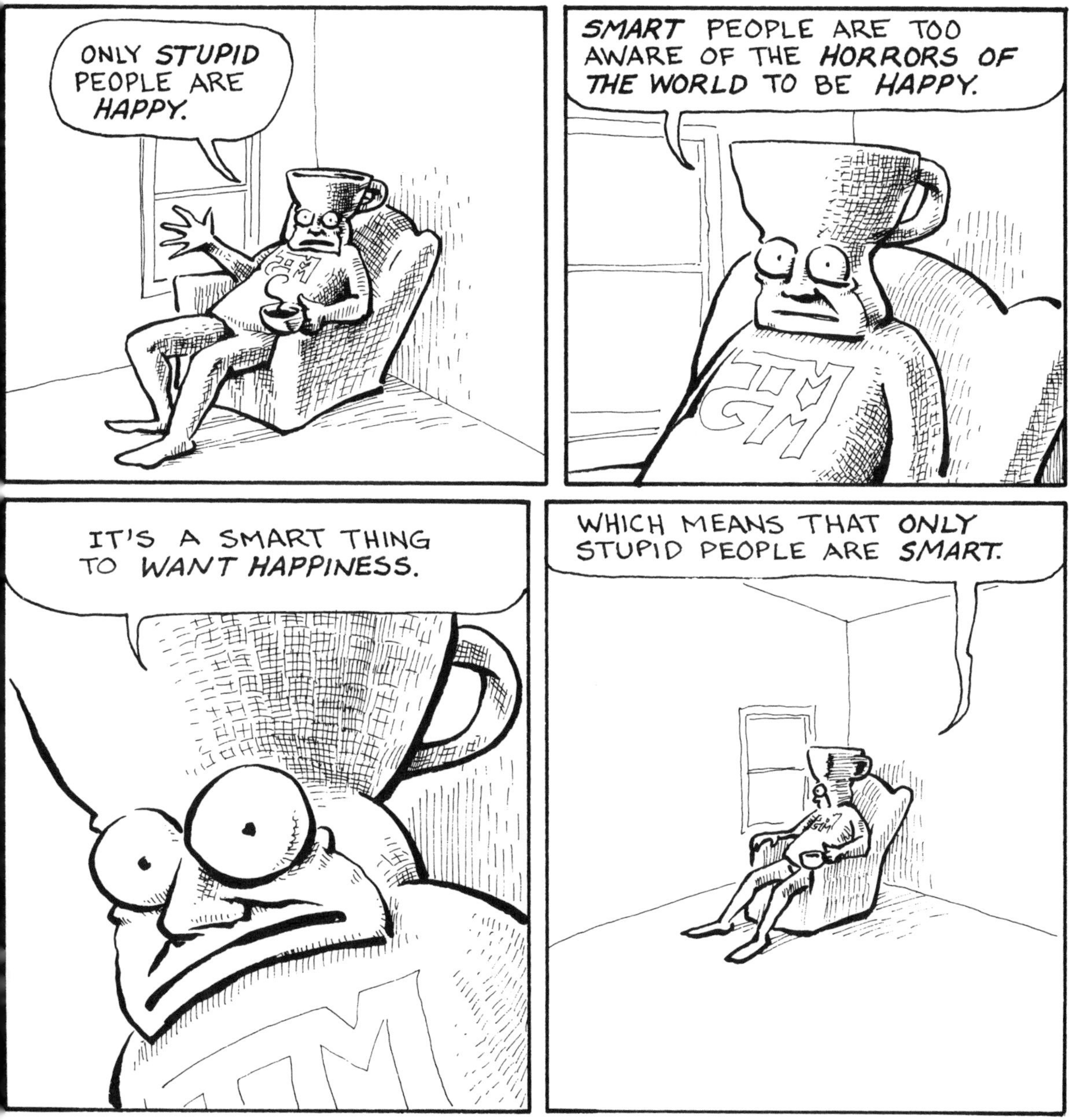

ONLY STUPID PEOPLE ARE HAPPY.
SMART PEOPLE ARE TOO AWARE OF THE HORRORS OF THE WORLD TO BE HAPPY.
IT'S A SMART THING TO WANT HAPPINESS.
WHICH MEANS THAT ONLY STUPID PEOPLE ARE SMART.

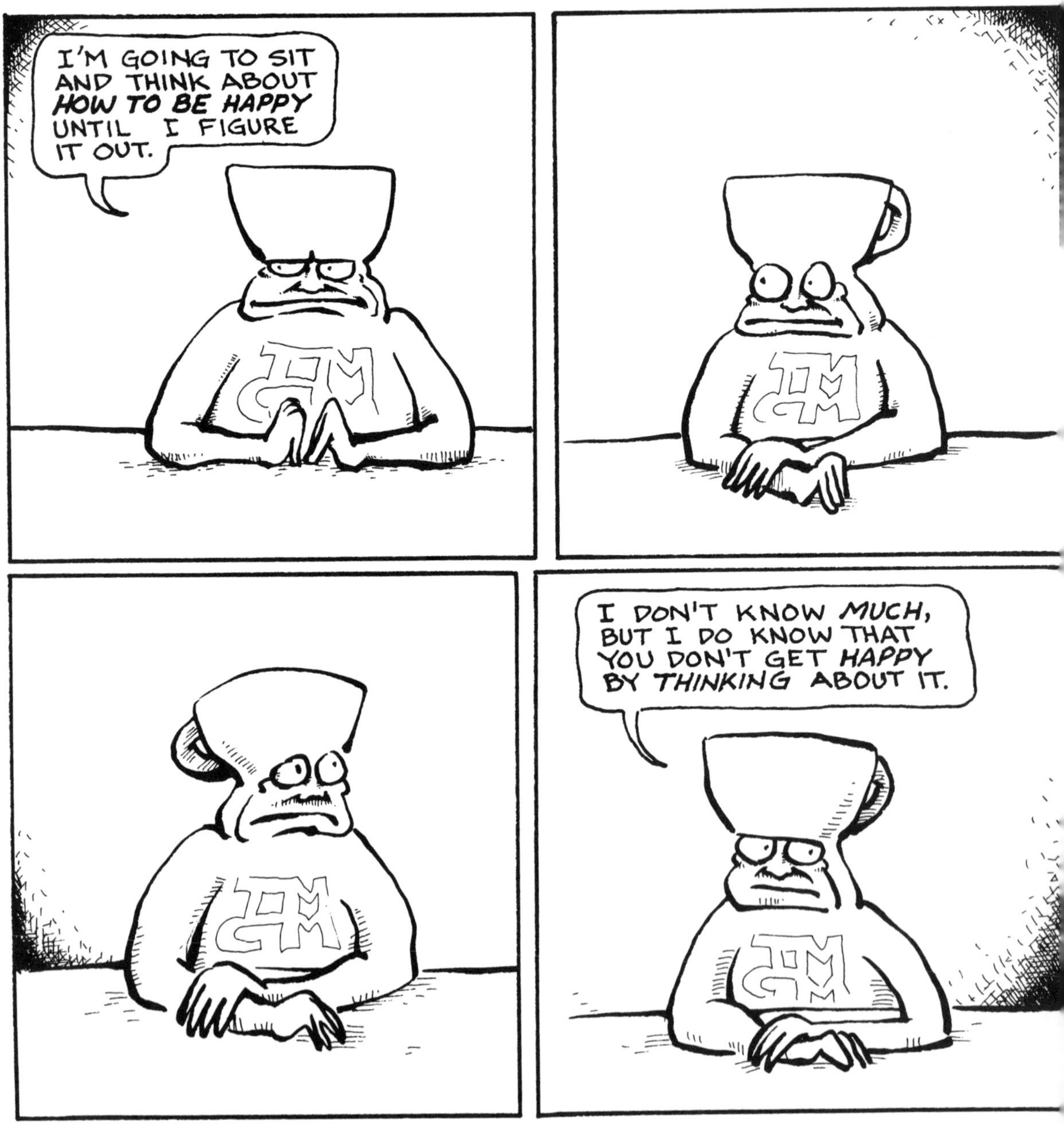
I'M GOING TO SIT AND THINK ABOUT *HOW TO BE HAPPY* UNTIL I FIGURE IT OUT.
I DON'T KNOW *MUCH*, BUT I DO KNOW THAT YOU DON'T GET *HAPPY* BY *THINKING* ABOUT IT.

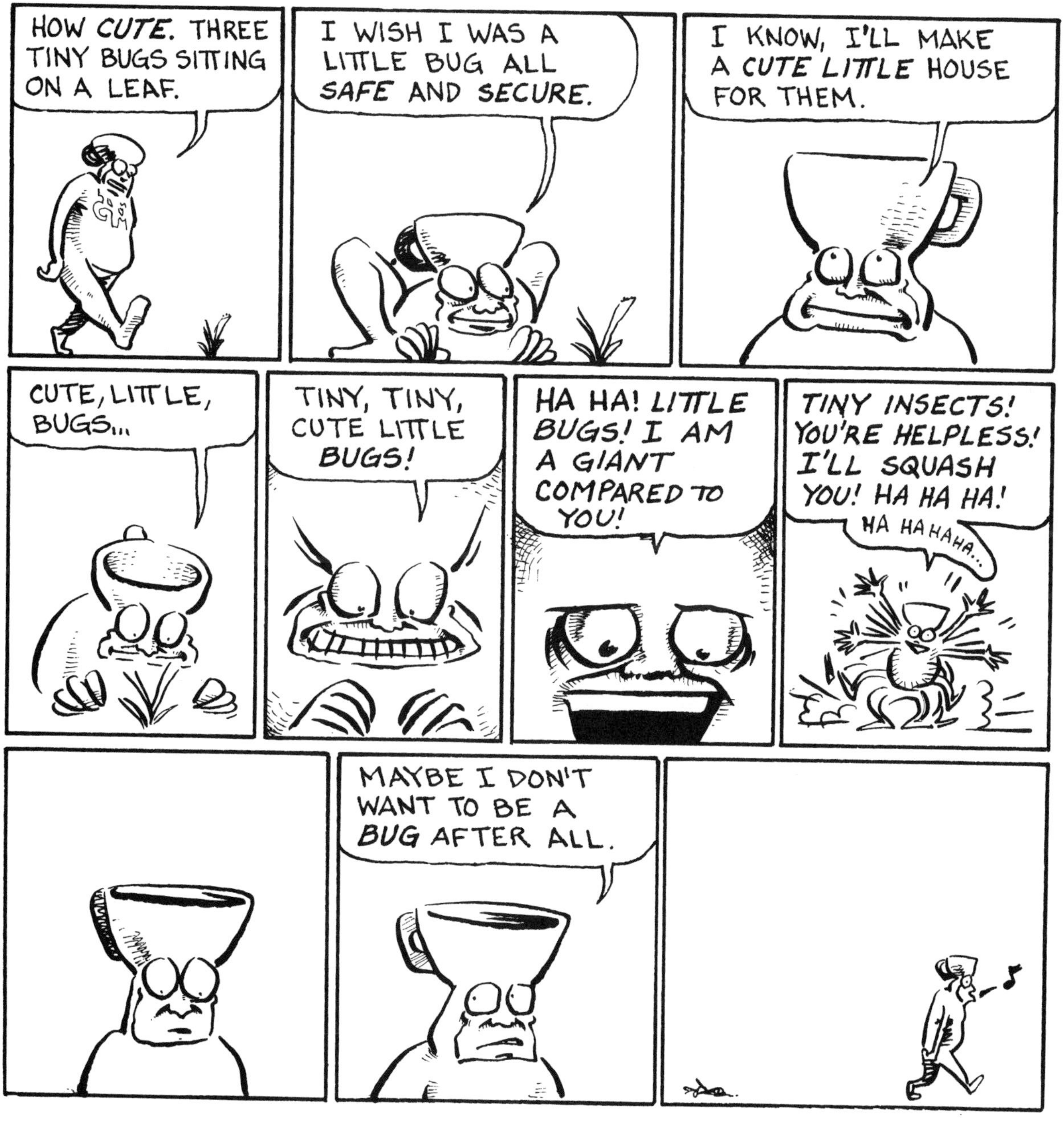
HOW *CUTE*. THREE TINY BUGS SITTING ON A LEAF.
I WISH I WAS A LITTLE BUG ALL *SAFE* AND *SECURE*.
I KNOW, I'LL MAKE A *CUTE LITTLE* HOUSE FOR THEM.
CUTE, LITTLE, BUGS...
TINY, TINY, CUTE LITTLE *BUGS!*
HA HA! *LITTLE BUGS! I AM A GIANT COMPARED TO YOU!*
TINY INSECTS! YOU'RE HELPLESS! I'LL SQUASH YOU! HA HA HA!
HA HA HAHAHA...
MAYBE I DON'T WANT TO BE A *BUG* AFTER ALL.

TO-DO LIST

1. GET PAPER AND PENCIL.

2. THINK ABOUT THINGS *TO-DO*.

3. START WRITING THE *TO-DO* LIST.

4. WATCH THE LIST GET *REALLY BIG*.

5. GET *OVERWHELMED*.

6. *PANIC.*

7. START DOING STUFF (THAT ISN'T THE STUFF YOU'RE TRYING TO DO) IN ORDER TO *AVOID* THE STUFF THAT YOU ARE *TRYING* TO DO.

8. HAVE *ANXIETY.*

9. WORK ON LIST AGAIN.

10. ADD INCREASINGLY *IMPOSSIBLE* THINGS TO THE LIST.

11. THINK ABOUT THE THINGS YOU'VE *WANTED* TO DO IN YOUR LIFE, BUT HAVEN'T DONE. REALIZE THAT YOUR LIFE IS A *WASTE* AND THAT ACHIEVING EVEN THE *SIMPLEST GOALS* IS BEYOND YOU.

12. ALLOW YOURSELF TO BE FILLED WITH *SHAME.*

13. FREAK OUT.

14. SPEND SO MUCH TIME ON THE *TO-DO LIST* THAT YOU RUN OUT OF TIME TO ACTUALLY DO *ANYTHING.*

15. GIVE UP.

16. GO OUTSIDE. IT'S A NICE DAY. LIFE IS SHORT.

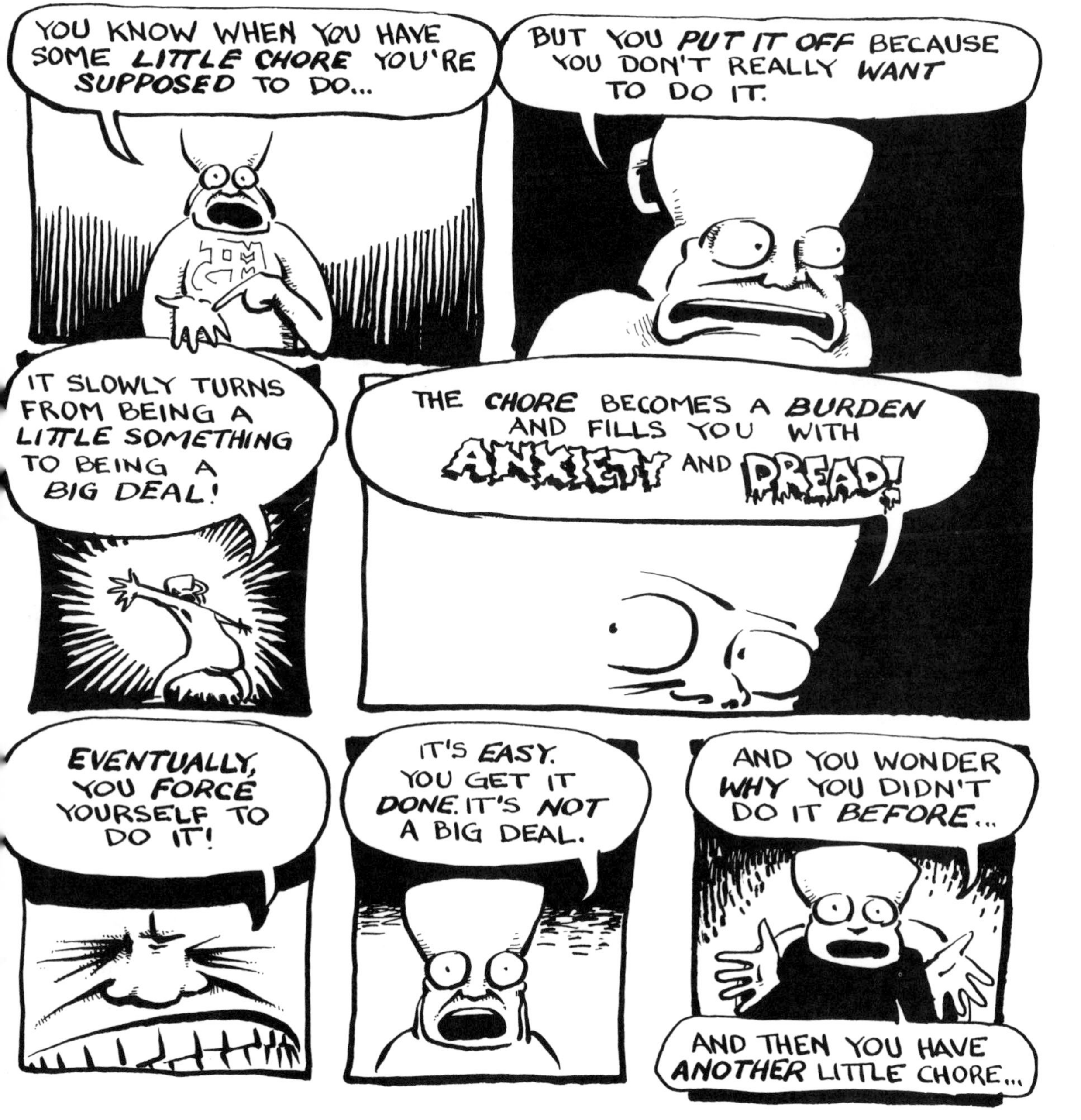
YOU KNOW WHEN YOU HAVE SOME LITTLE CHORE YOU'RE SUPPOSED TO DO...
BUT YOU PUT IT OFF BECAUSE YOU DON'T REALLY WANT TO DO IT.
IT SLOWLY TURNS FROM BEING A LITTLE SOMETHING TO BEING A BIG DEAL!
THE CHORE BECOMES A BURDEN AND FILLS YOU WITH ANXIETY AND DREAD!
EVENTUALLY, YOU FORCE YOURSELF TO DO IT!
IT'S EASY. YOU GET IT DONE. IT'S NOT A BIG DEAL.
AND YOU WONDER WHY YOU DIDN'T DO IT BEFORE...
AND THEN YOU HAVE ANOTHER LITTLE CHORE...

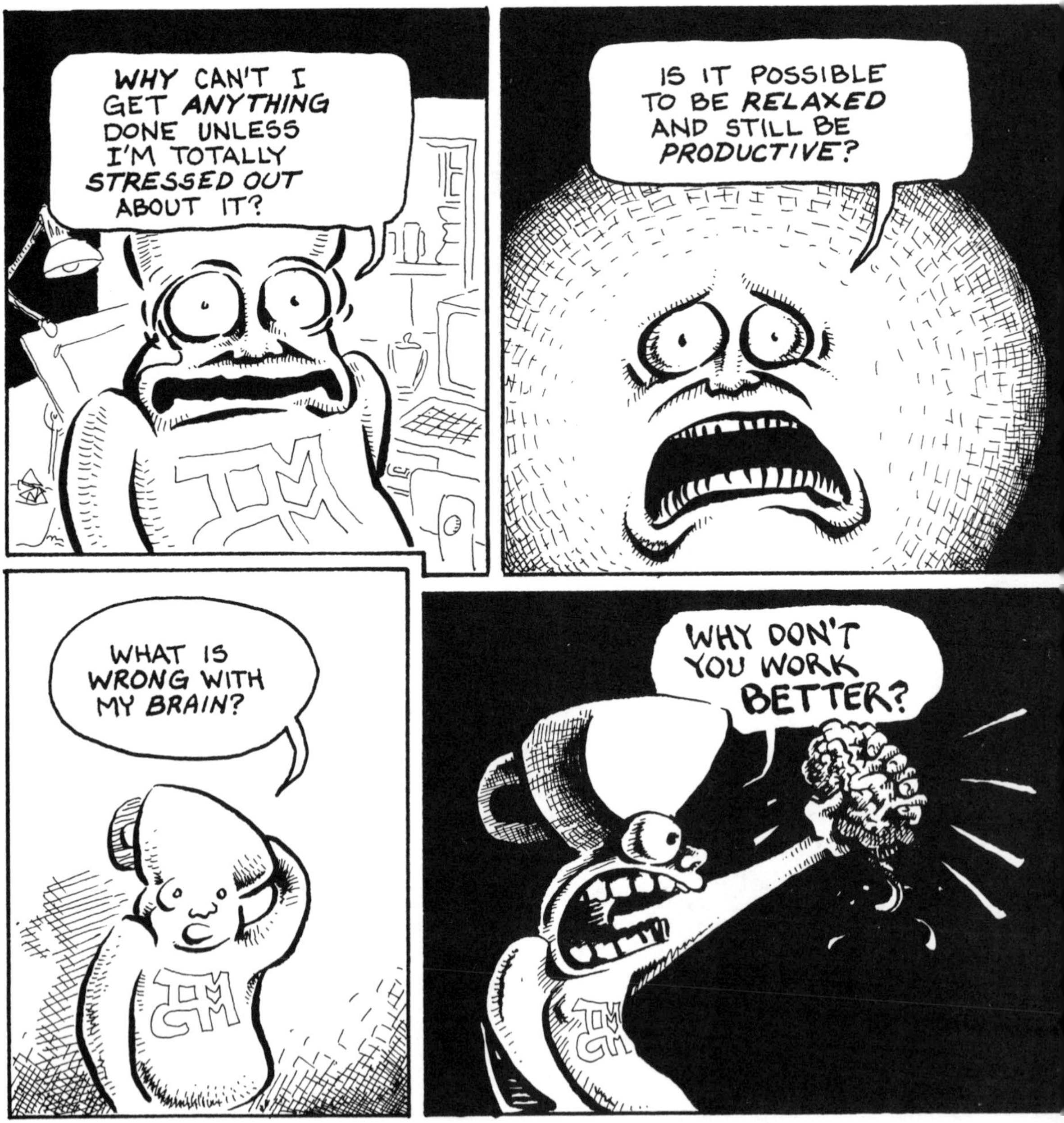
WHY CAN'T I GET ANYTHING DONE UNLESS I'M TOTALLY STRESSED OUT ABOUT IT?
IS IT POSSIBLE TO BE RELAXED AND STILL BE PRODUCTIVE?
WHAT IS WRONG WITH MY BRAIN?
WHY DON'T YOU WORK BETTER?

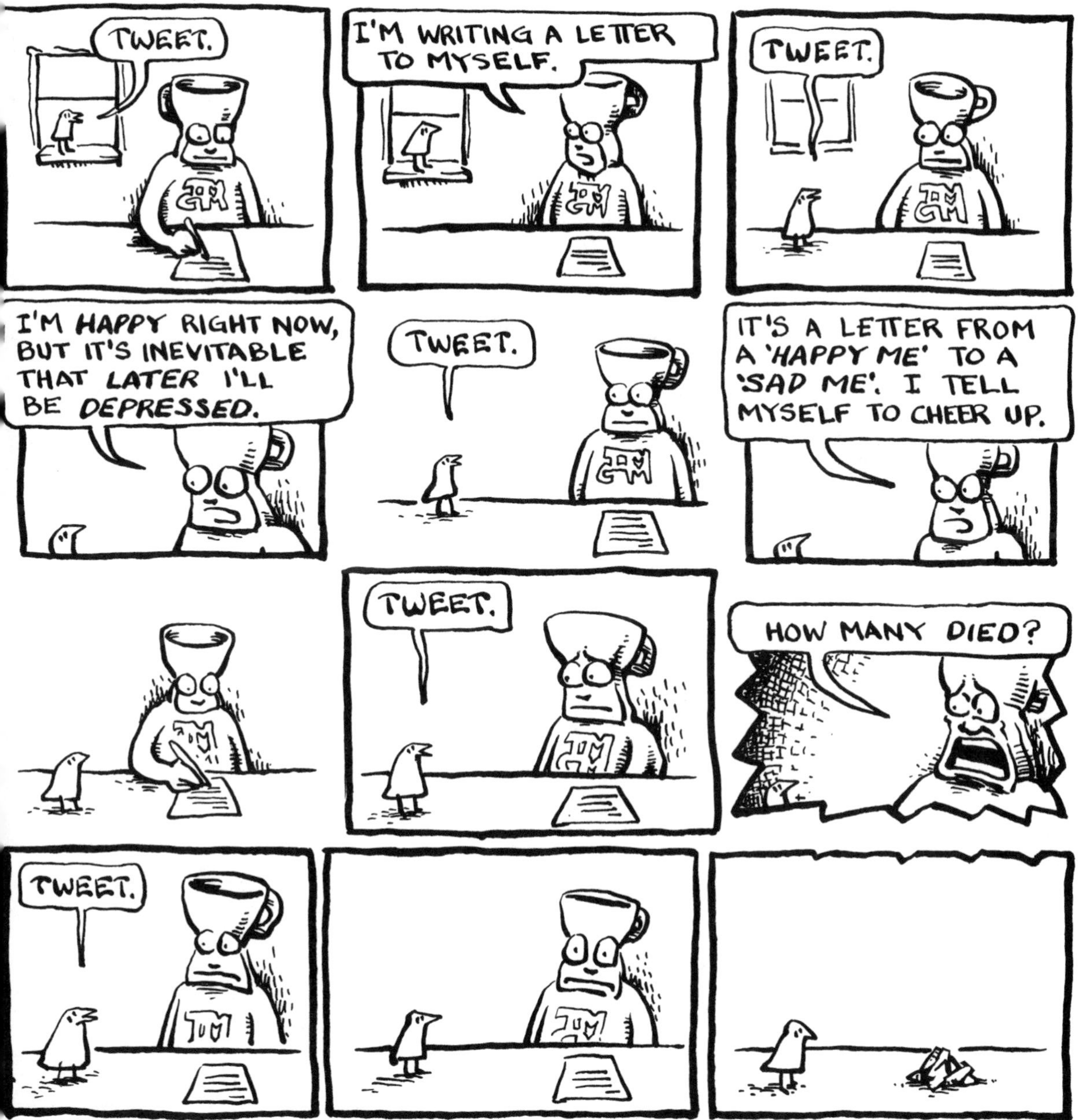
TWEET.
I'M WRITING A LETTER TO MYSELF.
TWEET.
I'M HAPPY RIGHT NOW, BUT IT'S INEVITABLE THAT LATER I'LL BE DEPRESSED.
TWEET.
IT'S A LETTER FROM A 'HAPPY ME' TO A 'SAD ME'. I TELL MYSELF TO CHEER UP.
TWEET.
HOW MANY DIED?
TWEET.

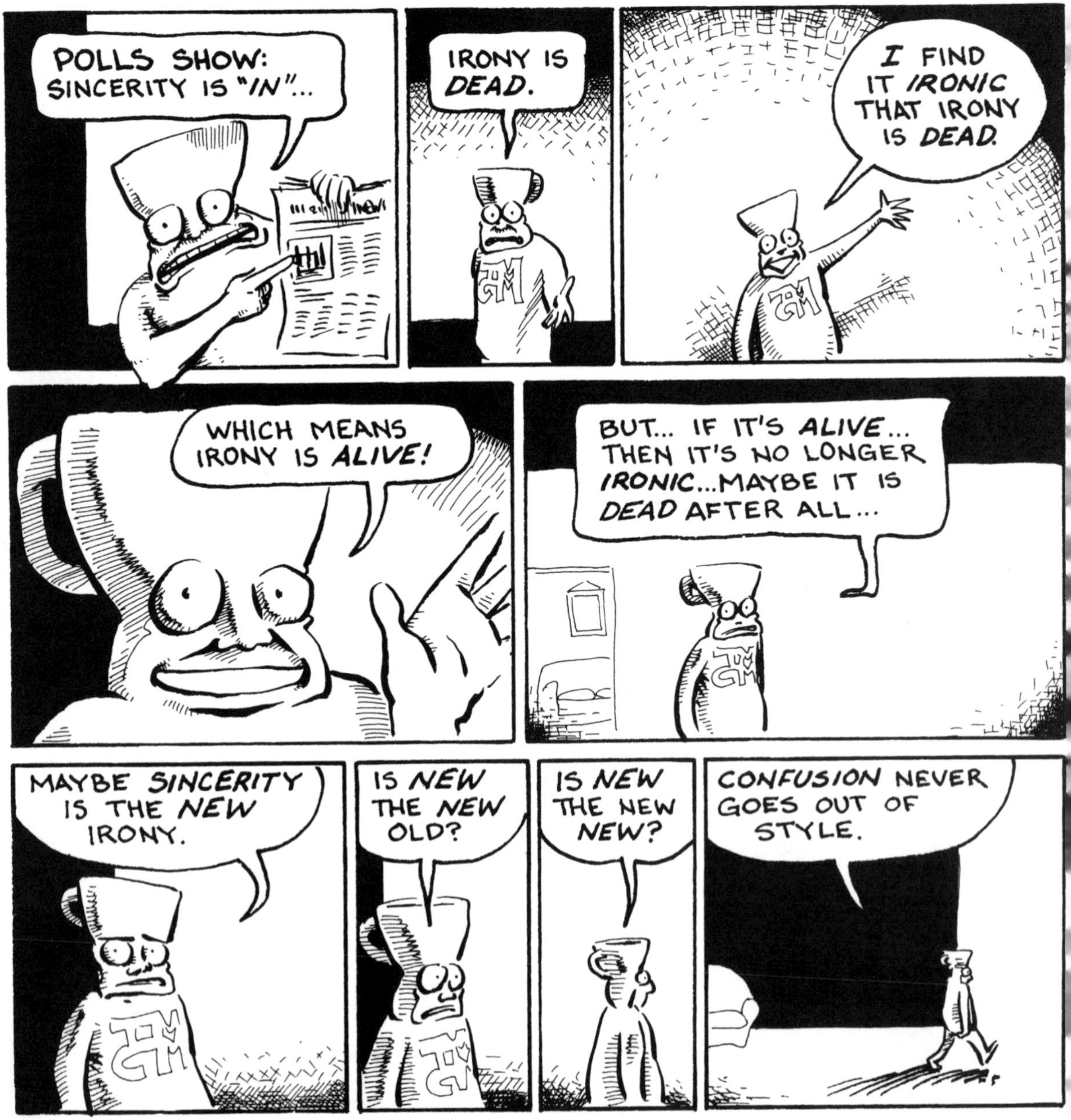
POLLS SHOW: SINCERITY IS "IN"...
IRONY IS DEAD.
I FIND IT IRONIC THAT IRONY IS DEAD.
WHICH MEANS IRONY IS ALIVE!
BUT... IF IT'S ALIVE... THEN IT'S NO LONGER IRONIC...MAYBE IT IS DEAD AFTER ALL...
MAYBE SINCERITY IS THE NEW IRONY.
IS NEW THE NEW OLD?
IS NEW THE NEW NEW?
CONFUSION NEVER GOES OUT OF STYLE.

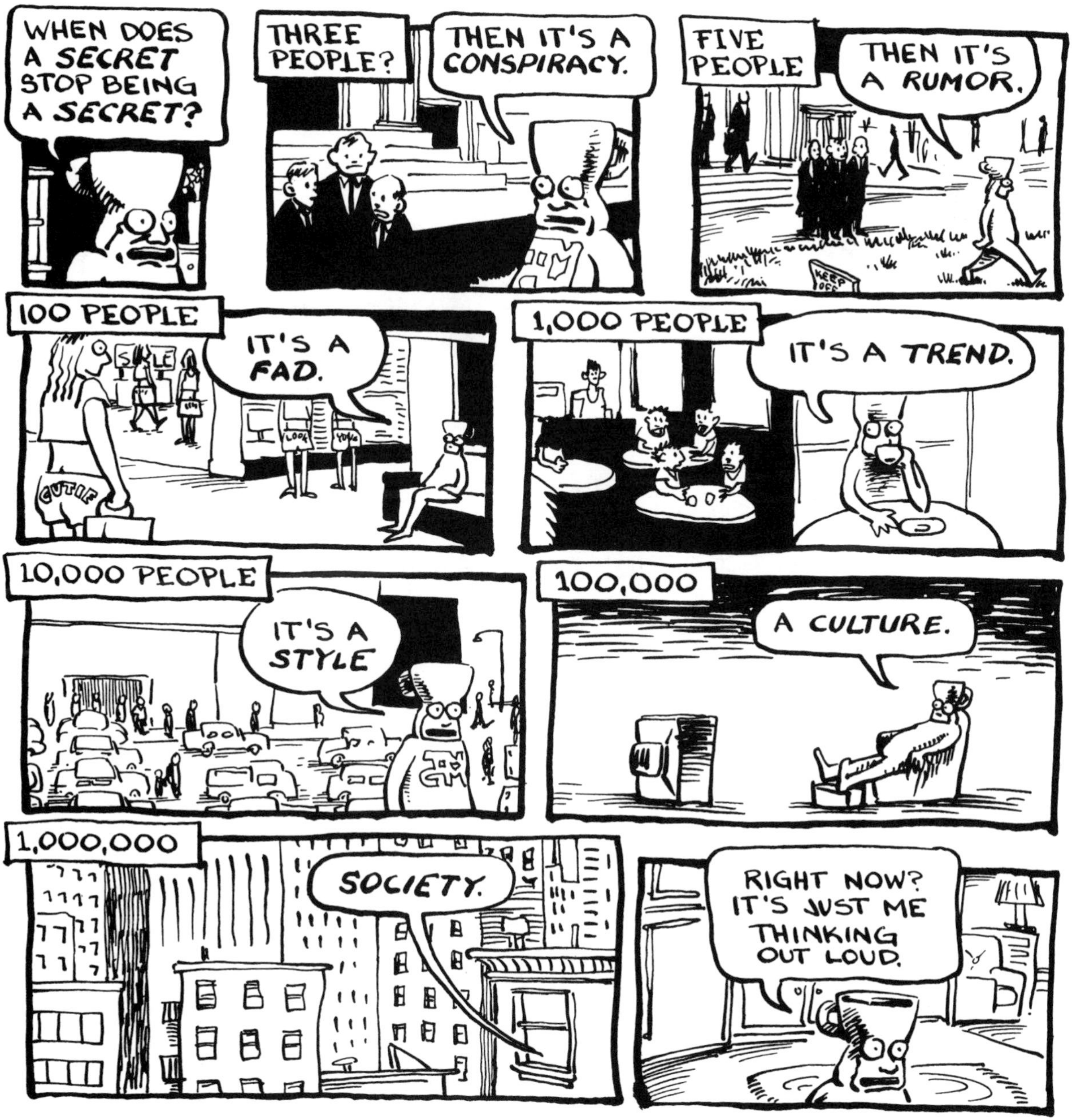
WHEN DOES A SECRET STOP BEING A SECRET?
THREE PEOPLE?
THEN IT'S A CONSPIRACY.
FIVE PEOPLE
THEN IT'S A RUMOR.
KEEP OFF
100 PEOPLE
IT'S A FAD.
CUTIE
1,000 PEOPLE
IT'S A TREND.
10,000 PEOPLE
IT'S A STYLE
100,000
A CULTURE.
1,000,000
SOCIETY.
RIGHT NOW? IT'S JUST ME THINKING OUT LOUD.

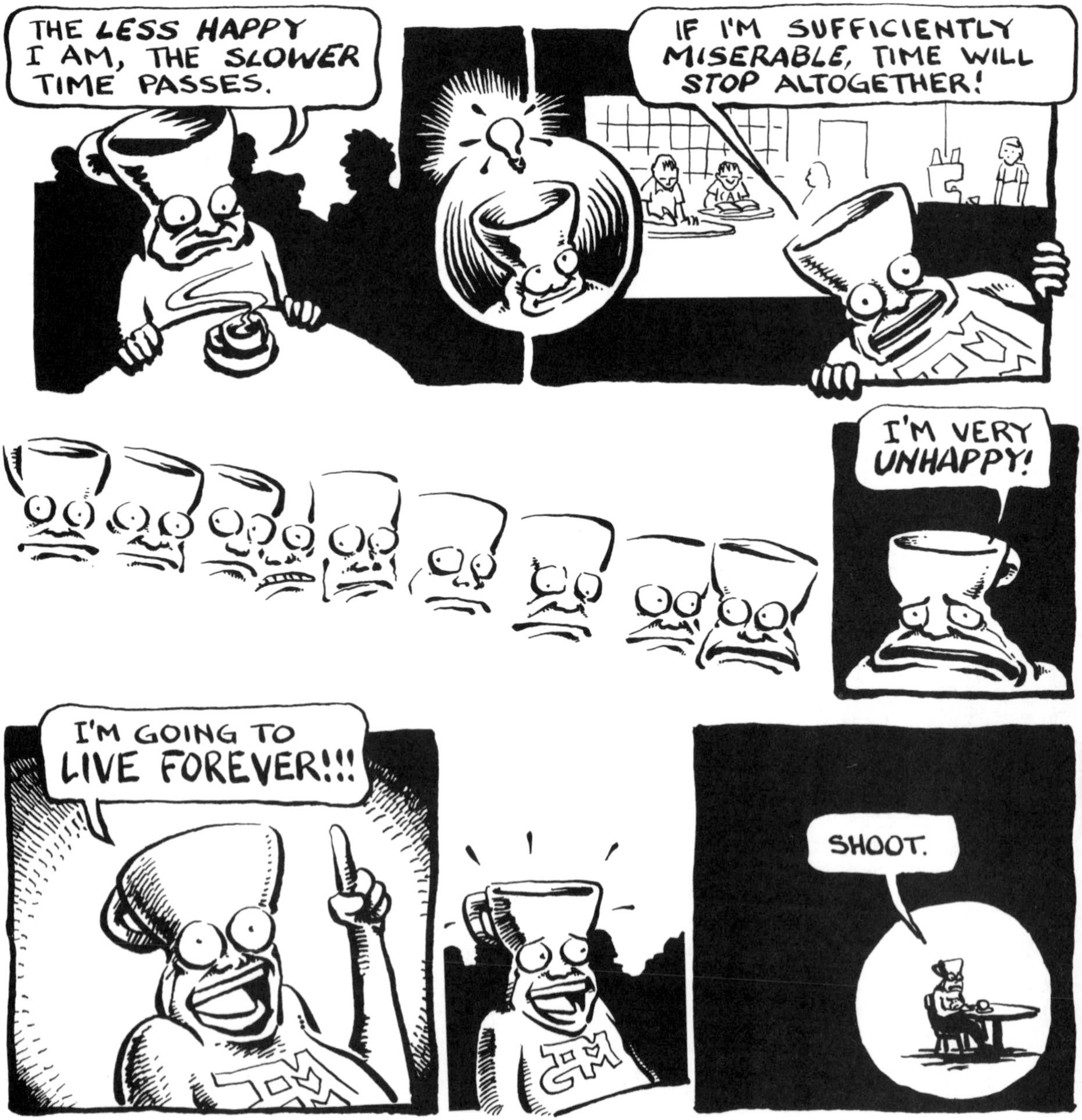
THE LESS HAPPY I AM, THE SLOWER TIME PASSES.
IF I'M SUFFICIENTLY MISERABLE, TIME WILL STOP ALTOGETHER!
I'M VERY UNHAPPY!
I'M GOING TO LIVE FOREVER!!!
SHOOT.

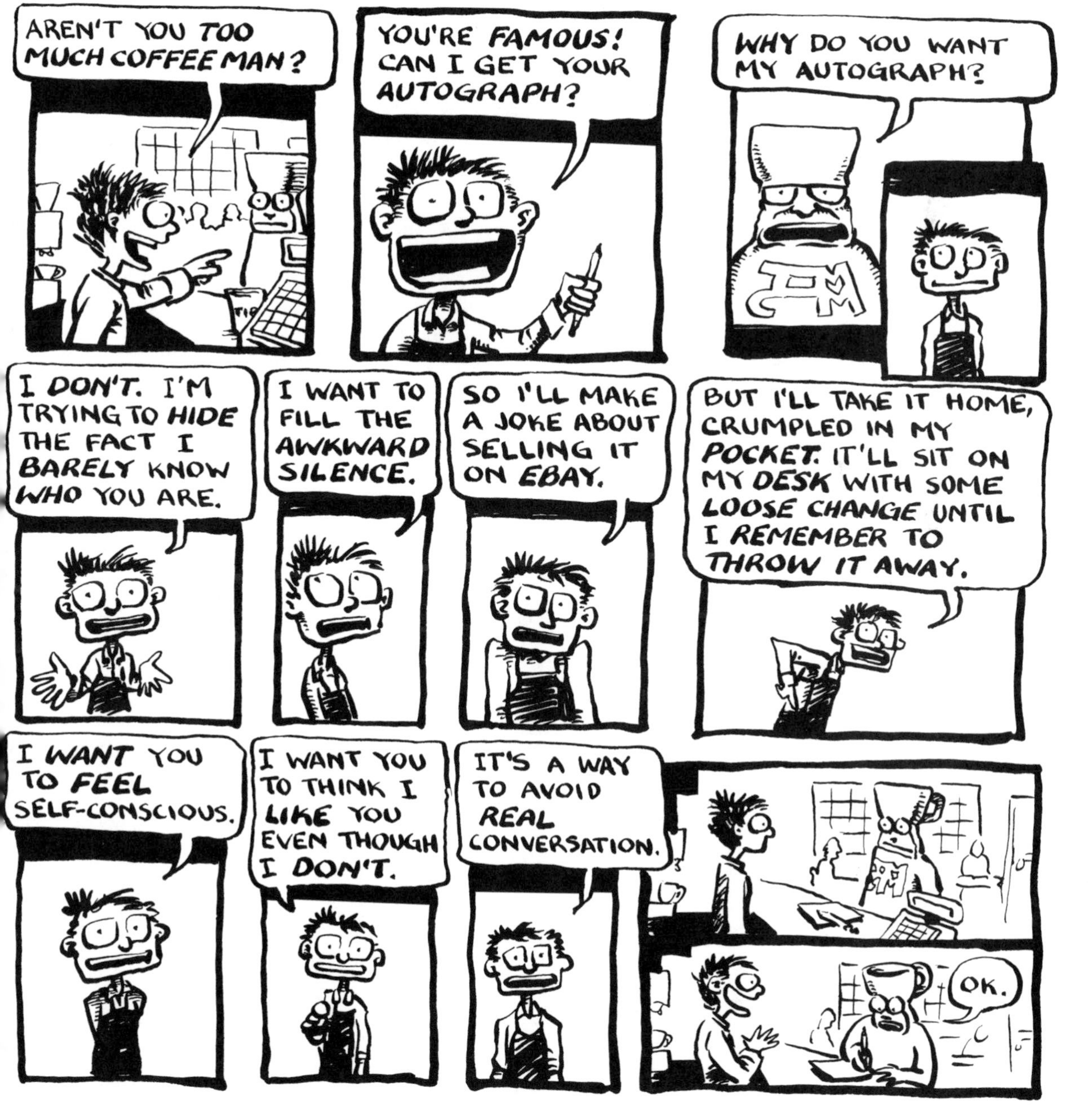
AREN'T YOU TOO MUCH COFFEE MAN?
YOU'RE FAMOUS! CAN I GET YOUR AUTOGRAPH?
WHY DO YOU WANT MY AUTOGRAPH?
I DON'T. I'M TRYING TO HIDE THE FACT I BARELY KNOW WHO YOU ARE.
I WANT TO FILL THE AWKWARD SILENCE.
SO I'LL MAKE A JOKE ABOUT SELLING IT ON EBAY.
BUT I'LL TAKE IT HOME, CRUMPLED IN MY POCKET. IT'LL SIT ON MY DESK WITH SOME LOOSE CHANGE UNTIL I REMEMBER TO THROW IT AWAY.
I WANT YOU TO FEEL SELF-CONSCIOUS.
I WANT YOU TO THINK I LIKE YOU EVEN THOUGH I DON'T.
IT'S A WAY TO AVOID REAL CONVERSATION.
OK.

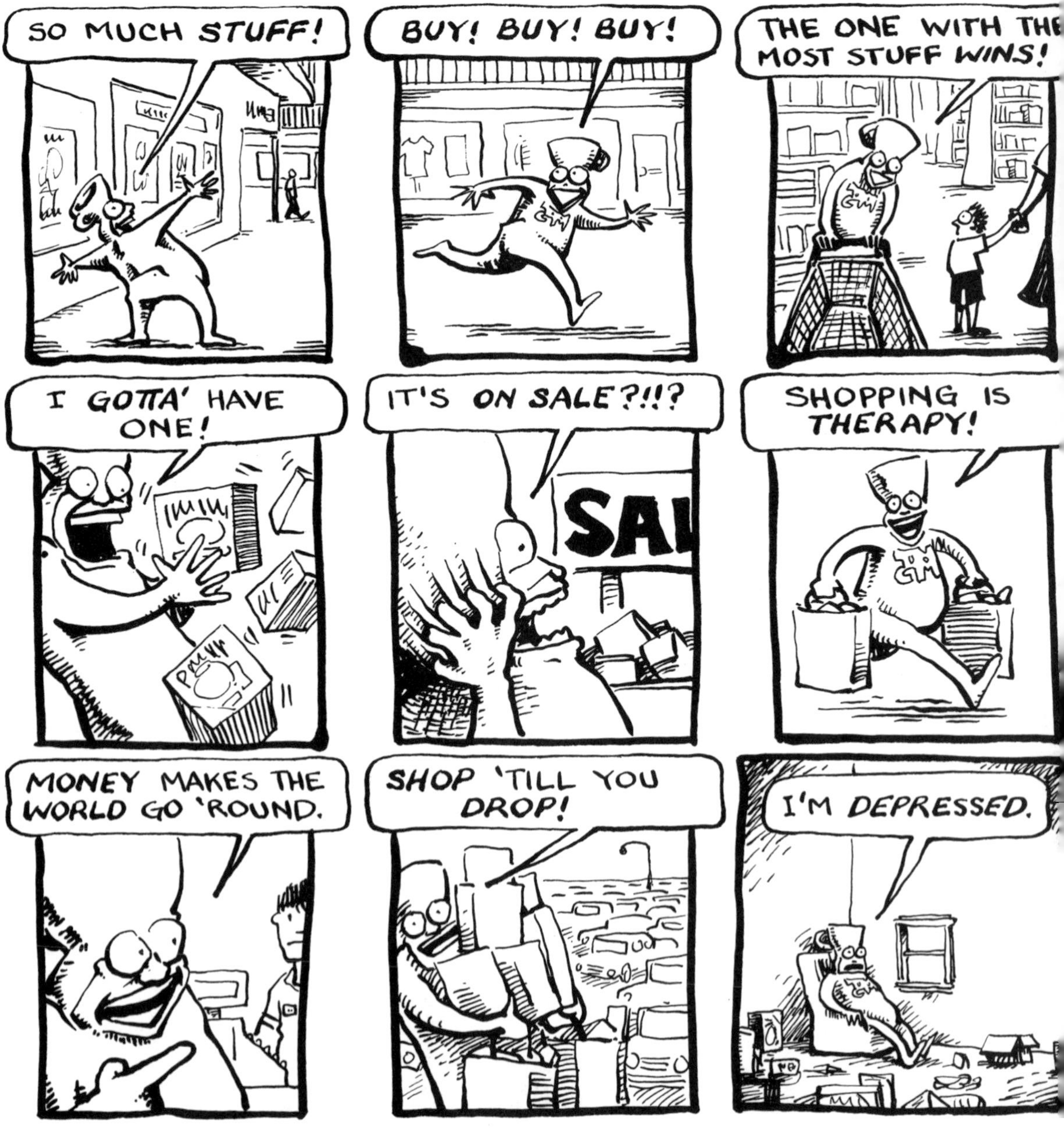
SO MUCH STUFF!
BUY! BUY! BUY!
THE ONE WITH THE MOST STUFF WINS!
I GOTTA' HAVE ONE!
IT'S ON SALE?!!?
SAL
SHOPPING IS THERAPY!
MONEY MAKES THE WORLD GO 'ROUND.
SHOP 'TILL YOU DROP!
I'M DEPRESSED.

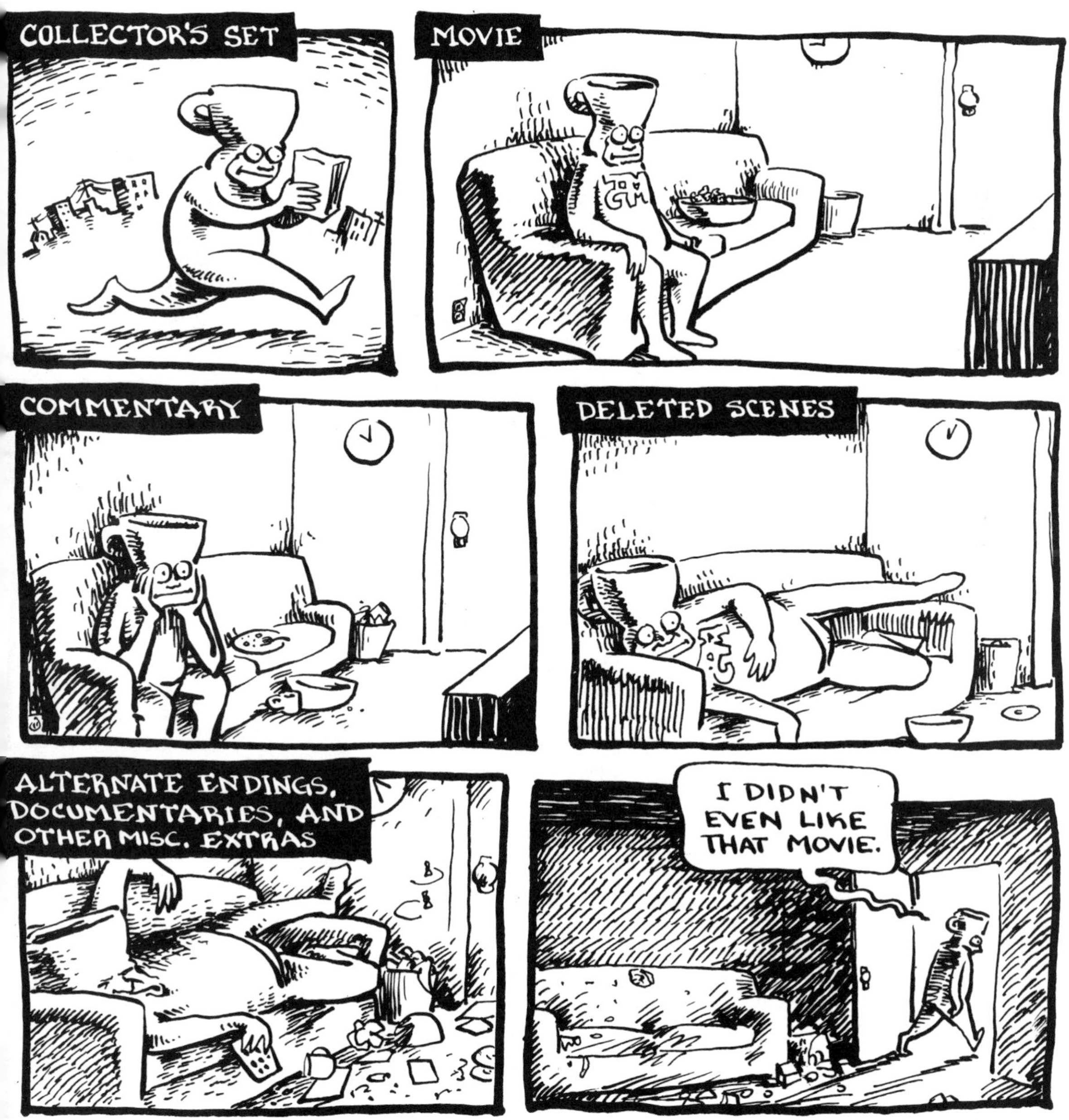
COLLECTOR'S SET
MOVIE
COMMENTARY
DELETED SCENES
ALTERNATE ENDINGS, DOCUMENTARIES, AND OTHER MISC. EXTRAS
I DIDN'T EVEN LIKE THAT MOVIE.

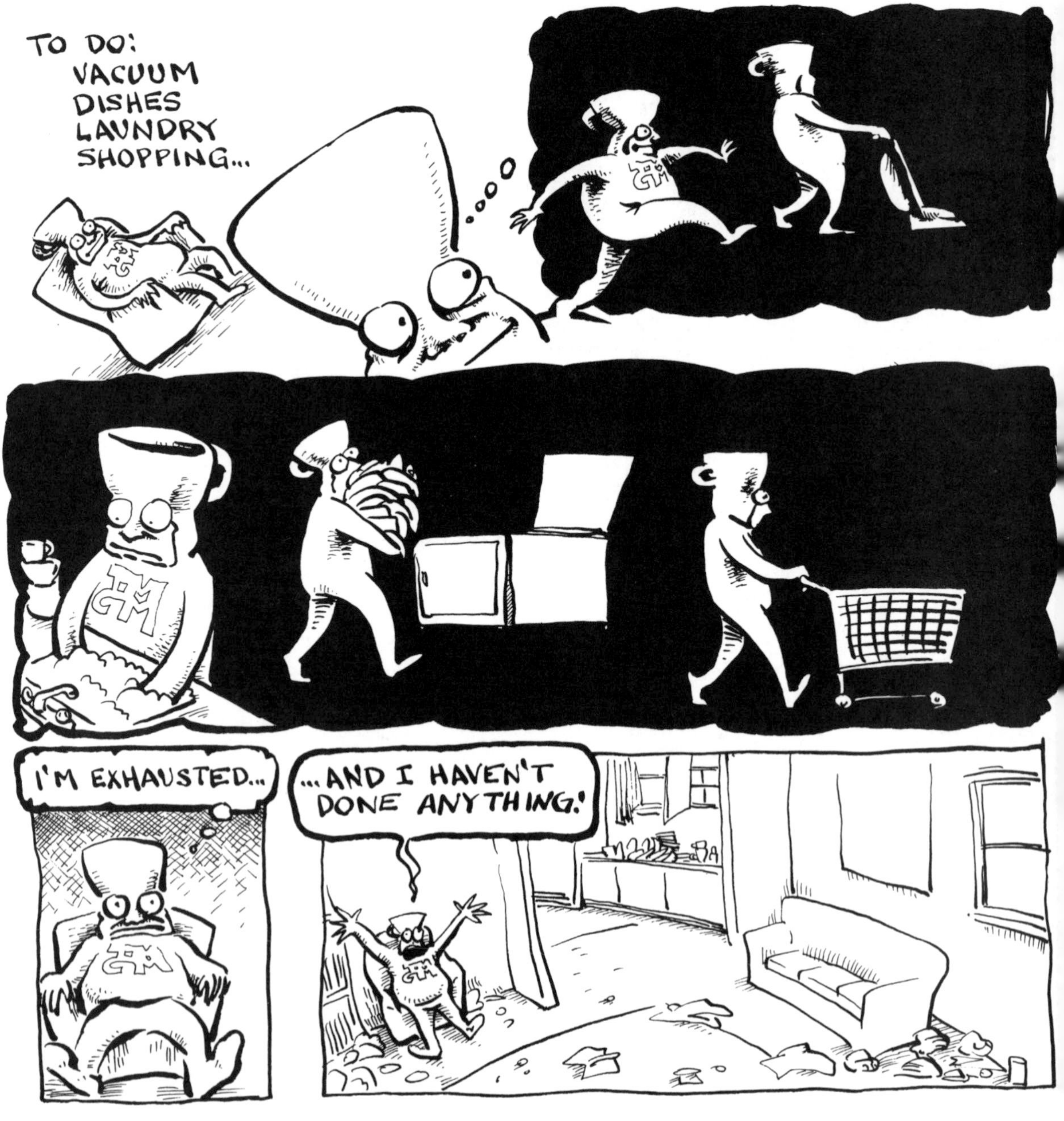
TO DO:
VACUUM
DISHES
LAUNDRY
SHOPPING...
I'M EXHAUSTED...
...AND I HAVEN'T DONE ANYTHING!

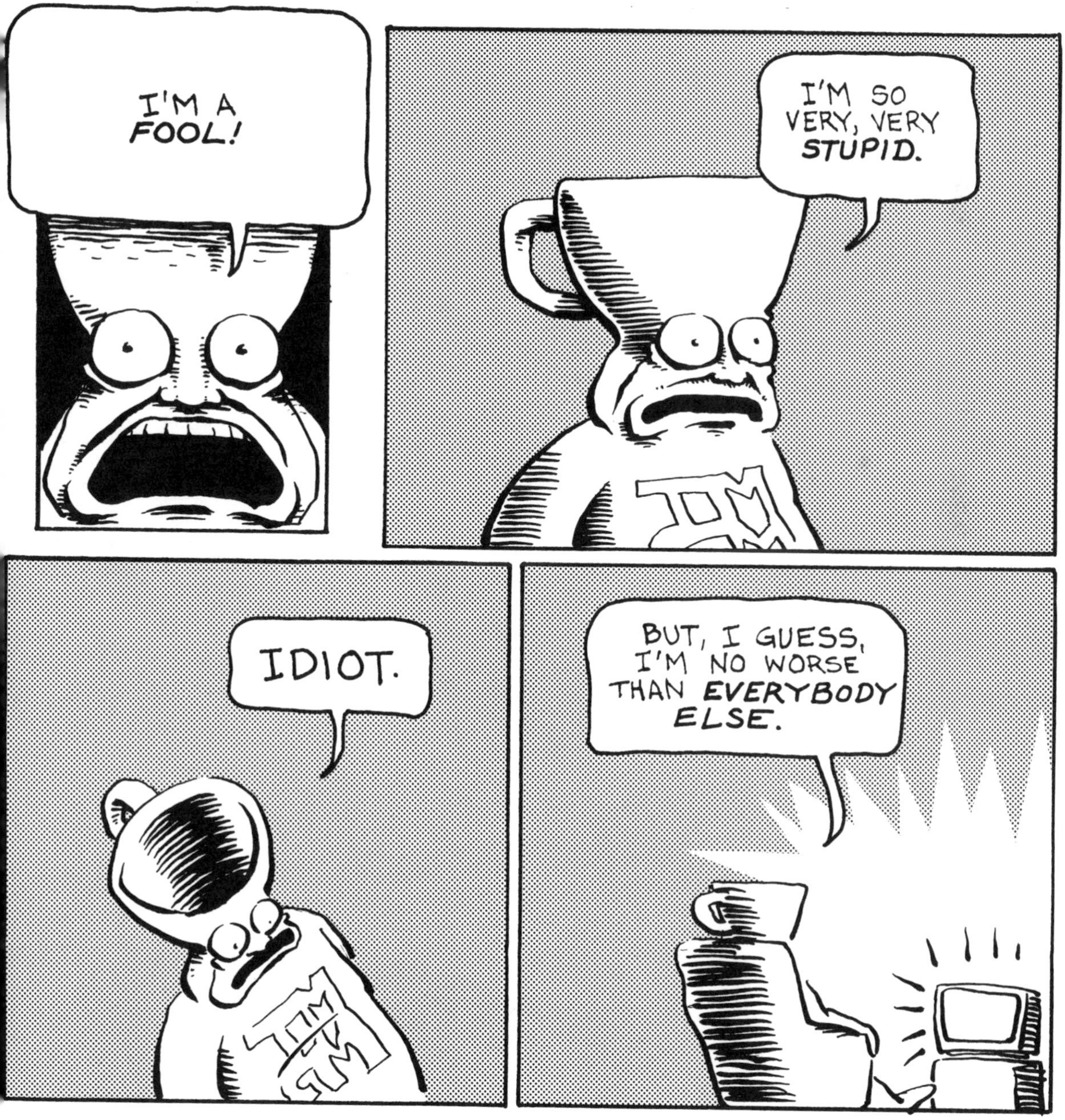
I'M A FOOL!
I'M SO VERY, VERY STUPID.
IDIOT.
BUT, I GUESS, I'M NO WORSE THAN EVERYBODY ELSE.

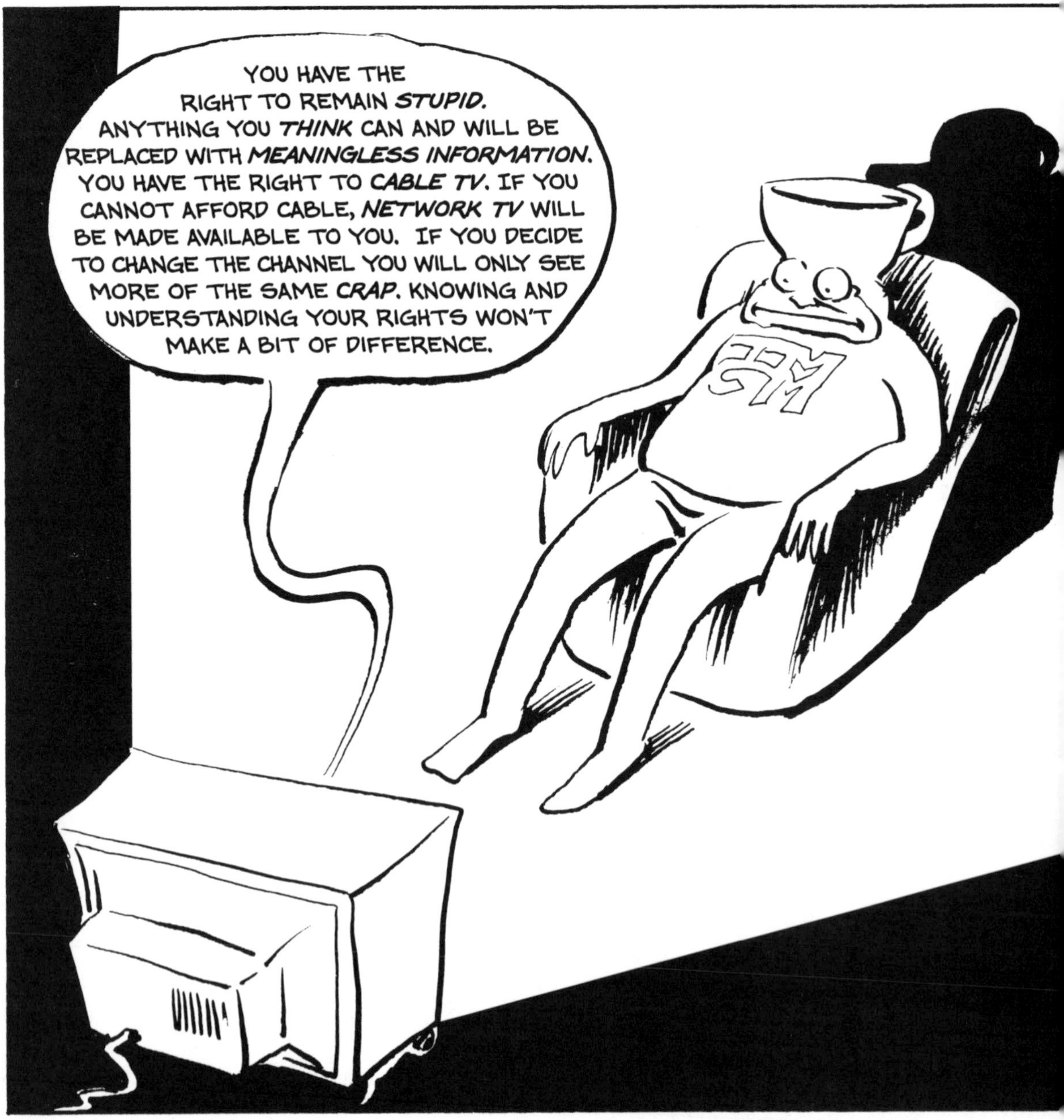
YOU HAVE THE RIGHT TO REMAIN STUPID. ANYTHING YOU THINK CAN AND WILL BE REPLACED WITH MEANINGLESS INFORMATION. YOU HAVE THE RIGHT TO CABLE TV. IF YOU CANNOT AFFORD CABLE, NETWORK TV WILL BE MADE AVAILABLE TO YOU. IF YOU DECIDE TO CHANGE THE CHANNEL YOU WILL ONLY SEE MORE OF THE SAME CRAP. KNOWING AND UNDERSTANDING YOUR RIGHTS WON'T MAKE A BIT OF DIFFERENCE.

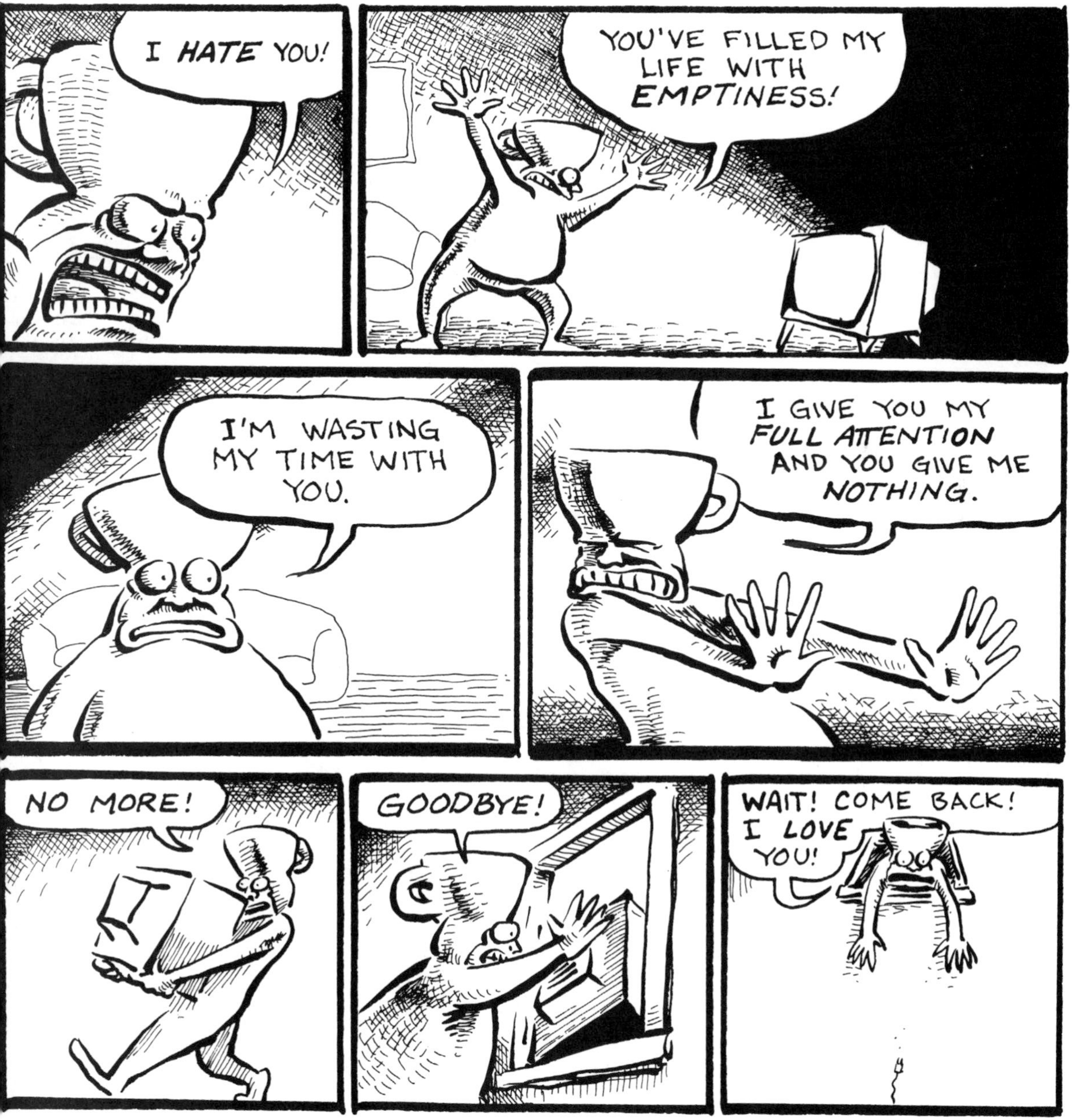
I HATE YOU!
YOU'VE FILLED MY LIFE WITH EMPTINESS!
I'M WASTING MY TIME WITH YOU.
I GIVE YOU MY FULL ATTENTION AND YOU GIVE ME NOTHING.
NO MORE!
GOODBYE!
WAIT! COME BACK! I LOVE YOU!

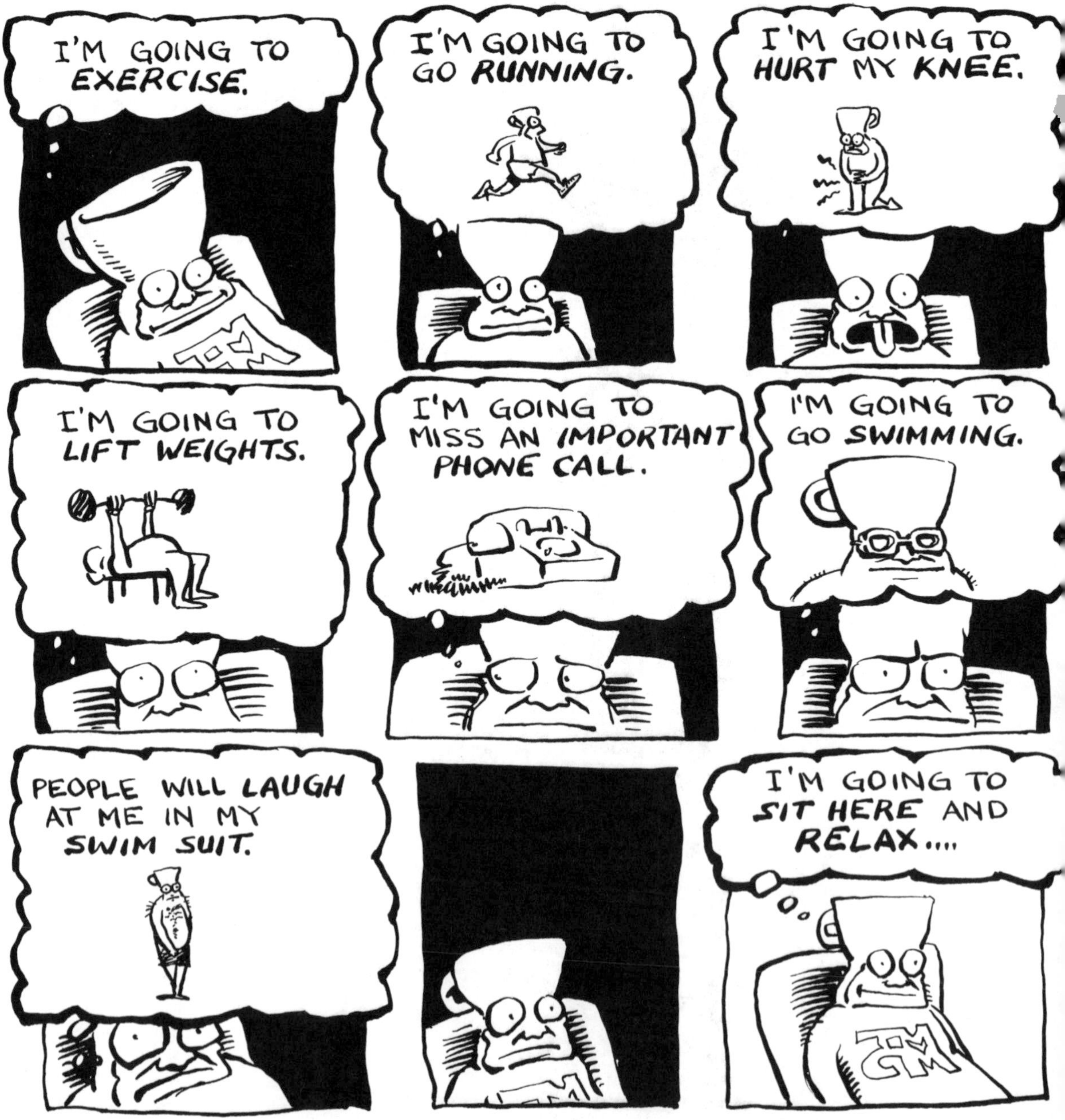

I'M GOING TO EXERCISE.
I'M GOING TO GO RUNNING.
I'M GOING TO HURT MY KNEE.
I'M GOING TO LIFT WEIGHTS.
I'M GOING TO MISS AN IMPORTANT PHONE CALL.
I'M GOING TO GO SWIMMING.
PEOPLE WILL LAUGH AT ME IN MY SWIM SUIT.
I'M GOING TO SIT HERE AND RELAX....

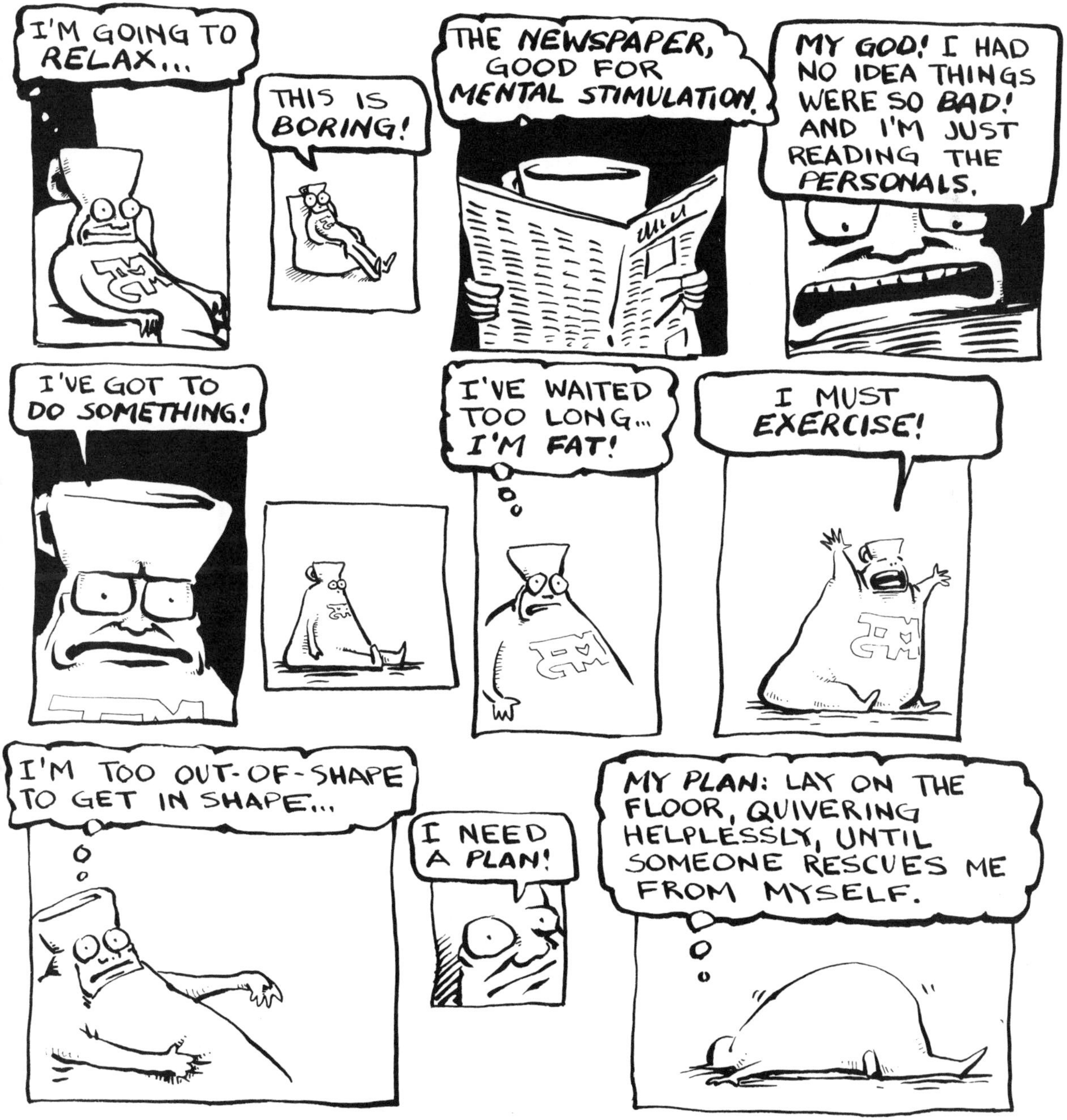
I'M GOING TO RELAX...
THIS IS BORING!
THE NEWSPAPER, GOOD FOR MENTAL STIMULATION.
MY GOD! I HAD NO IDEA THINGS WERE SO BAD! AND I'M JUST READING THE PERSONALS.
I'VE GOT TO DO SOMETHING!
I'VE WAITED TOO LONG... I'M FAT!
I MUST EXERCISE!
I'M TOO OUT-OF-SHAPE TO GET IN SHAPE...
I NEED A PLAN!
MY PLAN: LAY ON THE FLOOR, QUIVERING HELPLESSLY, UNTIL SOMEONE RESCUES ME FROM MYSELF.

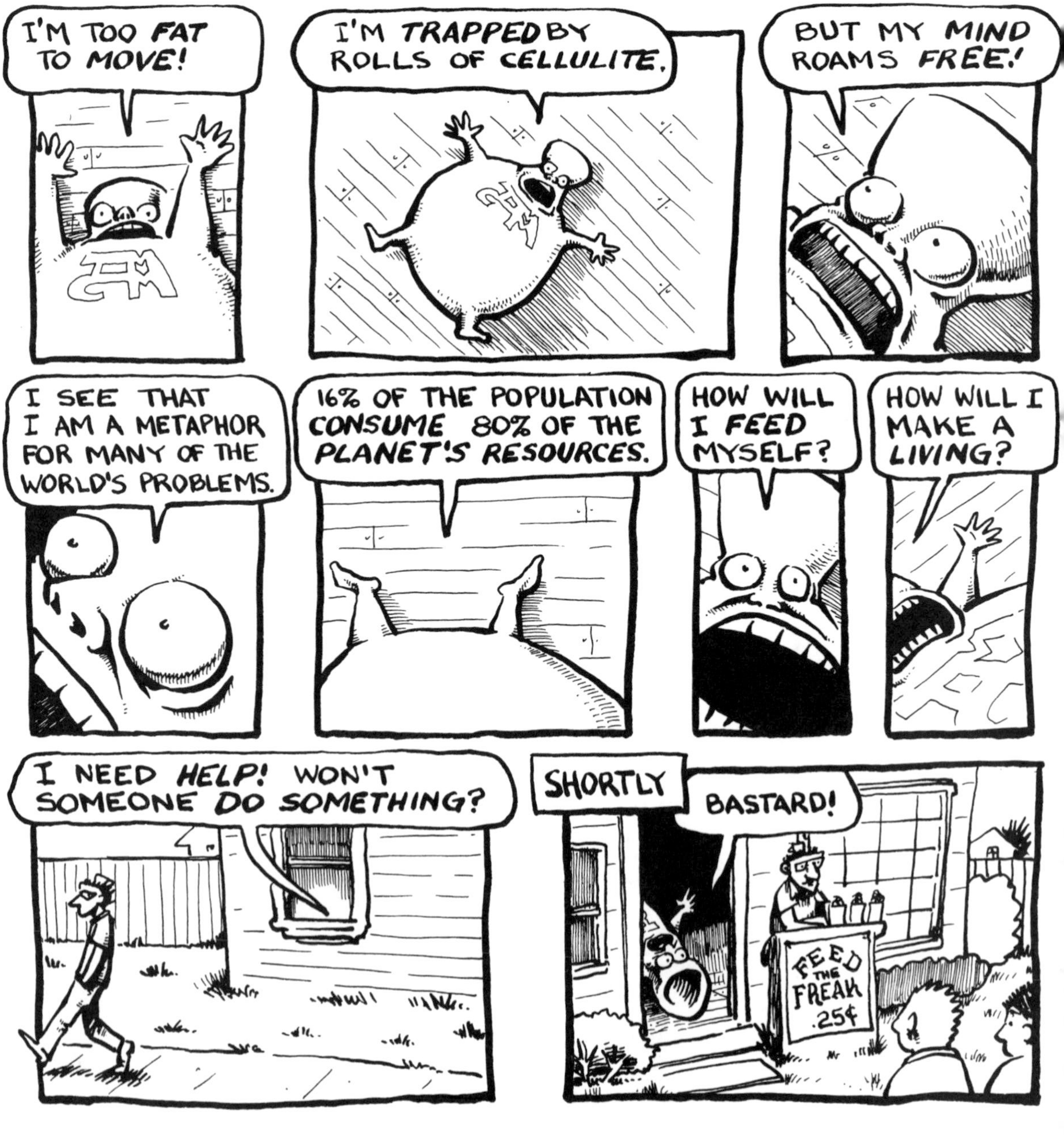
I'M TOO FAT TO MOVE!
I'M TRAPPED BY ROLLS OF CELLULITE.
BUT MY MIND ROAMS FREE!
I SEE THAT I AM A METAPHOR FOR MANY OF THE WORLD'S PROBLEMS.
16% OF THE POPULATION CONSUME 80% OF THE PLANET'S RESOURCES.
HOW WILL I FEED MYSELF?
HOW WILL I MAKE A LIVING?
I NEED HELP! WON'T SOMEONE DO SOMETHING?
SHORTLY
BASTARD!
FEED THE FREAK .25¢

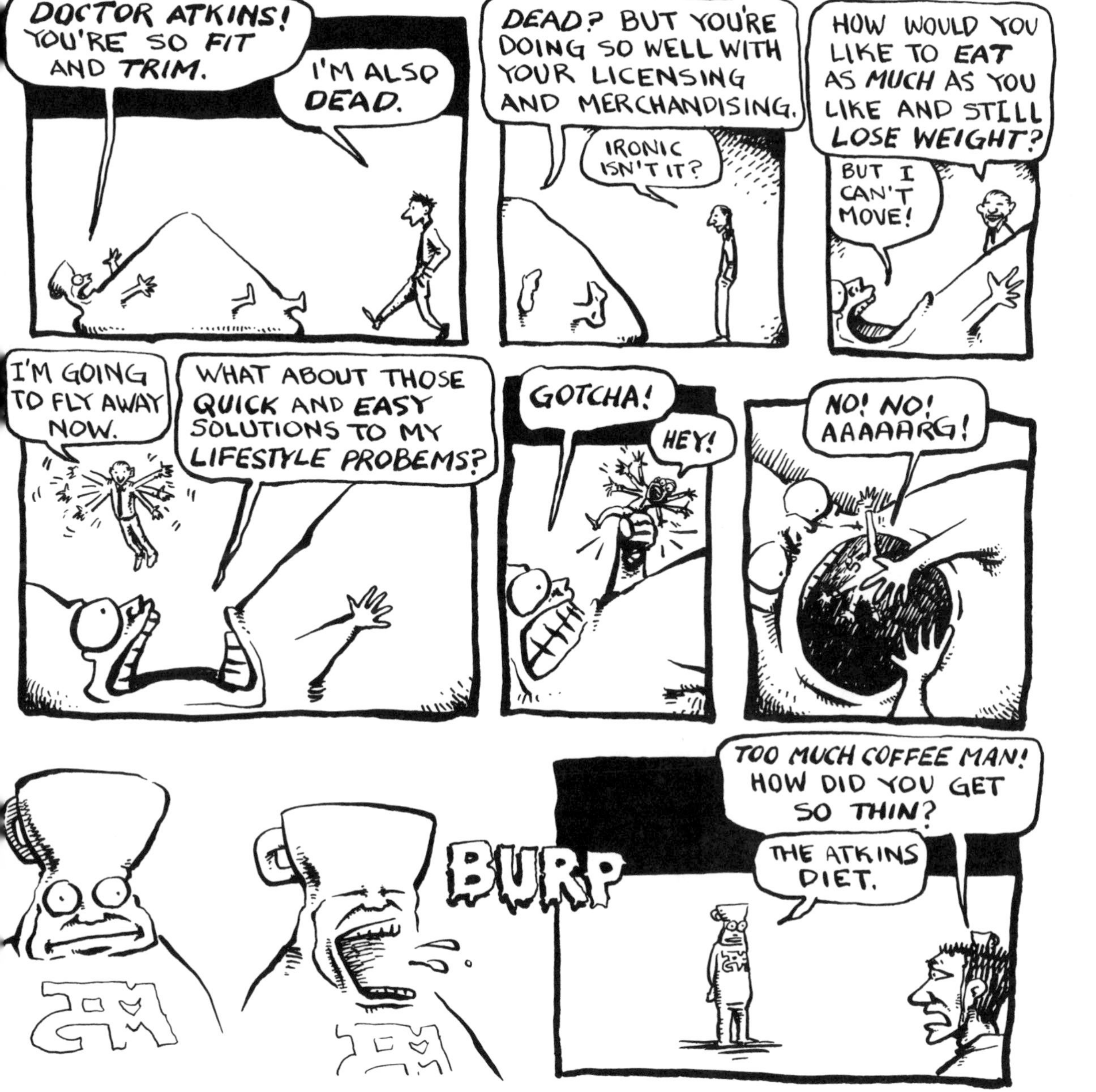
DOCTOR ATKINS! YOU'RE SO FIT AND TRIM.
I'M ALSO DEAD.
DEAD? BUT YOU'RE DOING SO WELL WITH YOUR LICENSING AND MERCHANDISING.
IRONIC ISN'T IT?
HOW WOULD YOU LIKE TO EAT AS MUCH AS YOU LIKE AND STILL LOSE WEIGHT?
BUT I CAN'T MOVE!
I'M GOING TO FLY AWAY NOW.
WHAT ABOUT THOSE QUICK AND EASY SOLUTIONS TO MY LIFESTYLE PROBEMS?
GOTCHA!
HEY!
NO! NO! AAAAARG!
BURP
TOO MUCH COFFEE MAN! HOW DID YOU GET SO THIN?
THE ATKINS DIET.

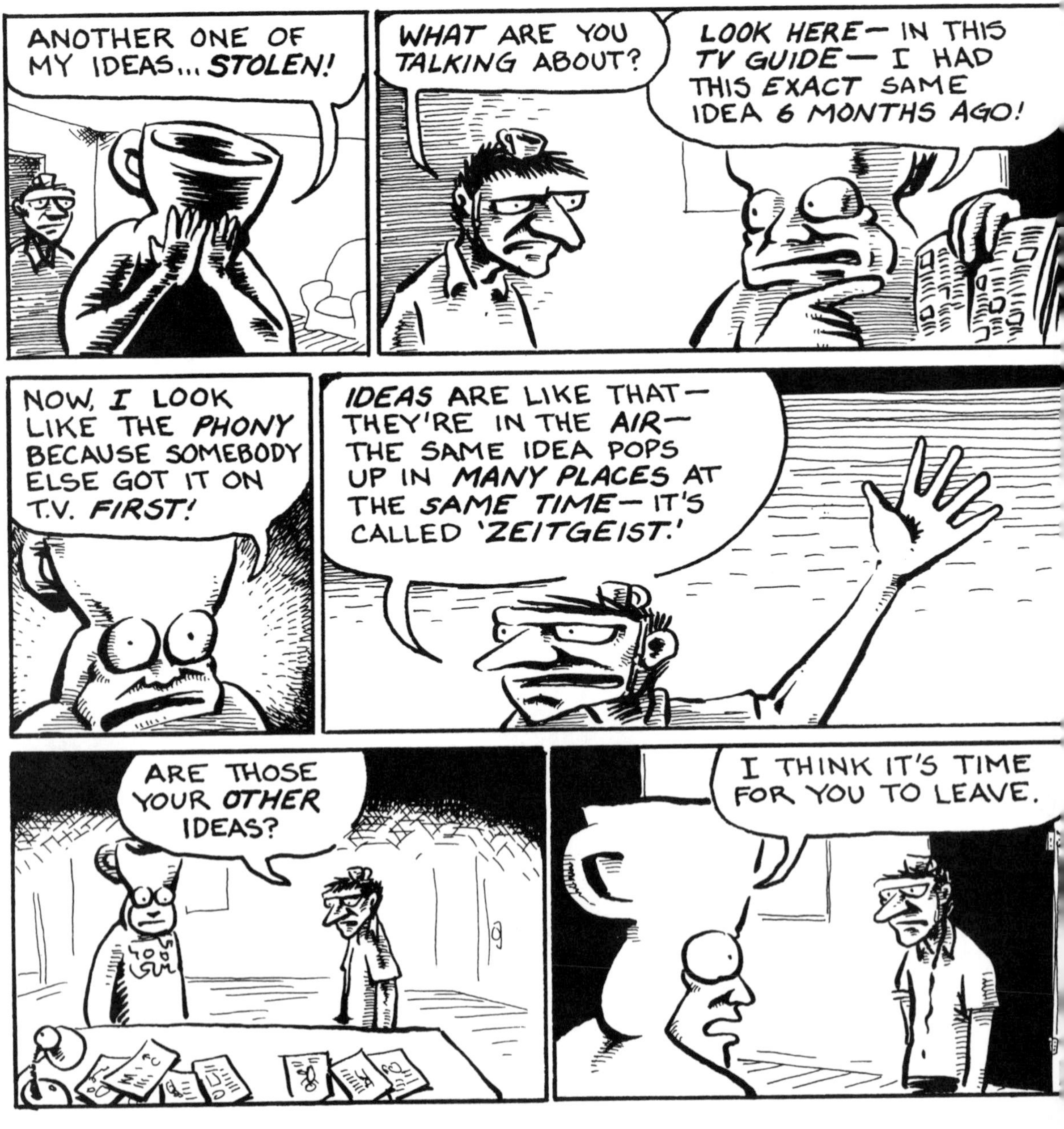
ANOTHER ONE OF MY IDEAS... STOLEN!
WHAT ARE YOU TALKING ABOUT?
LOOK HERE— IN THIS TV GUIDE— I HAD THIS EXACT SAME IDEA 6 MONTHS AGO!
NOW, I LOOK LIKE THE PHONY BECAUSE SOMEBODY ELSE GOT IT ON T.V. FIRST!
IDEAS ARE LIKE THAT— THEY'RE IN THE AIR— THE SAME IDEA POPS UP IN MANY PLACES AT THE SAME TIME— IT'S CALLED 'ZEITGEIST.'
ARE THOSE YOUR OTHER IDEAS?
I THINK IT'S TIME FOR YOU TO LEAVE.

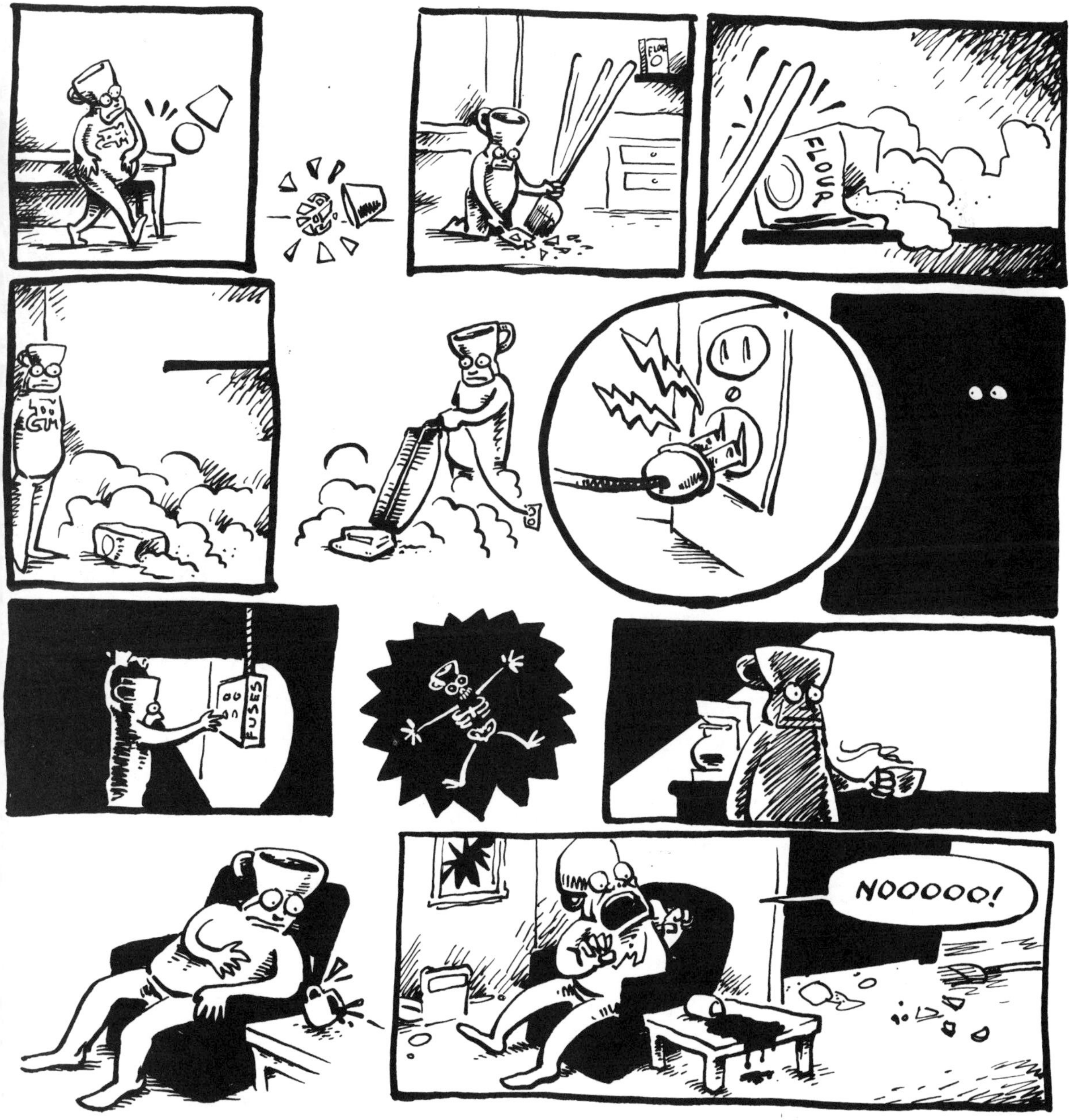
FLOUR
FLOUR
FUSES
NOOOOO!

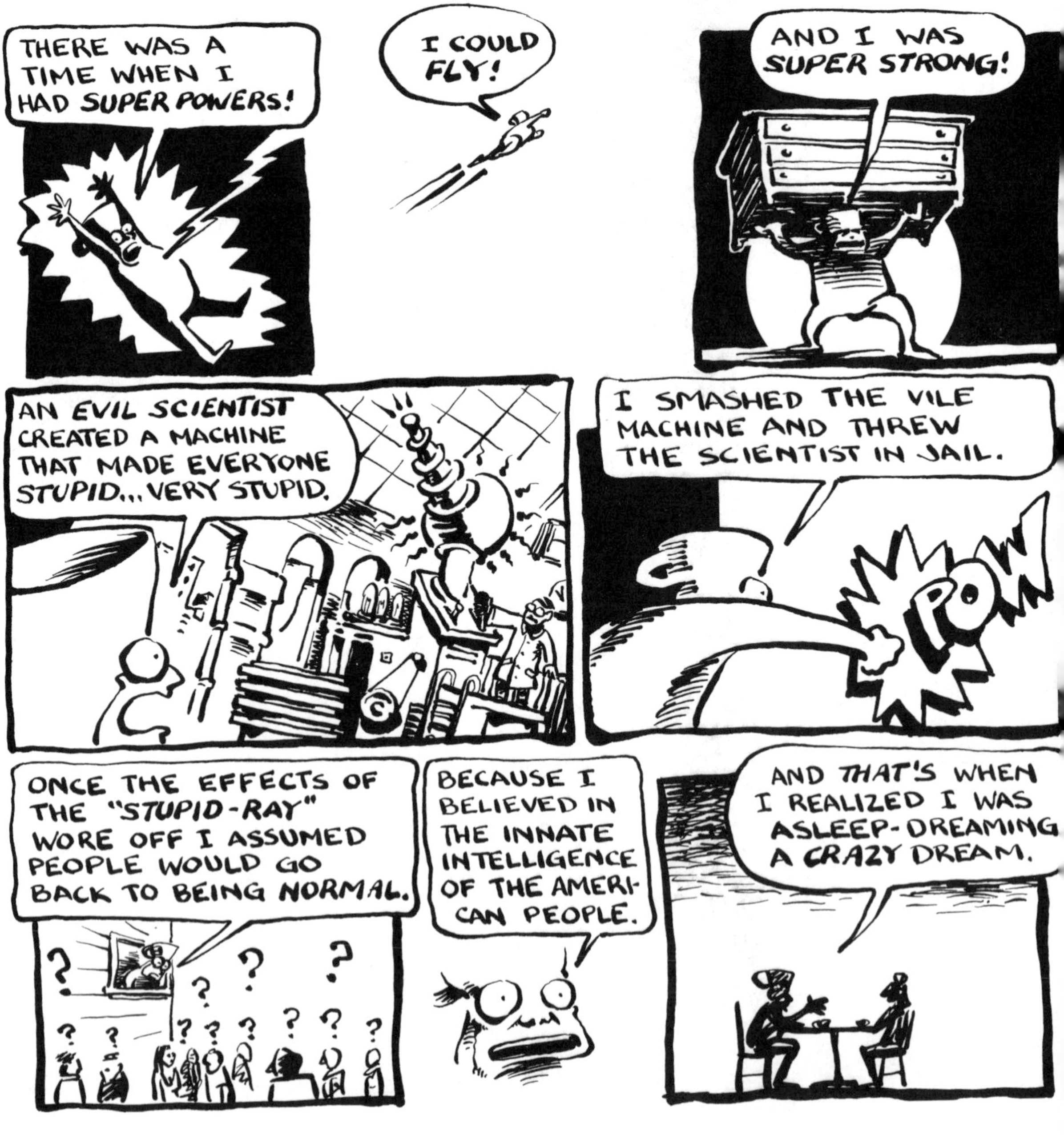
THERE WAS A TIME WHEN I HAD SUPER POWERS!
I COULD FLY!
AND I WAS SUPER STRONG!
AN EVIL SCIENTIST CREATED A MACHINE THAT MADE EVERYONE STUPID... VERY STUPID.
I SMASHED THE VILE MACHINE AND THREW THE SCIENTIST IN JAIL.
POW
ONCE THE EFFECTS OF THE "STUPID-RAY" WORE OFF I ASSUMED PEOPLE WOULD GO BACK TO BEING NORMAL.
BECAUSE I BELIEVED IN THE INNATE INTELLIGENCE OF THE AMERICAN PEOPLE.
AND THAT'S WHEN I REALIZED I WAS ASLEEP-DREAMING A CRAZY DREAM.

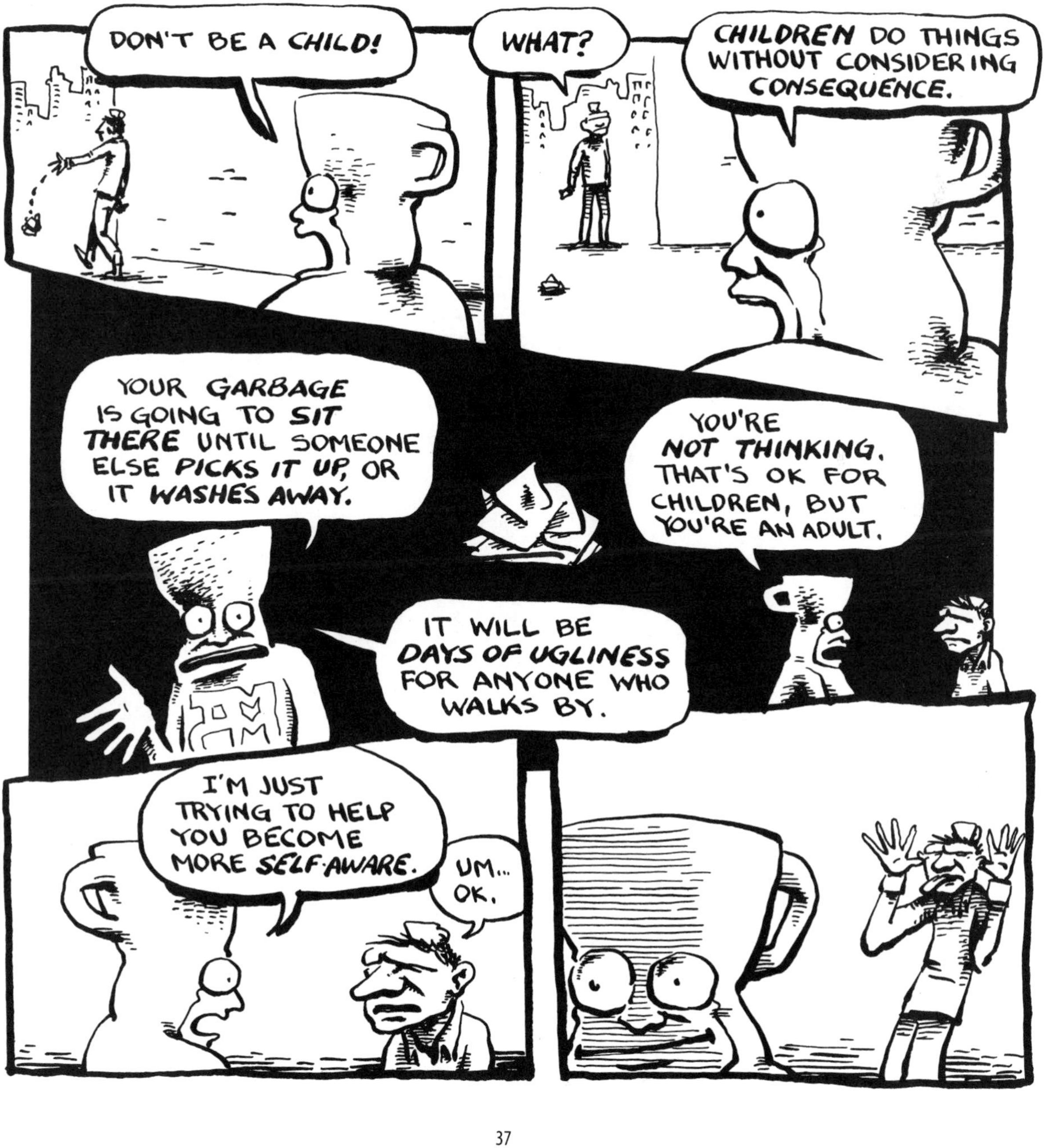
DON'T BE A CHILD!
WHAT?
CHILDREN DO THINGS WITHOUT CONSIDERING CONSEQUENCE.
YOUR GARBAGE IS GOING TO SIT THERE UNTIL SOMEONE ELSE PICKS IT UP, OR IT WASHES AWAY.
YOU'RE NOT THINKING. THAT'S OK FOR CHILDREN, BUT YOU'RE AN ADULT.
IT WILL BE DAYS OF UGLINESS FOR ANYONE WHO WALKS BY.
I'M JUST TRYING TO HELP YOU BECOME MORE SELF-AWARE.
UM... OK.

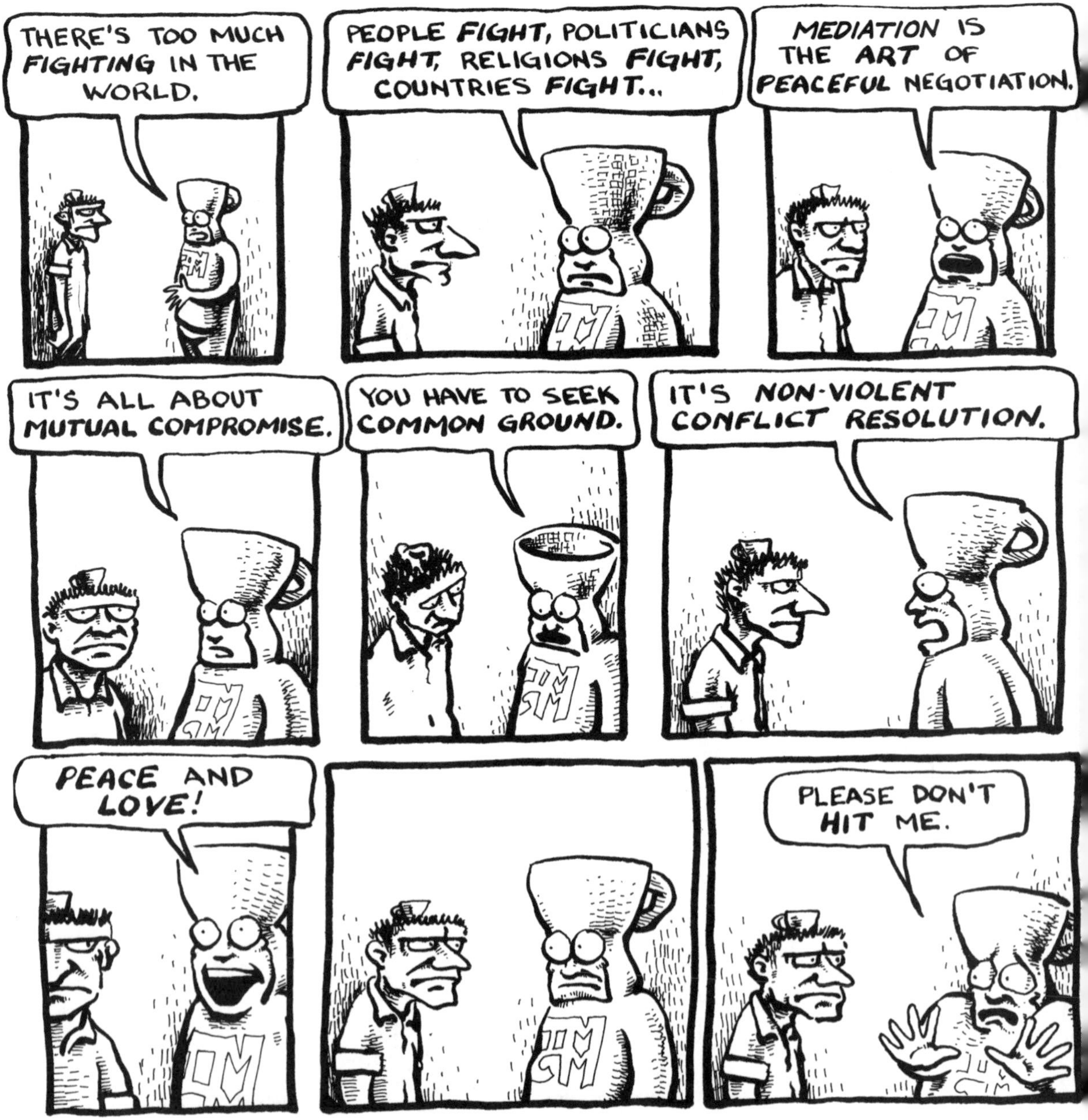
THERE'S TOO MUCH FIGHTING IN THE WORLD.
PEOPLE FIGHT, POLITICIANS FIGHT, RELIGIONS FIGHT, COUNTRIES FIGHT...
MEDIATION IS THE ART OF PEACEFUL NEGOTIATION.
IT'S ALL ABOUT MUTUAL COMPROMISE.
YOU HAVE TO SEEK COMMON GROUND.
IT'S NON-VIOLENT CONFLICT RESOLUTION.
PEACE AND LOVE!
PLEASE DON'T HIT ME.

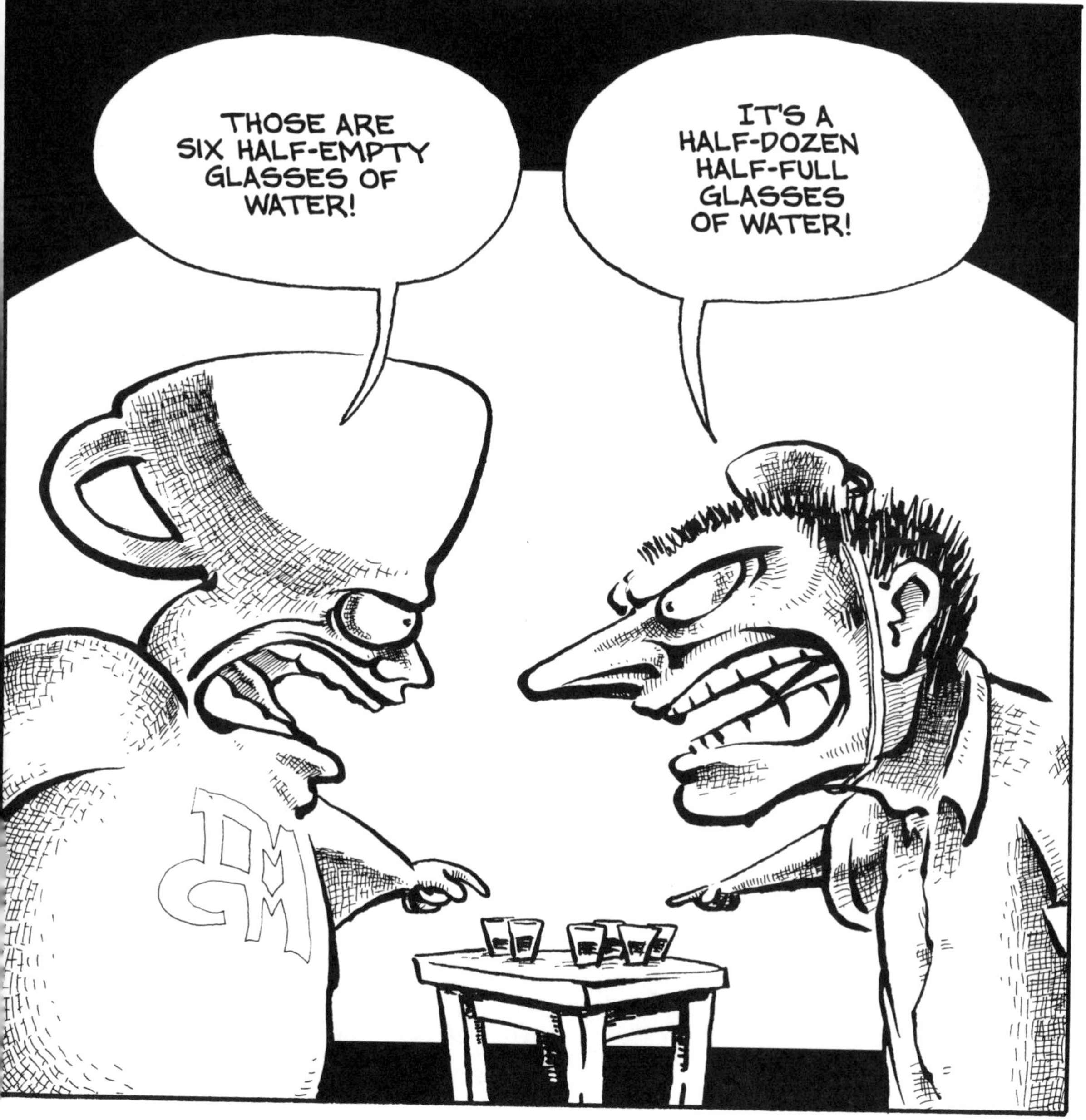
THOSE ARE SIX HALF-EMPTY GLASSES OF WATER!
IT'S A HALF-DOZEN HALF-FULL GLASSES OF WATER!
DM GM

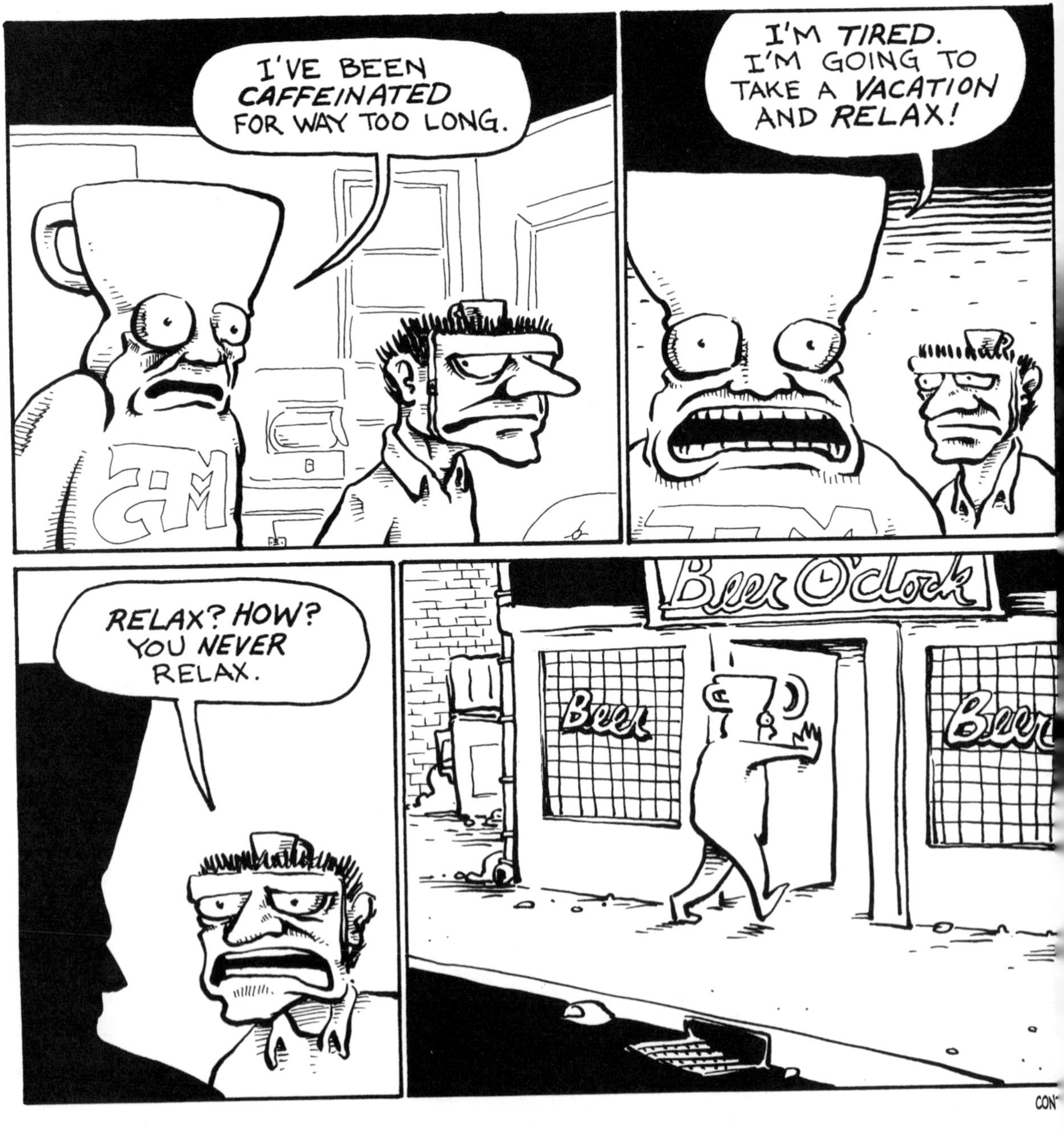
I'VE BEEN CAFFEINATED FOR WAY TOO LONG.
I'M TIRED. I'M GOING TO TAKE A VACATION AND RELAX!
RELAX? HOW? YOU NEVER RELAX.
Beer O'clock
Beer
CON

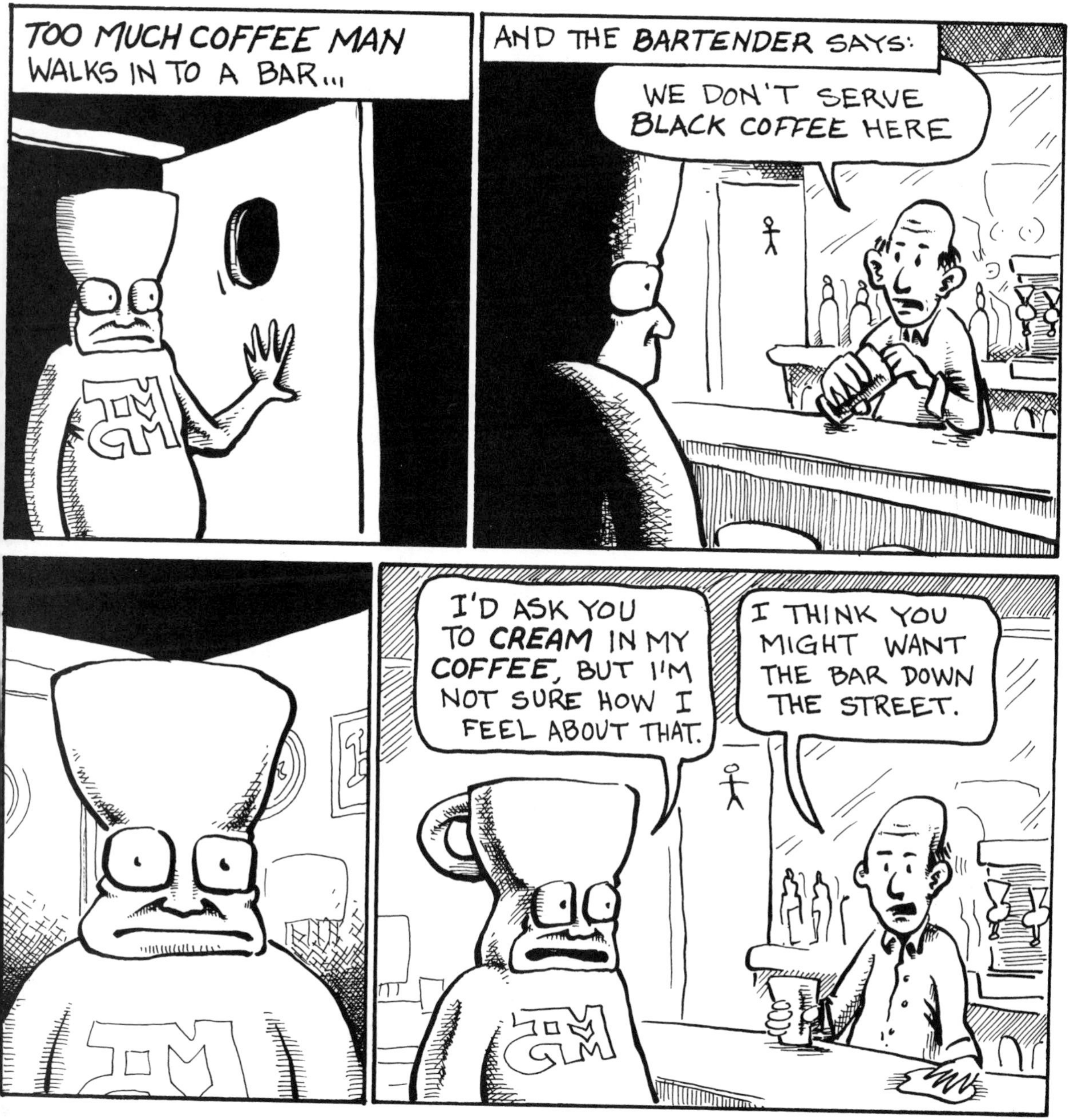
TOO MUCH COFFEE MAN WALKS IN TO A BAR...
AND THE BARTENDER SAYS:
WE DON'T SERVE BLACK COFFEE HERE
I'D ASK YOU TO CREAM IN MY COFFEE, BUT I'M NOT SURE HOW I FEEL ABOUT THAT.
I THINK YOU MIGHT WANT THE BAR DOWN THE STREET.

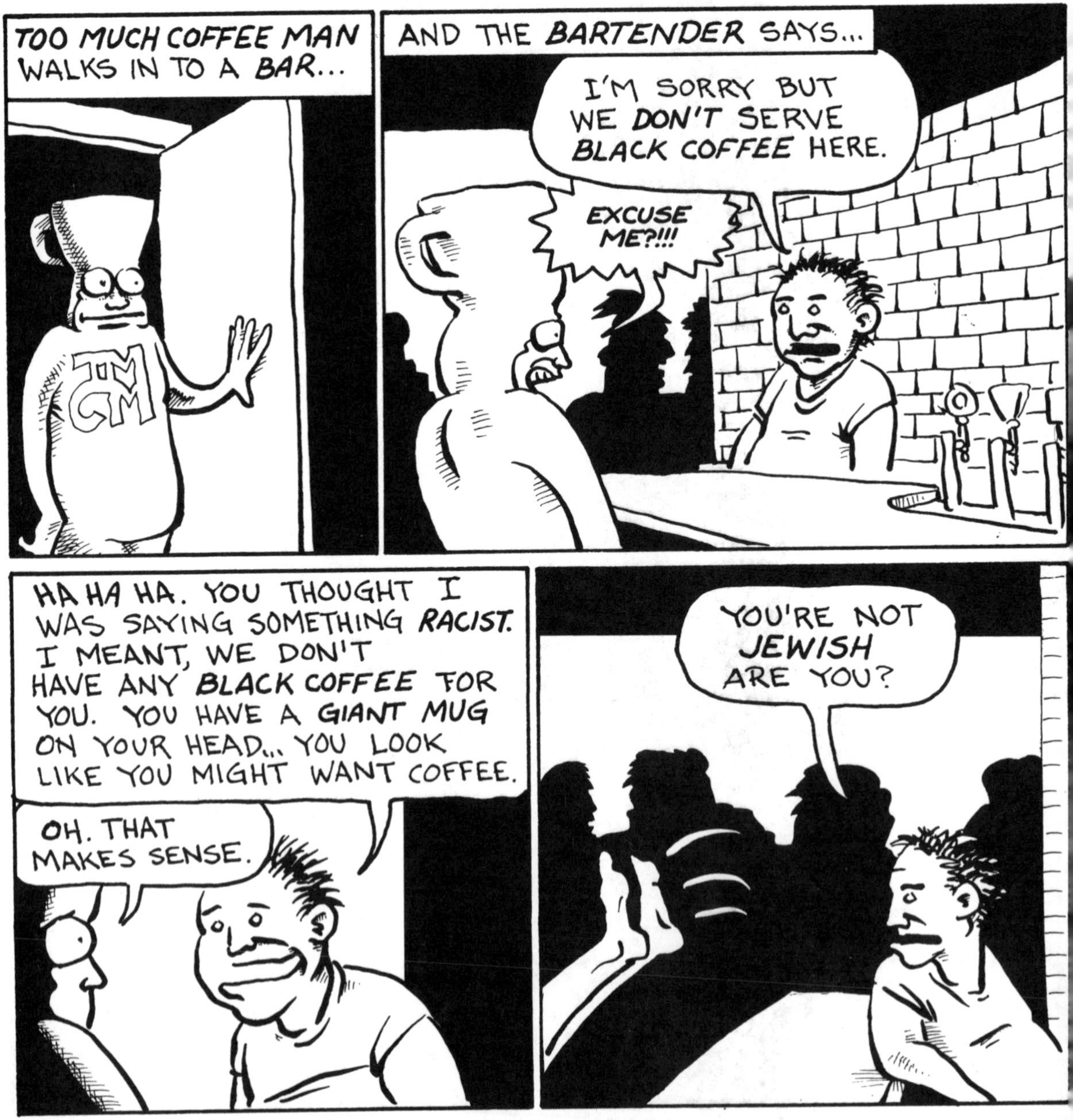
TOO MUCH COFFEE MAN WALKS IN TO A BAR...
TMCM
AND THE BARTENDER SAYS...
I'M SORRY BUT WE DON'T SERVE BLACK COFFEE HERE.
EXCUSE ME?!!!
HA HA HA. YOU THOUGHT I WAS SAYING SOMETHING RACIST. I MEANT, WE DON'T HAVE ANY BLACK COFFEE FOR YOU. YOU HAVE A GIANT MUG ON YOUR HEAD... YOU LOOK LIKE YOU MIGHT WANT COFFEE.
OH. THAT MAKES SENSE.
YOU'RE NOT JEWISH ARE YOU?

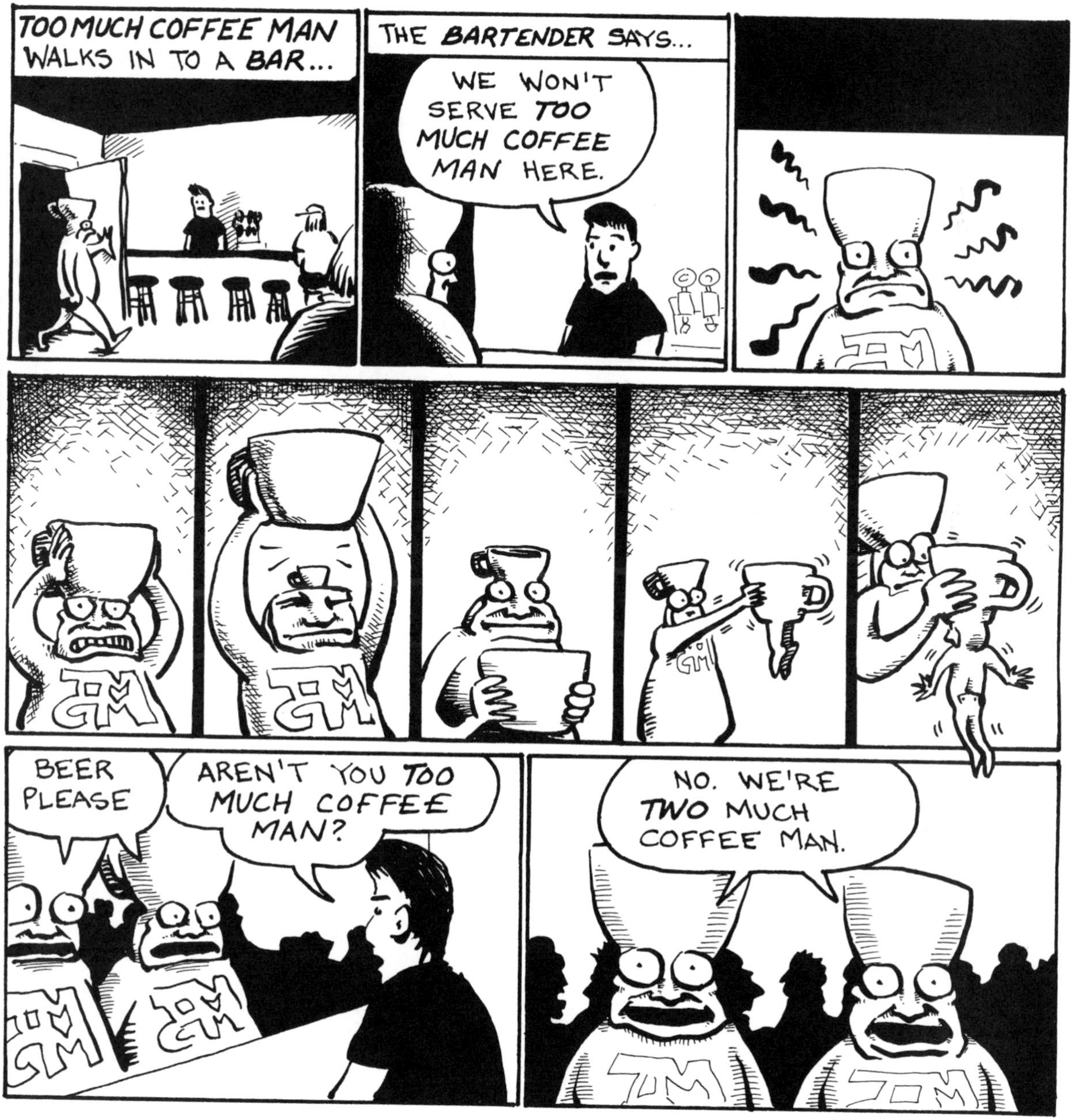
TOO MUCH COFFEE MAN WALKS IN TO A BAR...
THE BARTENDER SAYS...
WE WON'T SERVE TOO MUCH COFFEE MAN HERE.
BEER PLEASE
AREN'T YOU TOO MUCH COFFEE MAN?
NO. WE'RE TWO MUCH COFFEE MAN.

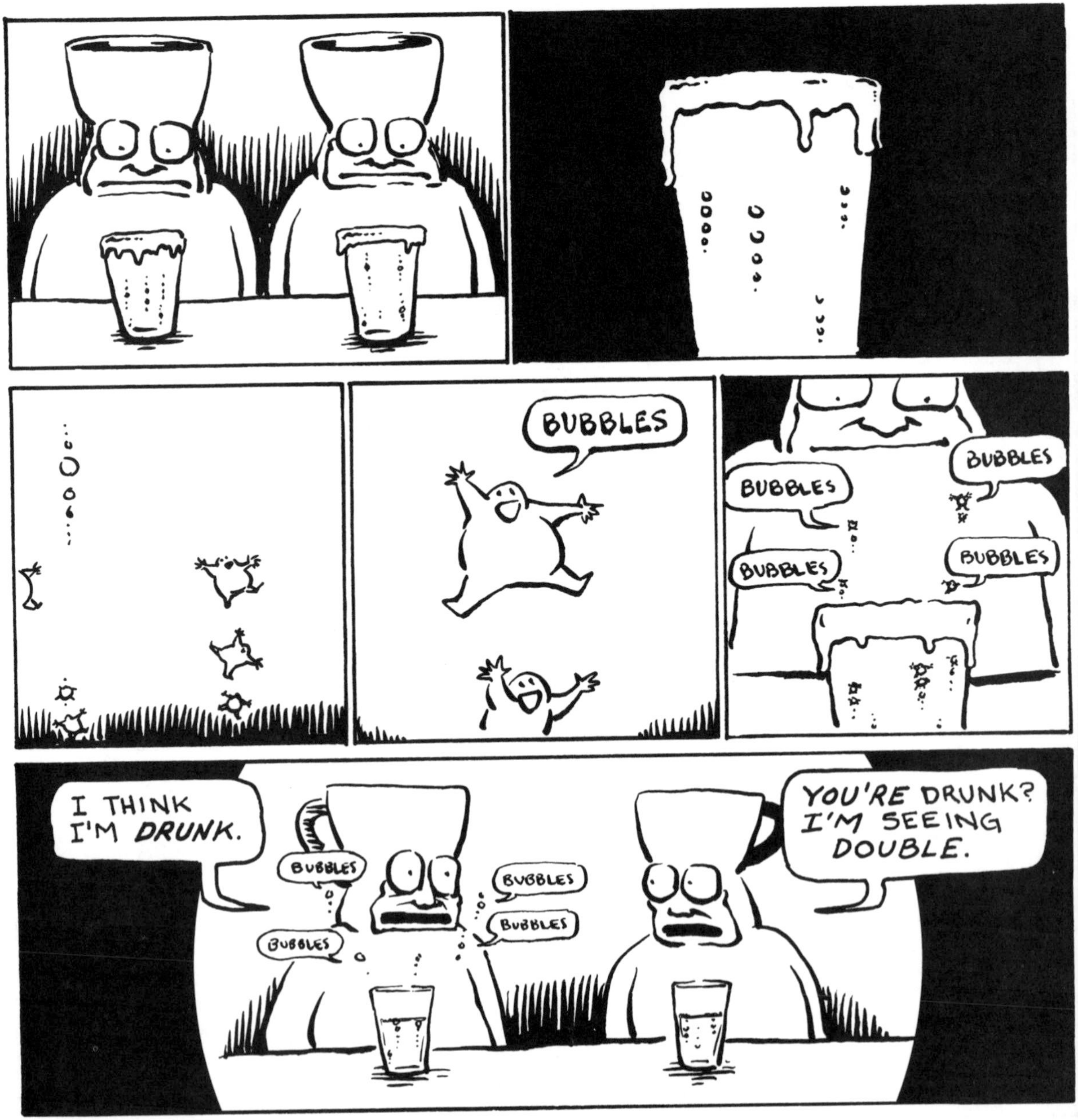
BUBBLES
BUBBLES
BUBBLES
BUBBLES
BUBBLES
I THINK I'M *DRUNK*.
BUBBLES
BUBBLES
BUBBLES
BUBBLES
YOU'RE DRUNK? I'M SEEING DOUBLE.

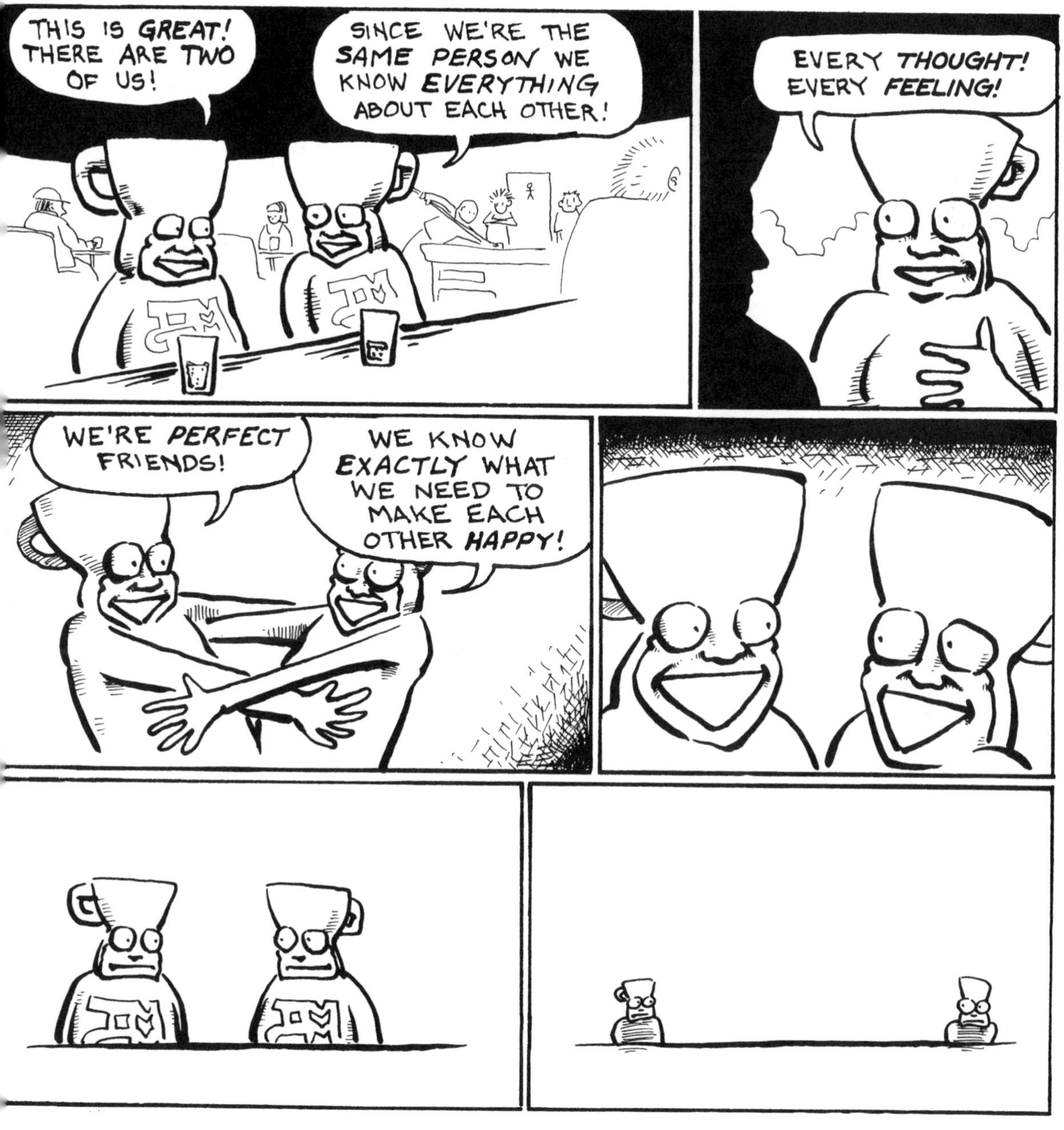
THIS IS GREAT! THERE ARE TWO OF US!
SINCE WE'RE THE SAME PERSON WE KNOW EVERYTHING ABOUT EACH OTHER!
EVERY THOUGHT! EVERY FEELING!
WE'RE PERFECT FRIENDS!
WE KNOW EXACTLY WHAT WE NEED TO MAKE EACH OTHER HAPPY!

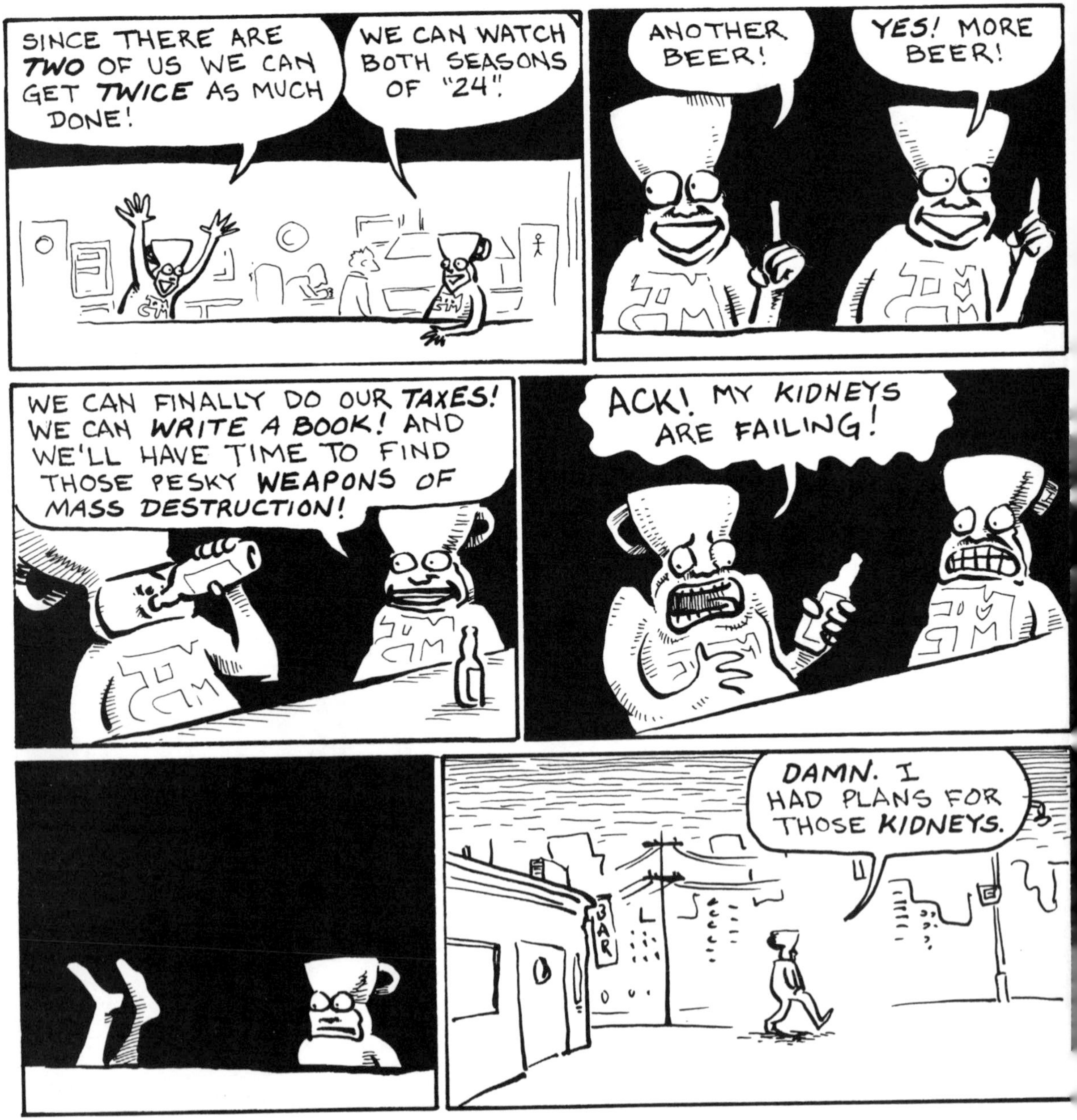
SINCE THERE ARE TWO OF US WE CAN GET TWICE AS MUCH DONE!
WE CAN WATCH BOTH SEASONS OF "24".
ANOTHER BEER!
YES! MORE BEER!
WE CAN FINALLY DO OUR TAXES! WE CAN WRITE A BOOK! AND WE'LL HAVE TIME TO FIND THOSE PESKY WEAPONS OF MASS DESTRUCTION!
ACK! MY KIDNEYS ARE FAILING!
BAR
DAMN. I HAD PLANS FOR THOSE KIDNEYS.

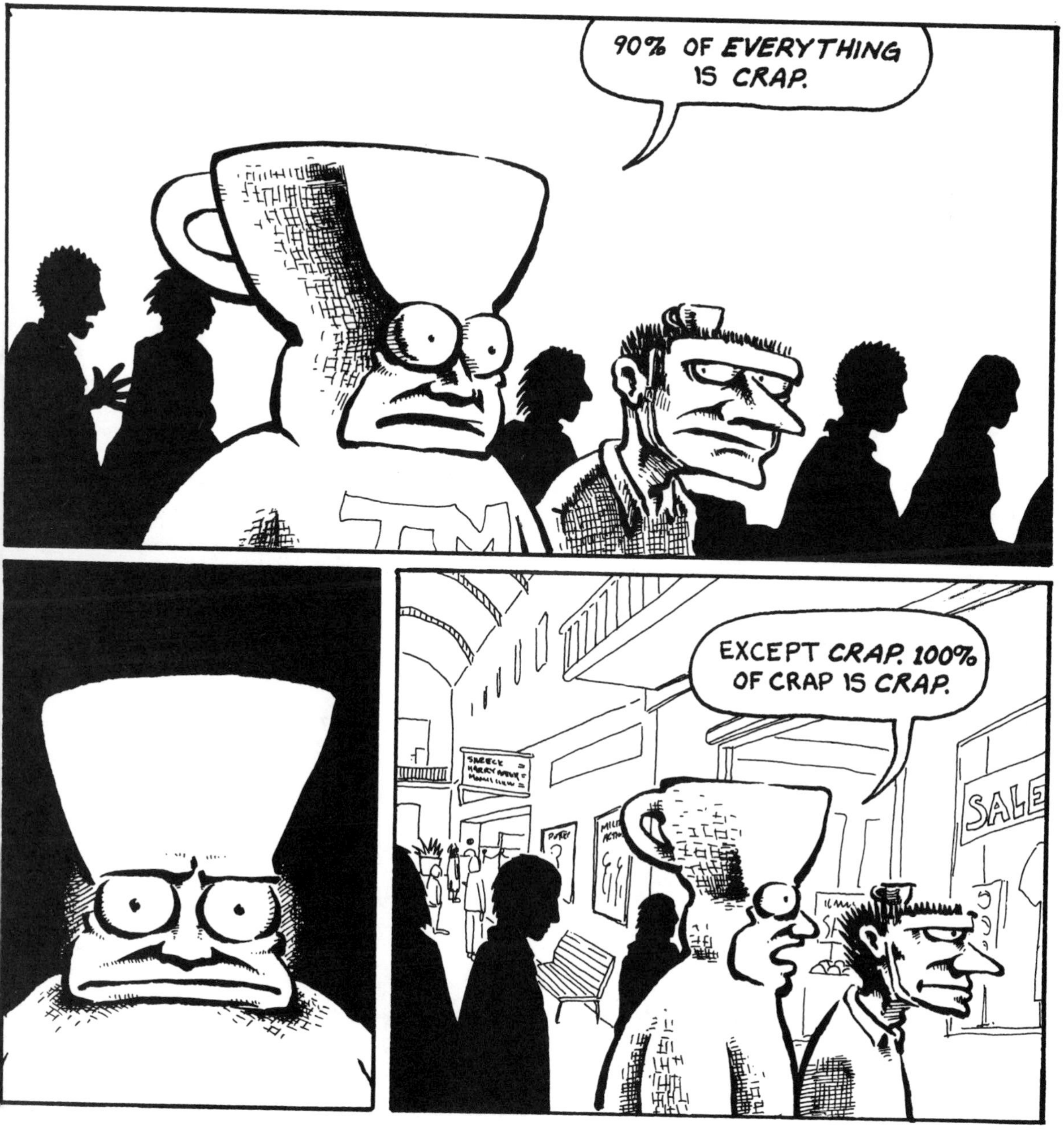
90% OF EVERYTHING IS CRAP.
EXCEPT CRAP. 100% OF CRAP IS CRAP.
SALE

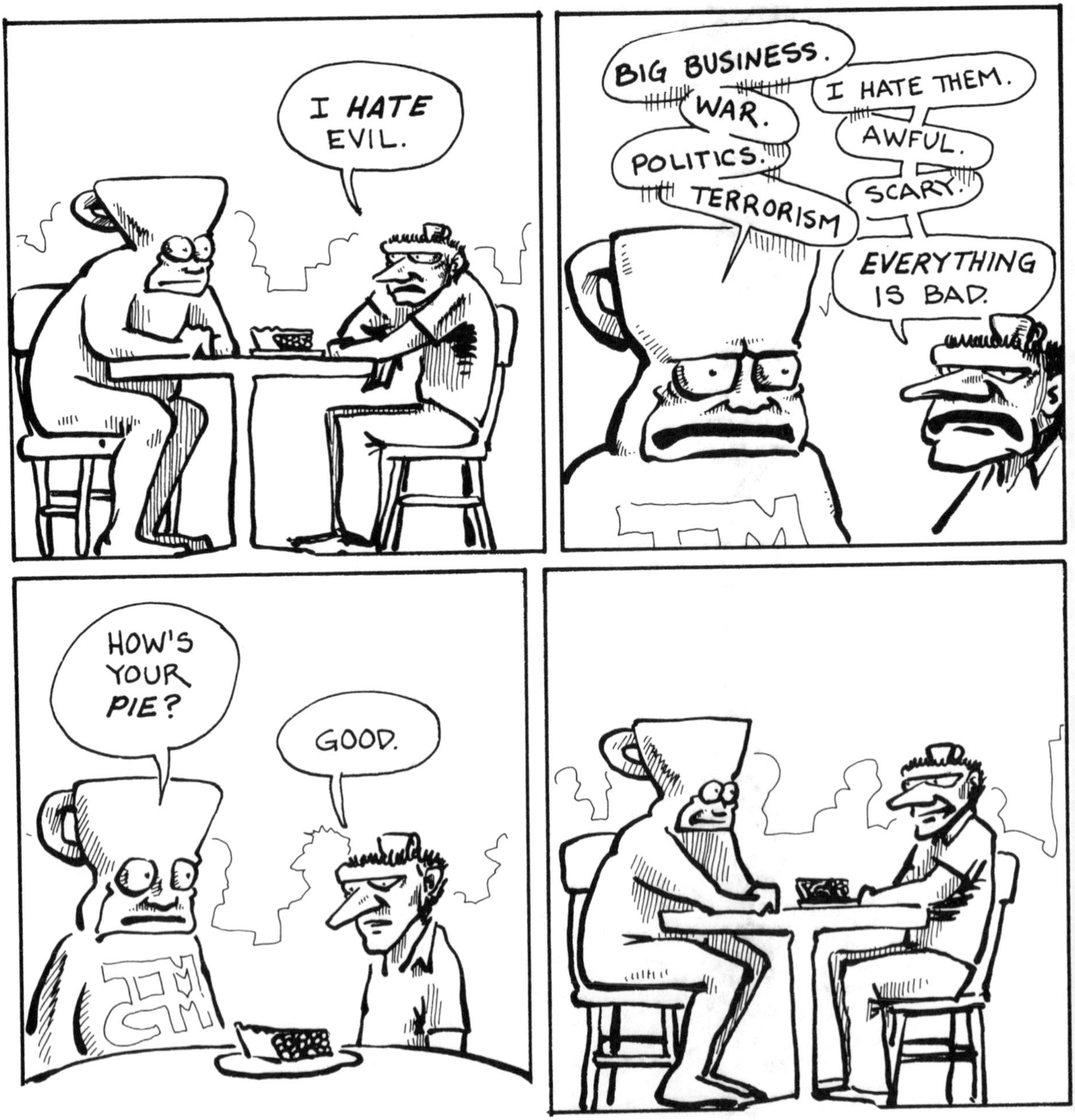
I HATE EVIL.
BIG BUSINESS.
WAR.
POLITICS.
TERRORISM
I HATE THEM.
AWFUL.
SCARY.
EVERYTHING IS BAD.
HOW'S YOUR PIE?
GOOD.

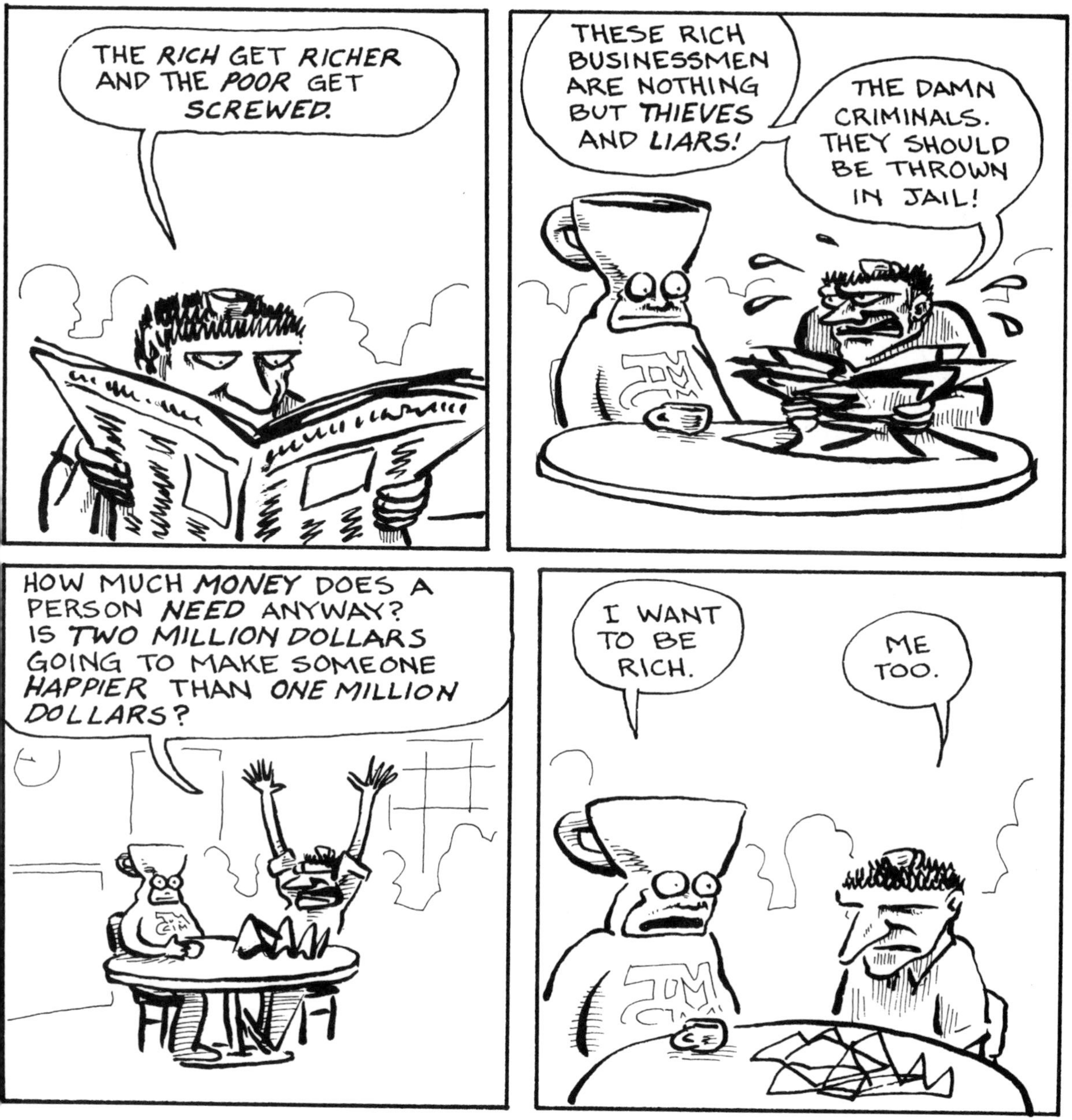
THE RICH GET RICHER AND THE POOR GET SCREWED.
THESE RICH BUSINESSMEN ARE NOTHING BUT THIEVES AND LIARS!
THE DAMN CRIMINALS. THEY SHOULD BE THROWN IN JAIL!
HOW MUCH MONEY DOES A PERSON NEED ANYWAY? IS TWO MILLION DOLLARS GOING TO MAKE SOMEONE HAPPIER THAN ONE MILLION DOLLARS?
I WANT TO BE RICH.
ME TOO.

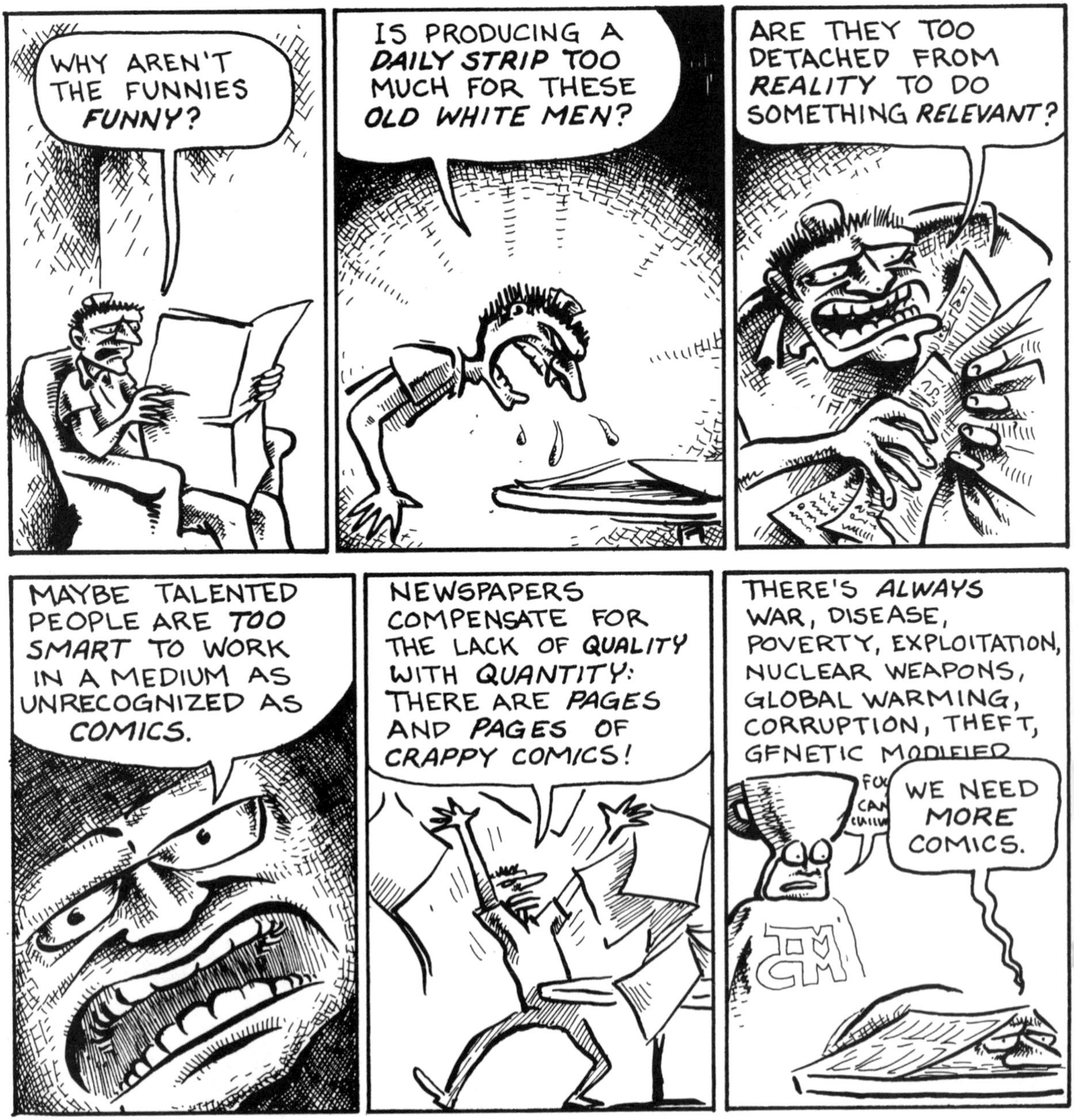

WHY AREN'T THE FUNNIES FUNNY?
IS PRODUCING A DAILY STRIP TOO MUCH FOR THESE OLD WHITE MEN?
ARE THEY TOO DETACHED FROM REALITY TO DO SOMETHING RELEVANT?
MAYBE TALENTED PEOPLE ARE TOO SMART TO WORK IN A MEDIUM AS UNRECOGNIZED AS COMICS.
NEWSPAPERS COMPENSATE FOR THE LACK OF QUALITY WITH QUANTITY: THERE ARE PAGES AND PAGES OF CRAPPY COMICS!
THERE'S ALWAYS WAR, DISEASE, POVERTY, EXPLOITATION, NUCLEAR WEAPONS, GLOBAL WARMING, CORRUPTION, THEFT, GENETIC MODIFIED
WE NEED MORE COMICS.

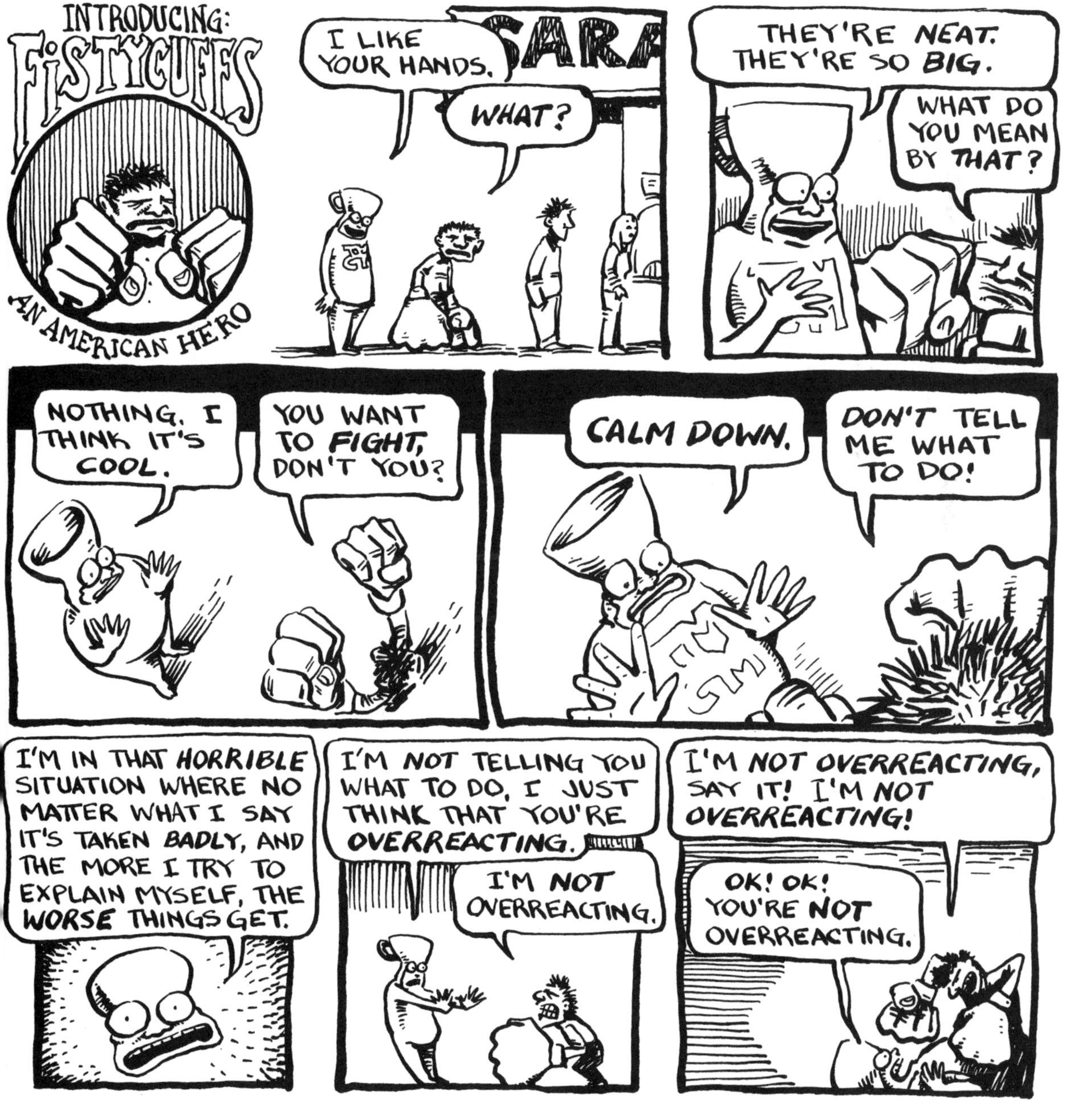
INTRODUCING:
FISTYCUFFS
AN AMERICAN HERO
I LIKE YOUR HANDS.
WHAT?
THEY'RE NEAT. THEY'RE SO BIG.
WHAT DO YOU MEAN BY THAT?
NOTHING. I THINK IT'S COOL.
YOU WANT TO FIGHT, DON'T YOU?
CALM DOWN.
DON'T TELL ME WHAT TO DO!
I'M IN THAT HORRIBLE SITUATION WHERE NO MATTER WHAT I SAY IT'S TAKEN BADLY, AND THE MORE I TRY TO EXPLAIN MYSELF, THE WORSE THINGS GET.
I'M NOT TELLING YOU WHAT TO DO, I JUST THINK THAT YOU'RE OVERREACTING.
I'M NOT OVERREACTING.
I'M NOT OVERREACTING, SAY IT! I'M NOT OVERREACTING!
OK! OK! YOU'RE NOT OVERREACTING.

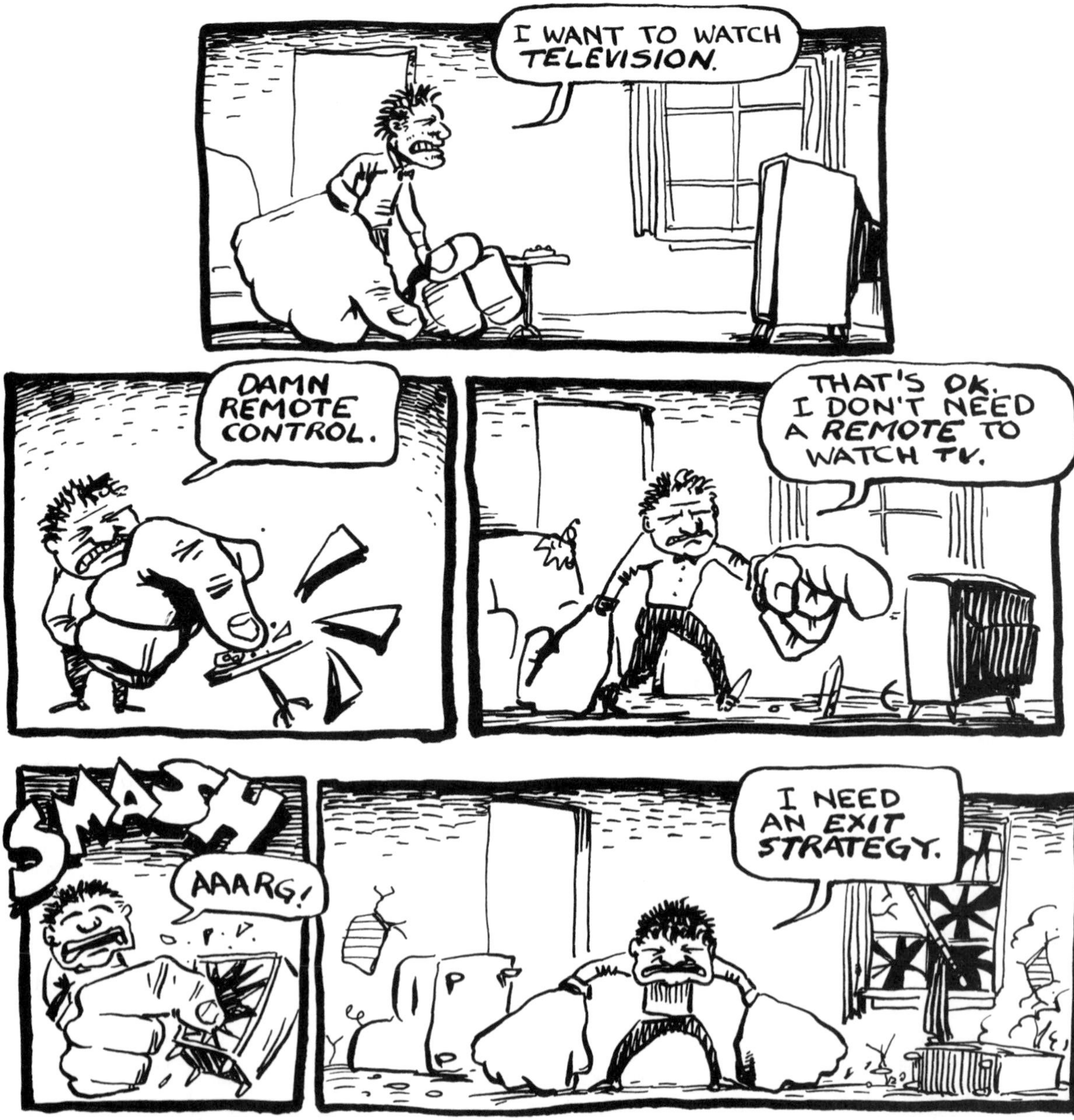
I WANT TO WATCH TELEVISION.
DAMN REMOTE CONTROL.
THAT'S OK. I DON'T NEED A REMOTE TO WATCH TV.
SMASH
AAARG!
I NEED AN EXIT STRATEGY.

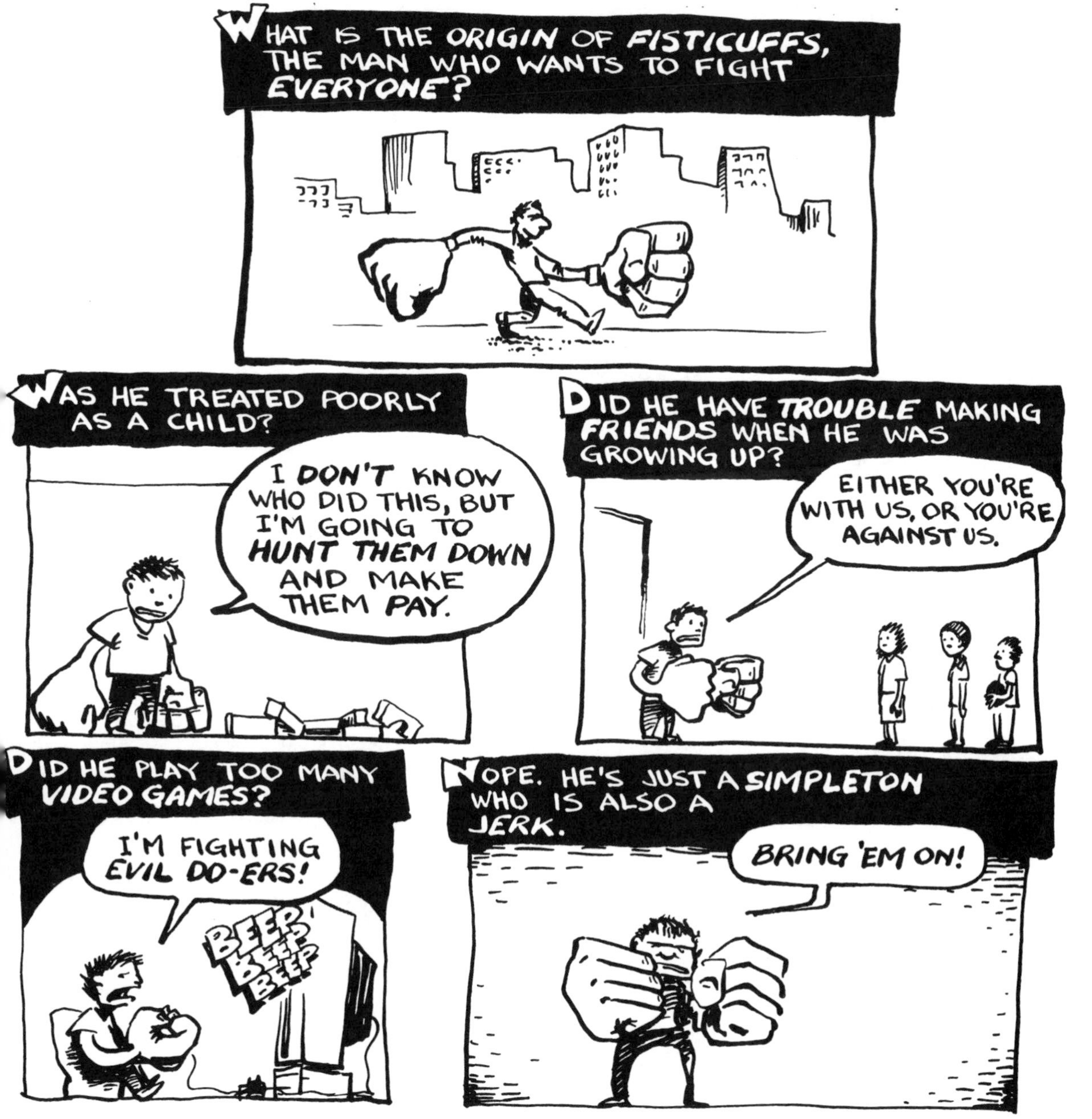
WHAT IS THE ORIGIN OF FISTICUFFS, THE MAN WHO WANTS TO FIGHT EVERYONE?
WAS HE TREATED POORLY AS A CHILD?
I DON'T KNOW WHO DID THIS, BUT I'M GOING TO HUNT THEM DOWN AND MAKE THEM PAY.
DID HE HAVE TROUBLE MAKING FRIENDS WHEN HE WAS GROWING UP?
EITHER YOU'RE WITH US, OR YOU'RE AGAINST US.
DID HE PLAY TOO MANY VIDEO GAMES?
I'M FIGHTING EVIL DO-ERS!
BEEP BEEP BEEP
NOPE. HE'S JUST A SIMPLETON WHO IS ALSO A JERK.
BRING 'EM ON!

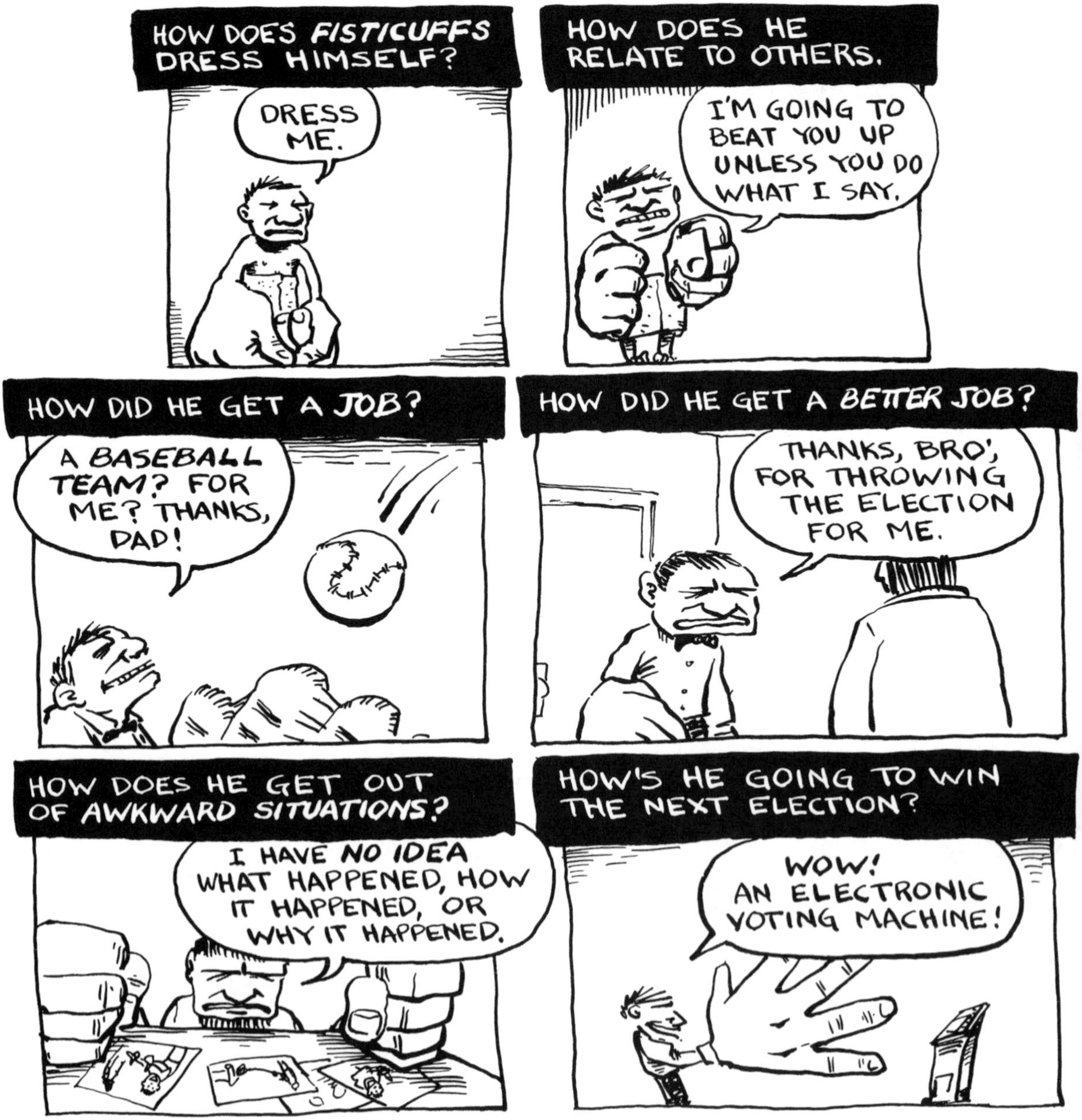
HOW DOES FISTICUFFS DRESS HIMSELF?
DRESS ME.
HOW DOES HE RELATE TO OTHERS.
I'M GOING TO BEAT YOU UP UNLESS YOU DO WHAT I SAY.
HOW DID HE GET A JOB?
A BASEBALL TEAM? FOR ME? THANKS, DAD!
HOW DID HE GET A BETTER JOB?
THANKS, BRO', FOR THROWING THE ELECTION FOR ME.
HOW DOES HE GET OUT OF AWKWARD SITUATIONS?
I HAVE NO IDEA WHAT HAPPENED, HOW IT HAPPENED, OR WHY IT HAPPENED.
HOW'S HE GOING TO WIN THE NEXT ELECTION?
WOW! AN ELECTRONIC VOTING MACHINE!

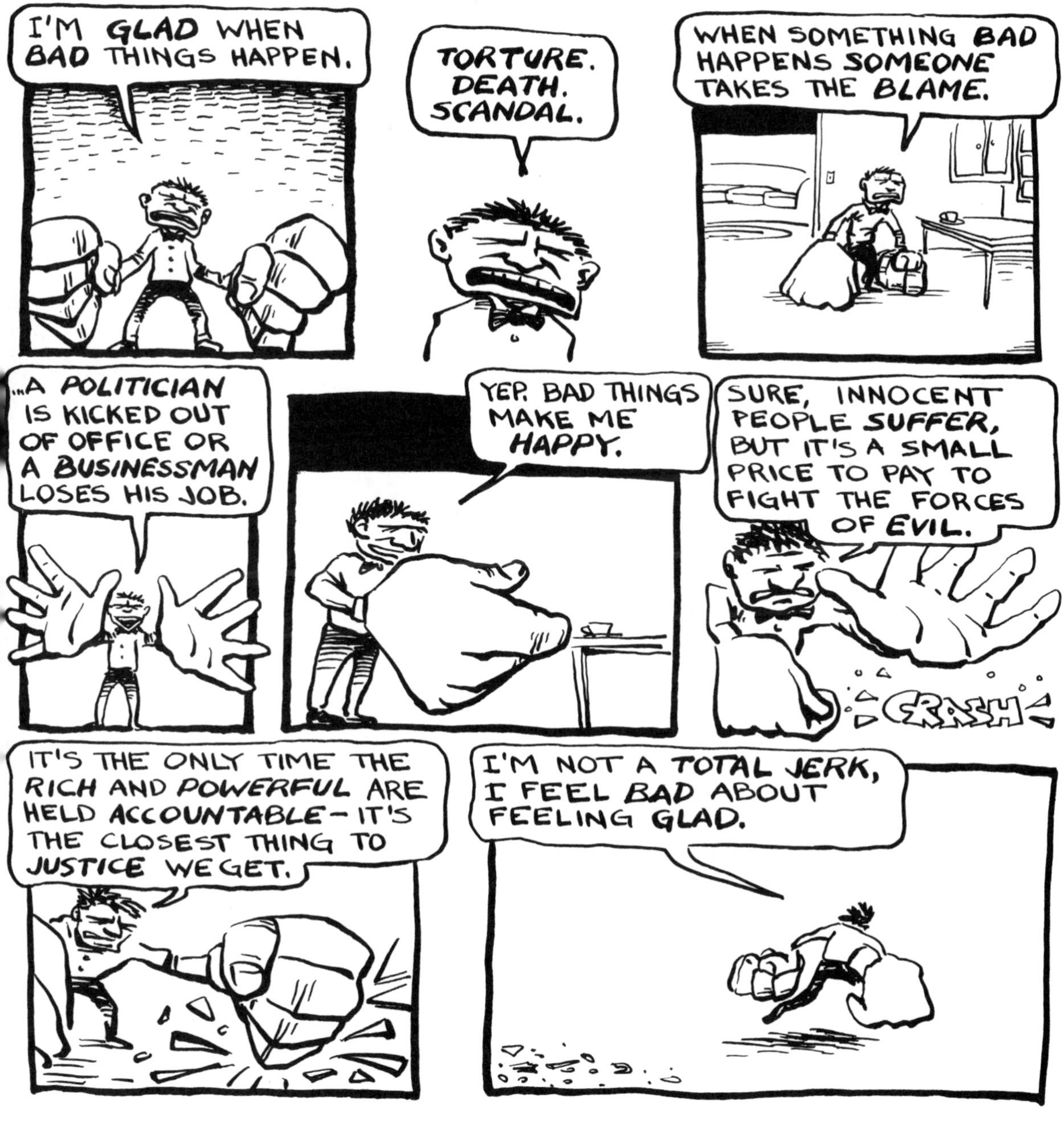
I'M GLAD WHEN BAD THINGS HAPPEN.
TORTURE. DEATH. SCANDAL.
WHEN SOMETHING BAD HAPPENS SOMEONE TAKES THE BLAME.
...A POLITICIAN IS KICKED OUT OF OFFICE OR A BUSINESSMAN LOSES HIS JOB.
YEP. BAD THINGS MAKE ME HAPPY.
SURE, INNOCENT PEOPLE SUFFER, BUT IT'S A SMALL PRICE TO PAY TO FIGHT THE FORCES OF EVIL.
CRASH
IT'S THE ONLY TIME THE RICH AND POWERFUL ARE HELD ACCOUNTABLE - IT'S THE CLOSEST THING TO JUSTICE WE GET.
I'M NOT A TOTAL JERK, I FEEL BAD ABOUT FEELING GLAD.

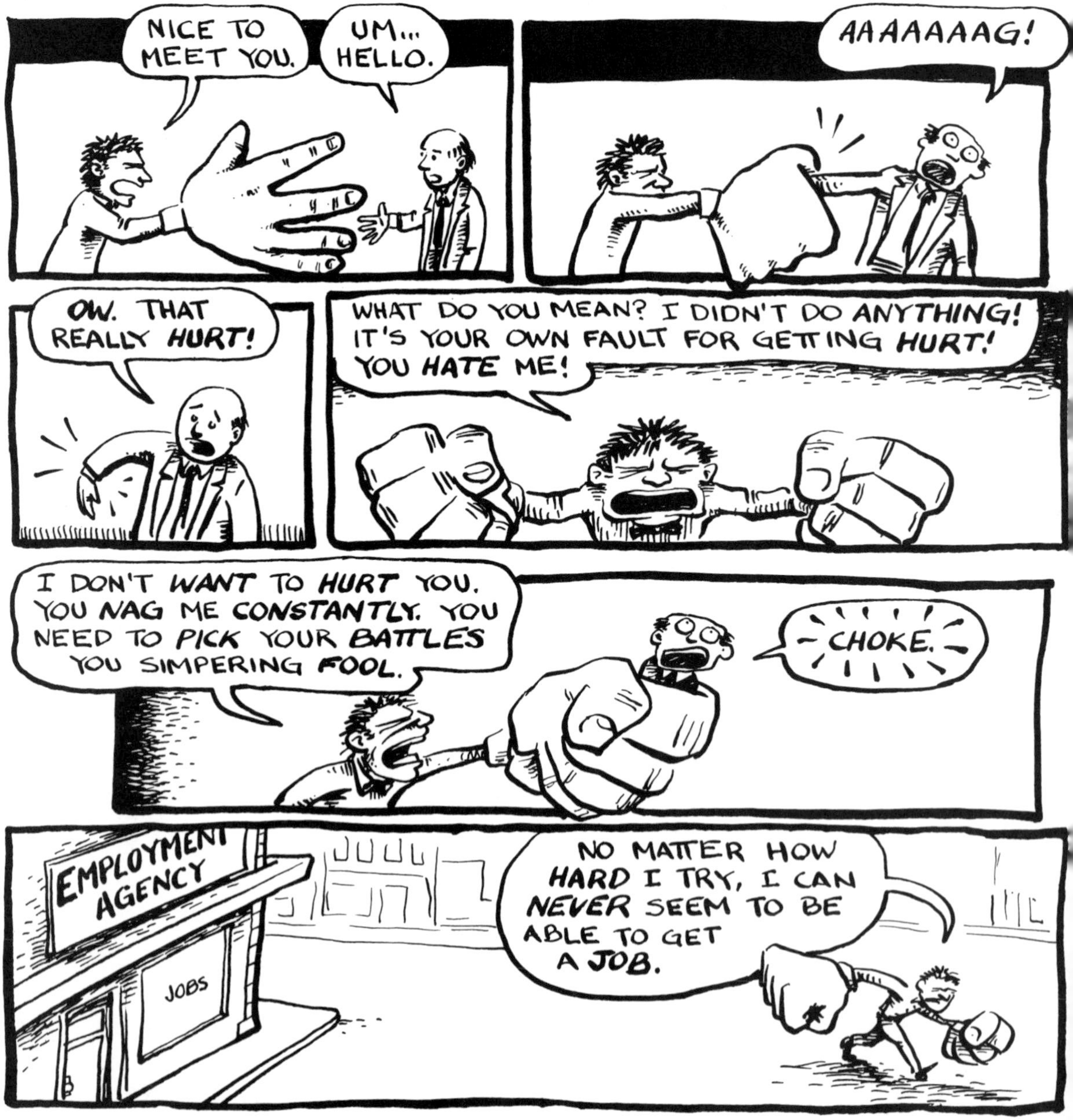
NICE TO MEET YOU.
UM... HELLO.
AAAAAAAG!
OW. THAT REALLY HURT!
WHAT DO YOU MEAN? I DIDN'T DO ANYTHING! IT'S YOUR OWN FAULT FOR GETTING HURT! YOU HATE ME!
I DON'T WANT TO HURT YOU. YOU NAG ME CONSTANTLY. YOU NEED TO PICK YOUR BATTLES YOU SIMPERING FOOL.
CHOKE.
EMPLOYMENT AGENCY
JOBS
NO MATTER HOW HARD I TRY, I CAN NEVER SEEM TO BE ABLE TO GET A JOB.

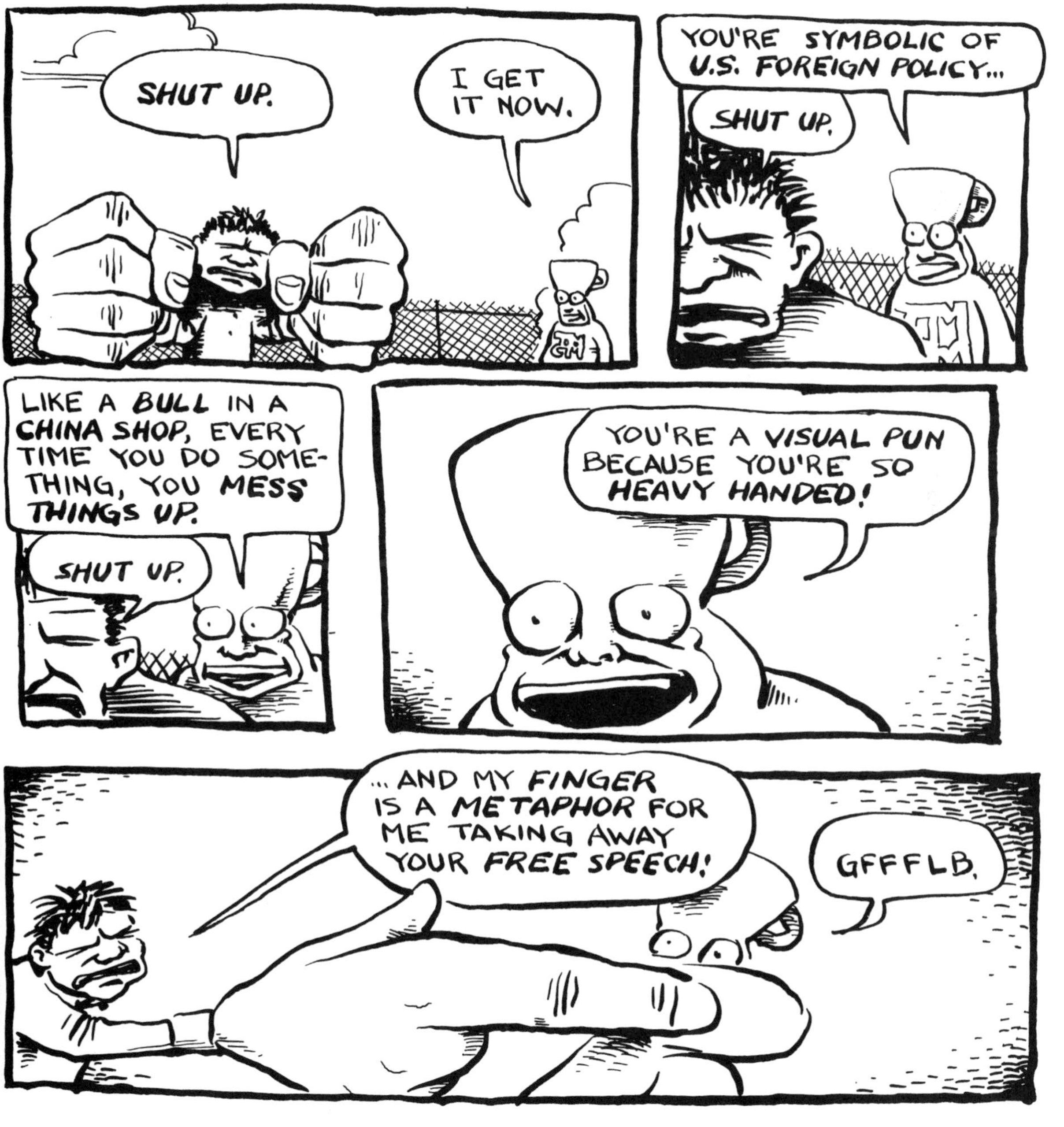
SHUT UP.
I GET IT NOW.
YOU'RE SYMBOLIC OF U.S. FOREIGN POLICY...
SHUT UP.
LIKE A BULL IN A CHINA SHOP, EVERY TIME YOU DO SOME-THING, YOU MESS THINGS UP.
SHUT UP.
YOU'RE A VISUAL PUN BECAUSE YOU'RE SO HEAVY HANDED!
...AND MY FINGER IS A METAPHOR FOR ME TAKING AWAY YOUR FREE SPEECH!
GFFFLB.

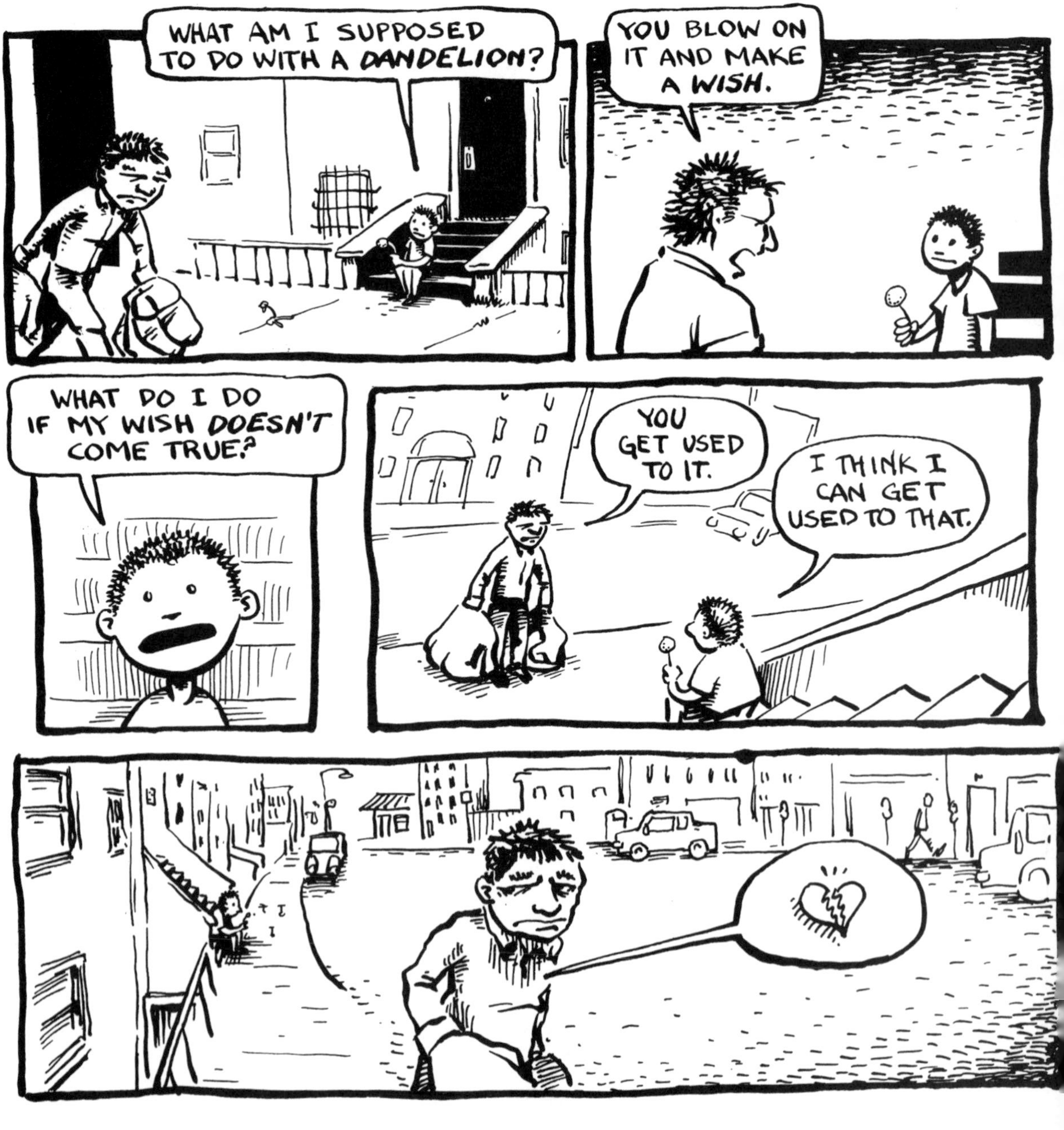
WHAT AM I SUPPOSED TO DO WITH A DANDELION?
YOU BLOW ON IT AND MAKE A WISH.
WHAT DO I DO IF MY WISH DOESN'T COME TRUE?
YOU GET USED TO IT.
I THINK I CAN GET USED TO THAT.

CHAPTER TWO

WINNING THE WAR WITHIN

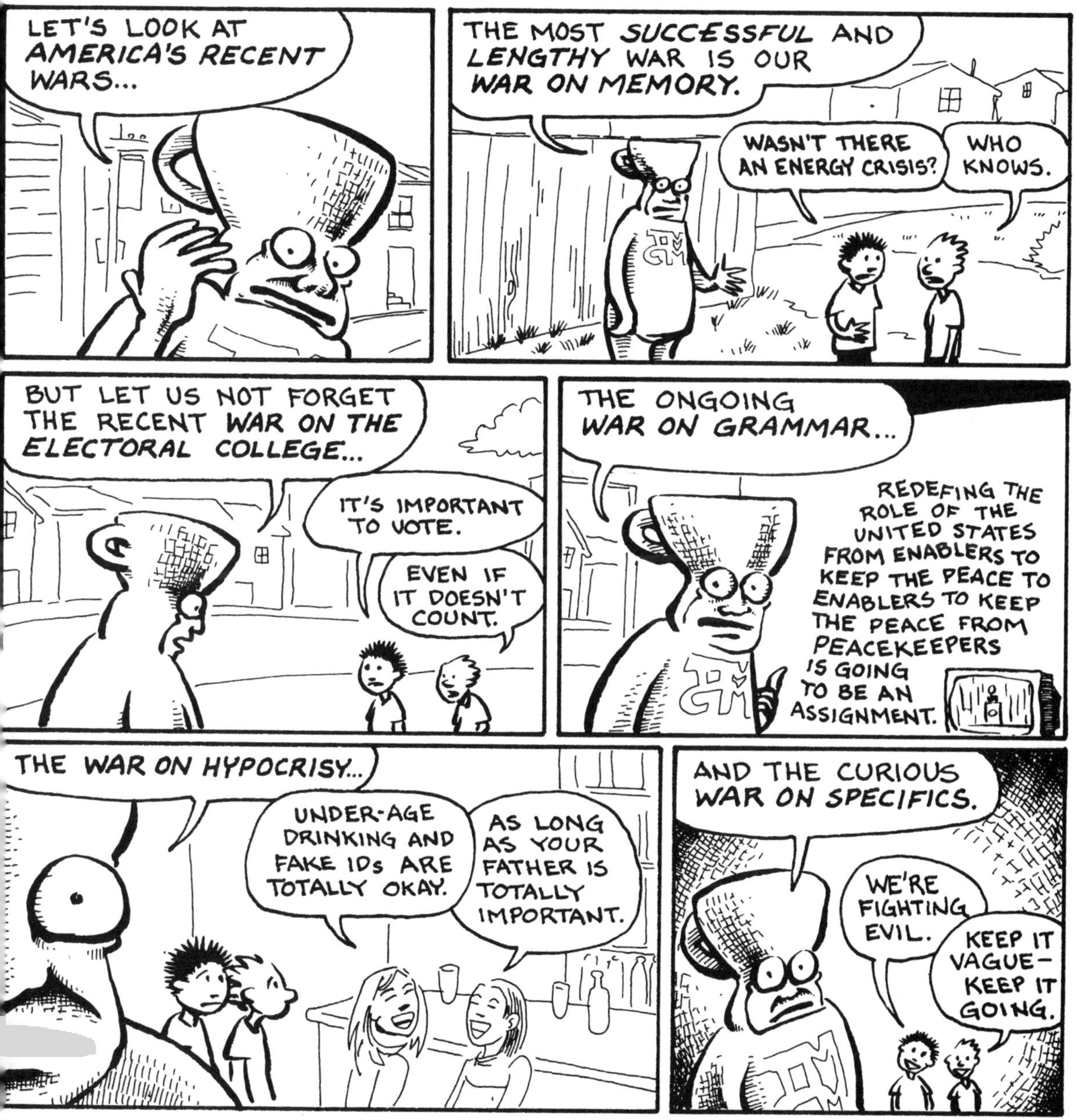

LET'S LOOK AT AMERICA'S RECENT WARS...
THE MOST SUCCESSFUL AND LENGTHY WAR IS OUR WAR ON MEMORY.
WASN'T THERE AN ENERGY CRISIS?
WHO KNOWS.
BUT LET US NOT FORGET THE RECENT WAR ON THE ELECTORAL COLLEGE...
IT'S IMPORTANT TO VOTE.
EVEN IF IT DOESN'T COUNT.
THE ONGOING WAR ON GRAMMAR...
REDEFING THE ROLE OF THE UNITED STATES FROM ENABLERS TO KEEP THE PEACE TO ENABLERS TO KEEP THE PEACE FROM PEACEKEEPERS IS GOING TO BE AN ASSIGNMENT.
THE WAR ON HYPOCRISY...
UNDER-AGE DRINKING AND FAKE IDs ARE TOTALLY OKAY.
AS LONG AS YOUR FATHER IS TOTALLY IMPORTANT.
AND THE CURIOUS WAR ON SPECIFICS.
WE'RE FIGHTING EVIL.
KEEP IT VAGUE— KEEP IT GOING.

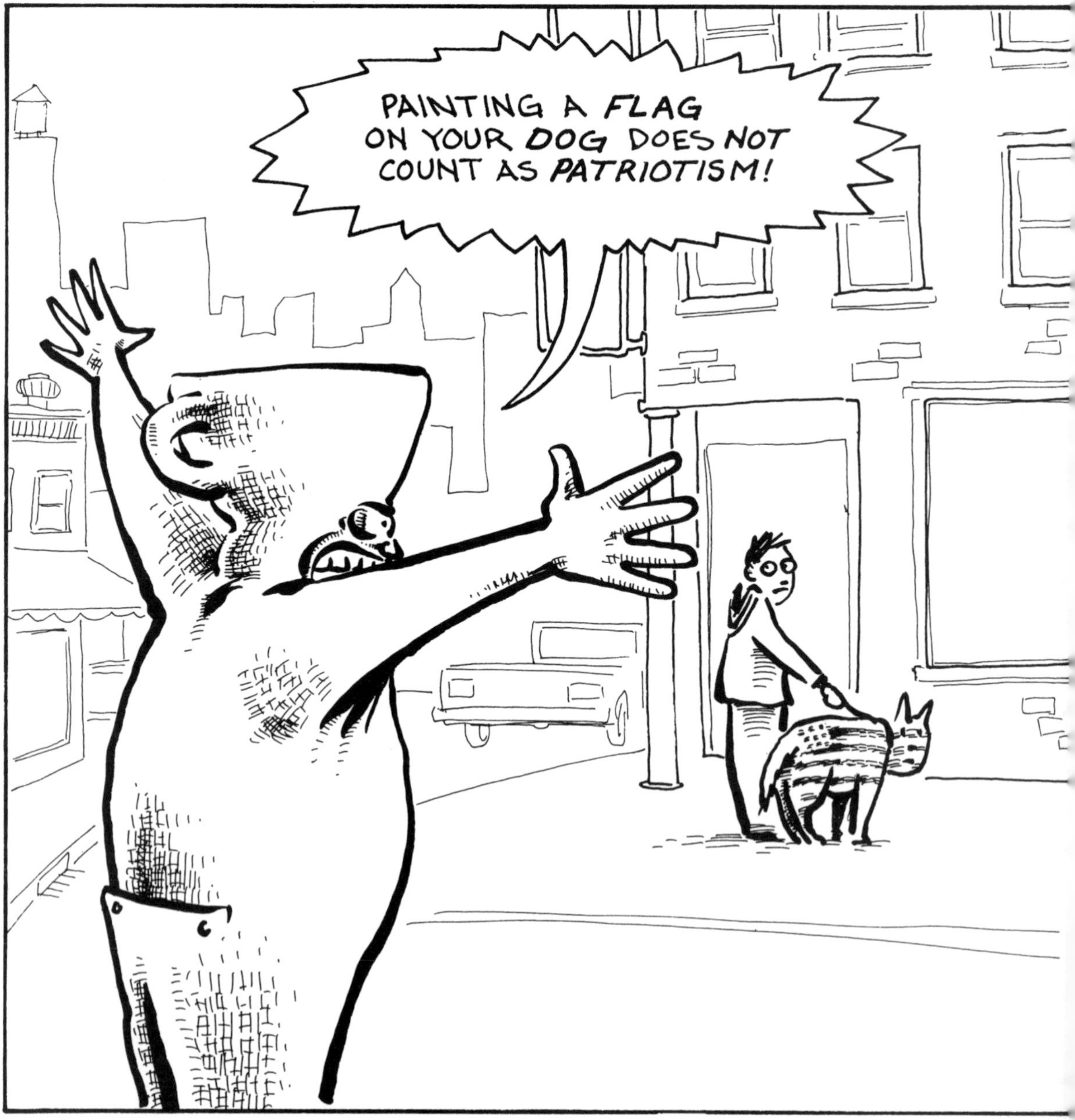
PAINTING A FLAG ON YOUR DOG DOES NOT COUNT AS PATRIOTISM!

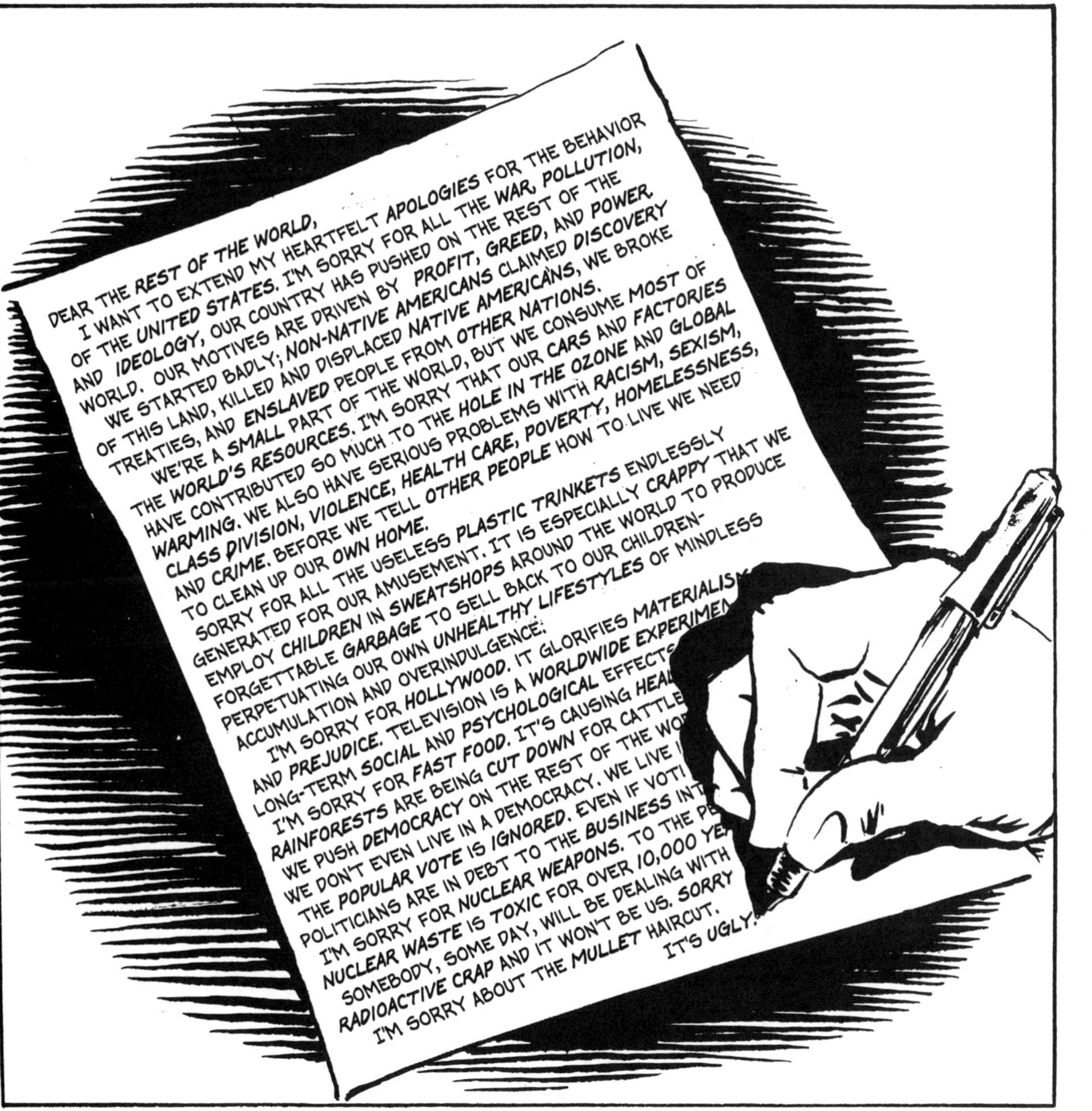
DEAR THE REST OF THE WORLD,
I WANT TO EXTEND MY HEARTFELT APOLOGIES FOR THE BEHAVIOR
OF THE UNITED STATES. I'M SORRY FOR ALL THE WAR, POLLUTION,
AND IDEOLOGY, OUR COUNTRY HAS PUSHED ON THE REST OF THE
WORLD. OUR MOTIVES ARE DRIVEN BY PROFIT, GREED, AND POWER.
WE STARTED BADLY; NON-NATIVE AMERICANS CLAIMED DISCOVERY
OF THIS LAND, KILLED AND DISPLACED NATIVE AMERICANS, WE BROKE
TREATIES, AND ENSLAVED PEOPLE FROM OTHER NATIONS.
WE'RE A SMALL PART OF THE WORLD, BUT WE CONSUME MOST OF
THE WORLD'S RESOURCES. I'M SORRY THAT OUR CARS AND FACTORIES
HAVE CONTRIBUTED SO MUCH TO THE HOLE IN THE OZONE AND GLOBAL
WARMING. WE ALSO HAVE SERIOUS PROBLEMS WITH RACISM, SEXISM,
CLASS DIVISION, VIOLENCE, HEALTH CARE, POVERTY, HOMELESSNESS,
AND CRIME. BEFORE WE TELL OTHER PEOPLE HOW TO LIVE WE NEED
TO CLEAN UP OUR OWN HOME.
SORRY FOR ALL THE USELESS PLASTIC TRINKETS ENDLESSLY
GENERATED FOR OUR AMUSEMENT. IT IS ESPECIALLY CRAPPY THAT WE
EMPLOY CHILDREN IN SWEATSHOPS AROUND THE WORLD TO PRODUCE
FORGETTABLE GARBAGE TO SELL BACK TO OUR CHILDREN-
PERPETUATING OUR OWN UNHEALTHY LIFESTYLES OF MINDLESS
ACCUMULATION AND OVERINDULGENCE.
I'M SORRY FOR HOLLYWOOD. IT GLORIFIES MATERIALIS
AND PREJUDICE. TELEVISION IS A WORLDWIDE EXPERIMEN
LONG-TERM SOCIAL AND PSYCHOLOGICAL EFFECTS
I'M SORRY FOR FAST FOOD. IT'S CAUSING HEAL
RAINFORESTS ARE BEING CUT DOWN FOR CATTLE
WE PUSH DEMOCRACY ON THE REST OF THE WO
WE DON'T EVEN LIVE IN A DEMOCRACY. WE LIVE I
THE POPULAR VOTE IS IGNORED. EVEN IF VOTI
POLITICIANS ARE IN DEBT TO THE BUSINESS INT
I'M SORRY FOR NUCLEAR WEAPONS. TO THE PE
NUCLEAR WASTE IS TOXIC FOR OVER 10,000 YE
SOMEBODY, SOME DAY, WILL BE DEALING WITH
RADIOACTIVE CRAP AND IT WON'T BE US. SORRY
I'M SORRY ABOUT THE MULLET HAIRCUT.
IT'S UGLY.

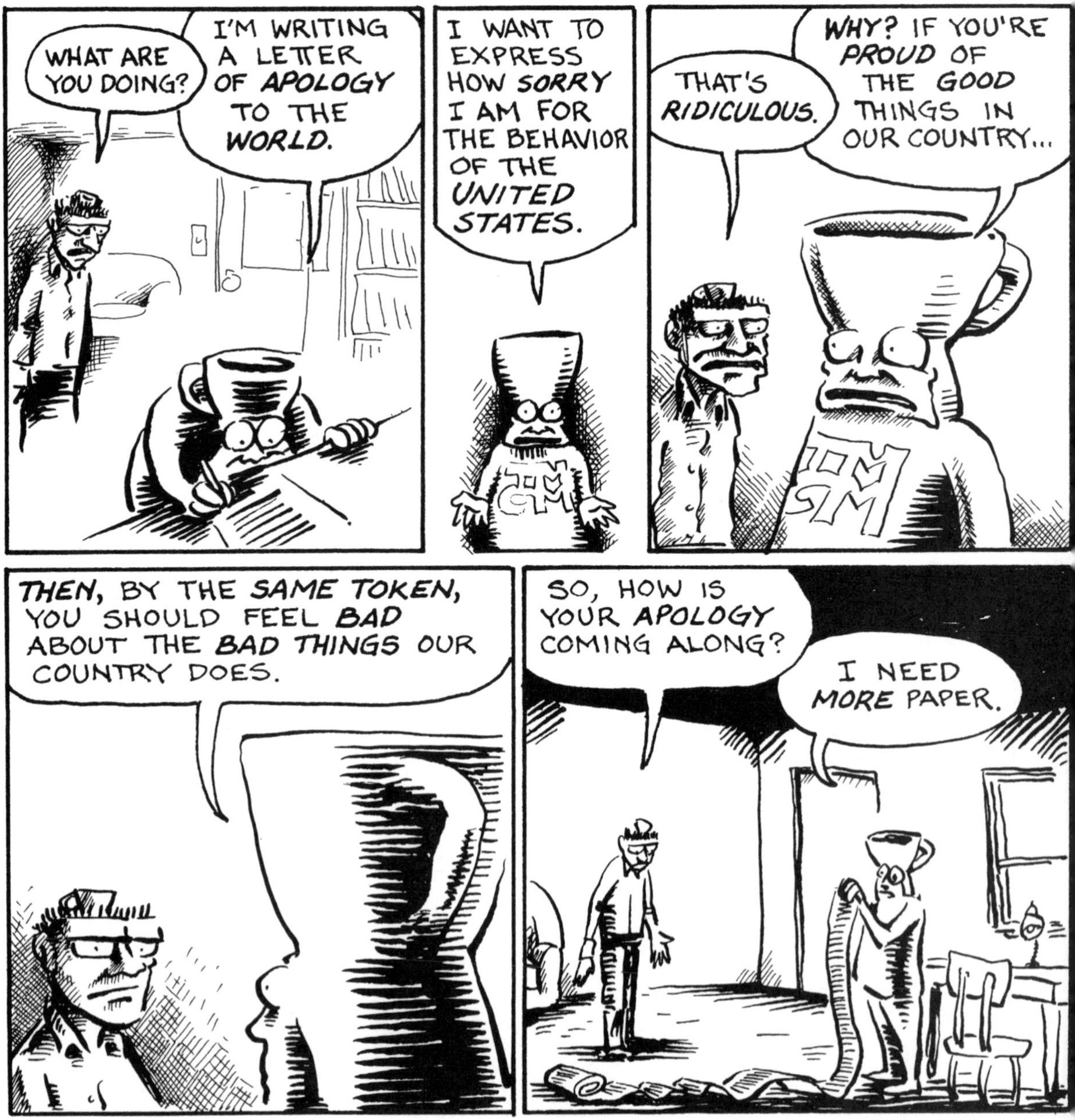
WHAT ARE YOU DOING?
I'M WRITING A LETTER OF APOLOGY TO THE WORLD.
I WANT TO EXPRESS HOW SORRY I AM FOR THE BEHAVIOR OF THE UNITED STATES.
THAT'S RIDICULOUS.
WHY? IF YOU'RE PROUD OF THE GOOD THINGS IN OUR COUNTRY...
THEN, BY THE SAME TOKEN, YOU SHOULD FEEL BAD ABOUT THE BAD THINGS OUR COUNTRY DOES.
SO, HOW IS YOUR APOLOGY COMING ALONG?
I NEED MORE PAPER.

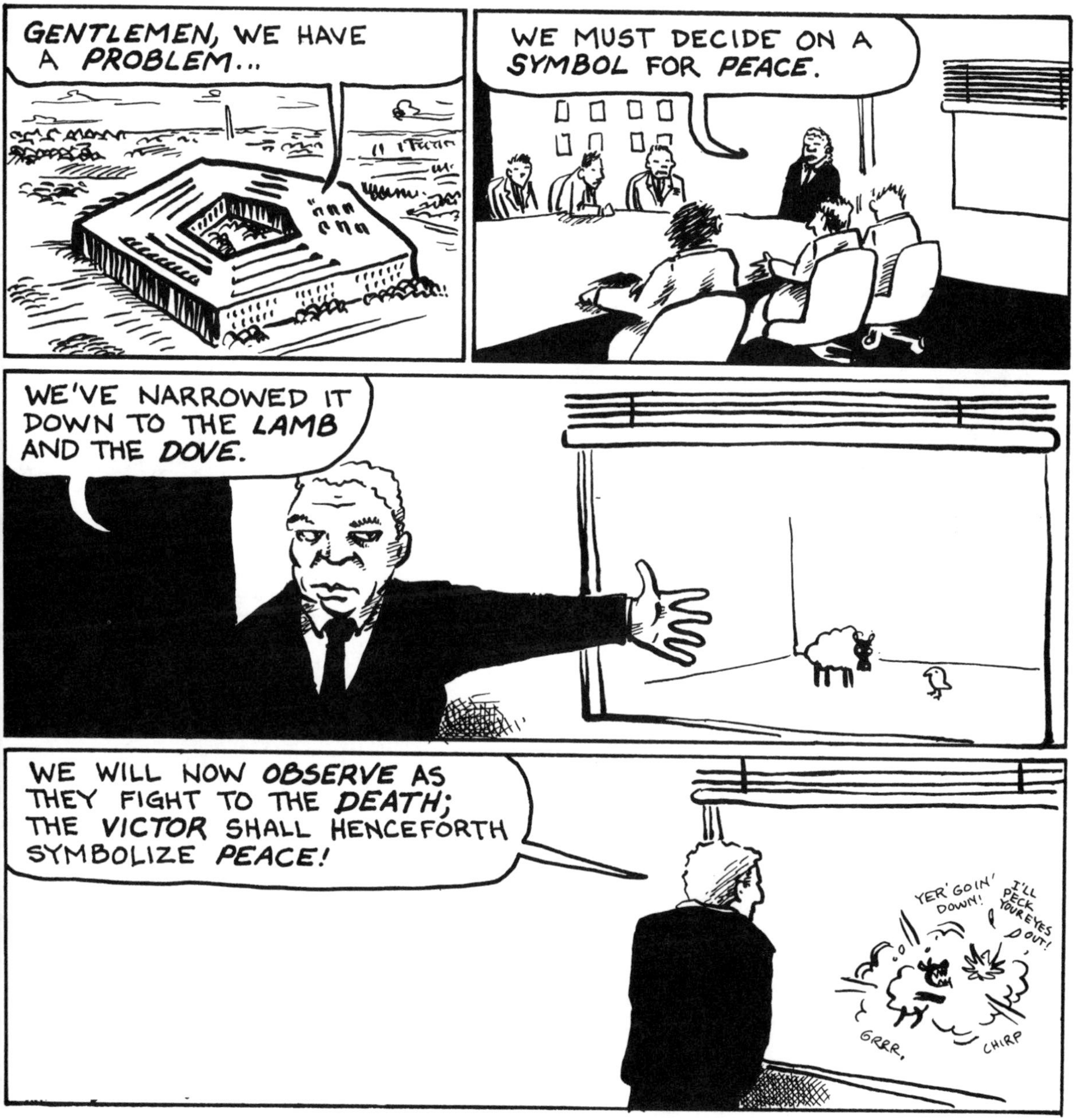
GENTLEMEN, WE HAVE A PROBLEM...
WE MUST DECIDE ON A SYMBOL FOR PEACE.
WE'VE NARROWED IT DOWN TO THE LAMB AND THE DOVE.
WE WILL NOW OBSERVE AS THEY FIGHT TO THE DEATH; THE VICTOR SHALL HENCEFORTH SYMBOLIZE PEACE!
YER' GOIN' DOWN!
I'LL PECK YOUR EYES OUT!
GRRR.
CHIRP

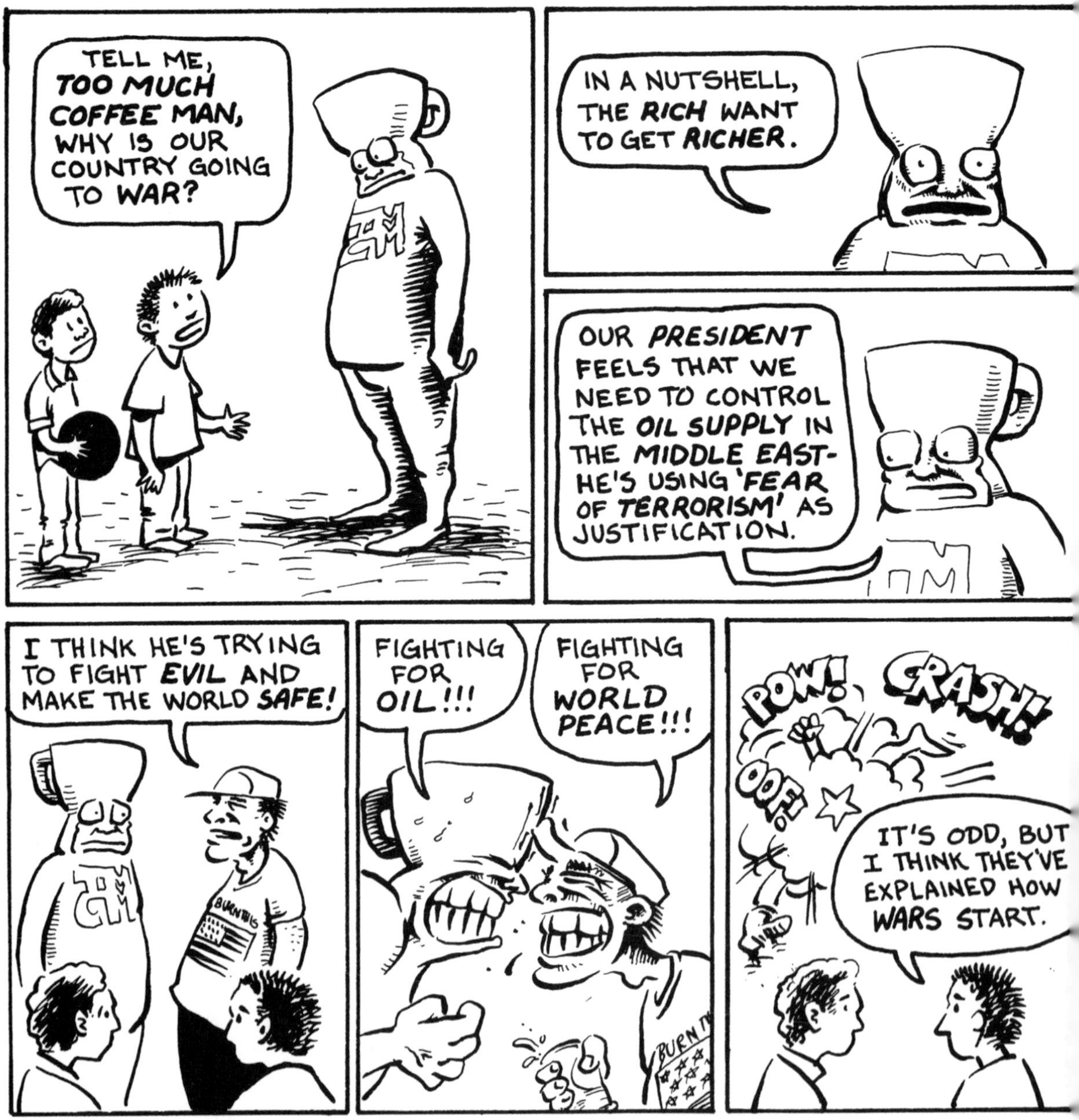
TELL ME, TOO MUCH COFFEE MAN, WHY IS OUR COUNTRY GOING TO WAR?
IN A NUTSHELL, THE RICH WANT TO GET RICHER.
OUR PRESIDENT FEELS THAT WE NEED TO CONTROL THE OIL SUPPLY IN THE MIDDLE EAST- HE'S USING 'FEAR OF TERRORISM' AS JUSTIFICATION.
I THINK HE'S TRYING TO FIGHT EVIL AND MAKE THE WORLD SAFE!
FIGHTING FOR OIL!!!
FIGHTING FOR WORLD PEACE!!!
POW!
CRASH!
OOF!
IT'S ODD, BUT I THINK THEY'VE EXPLAINED HOW WARS START.

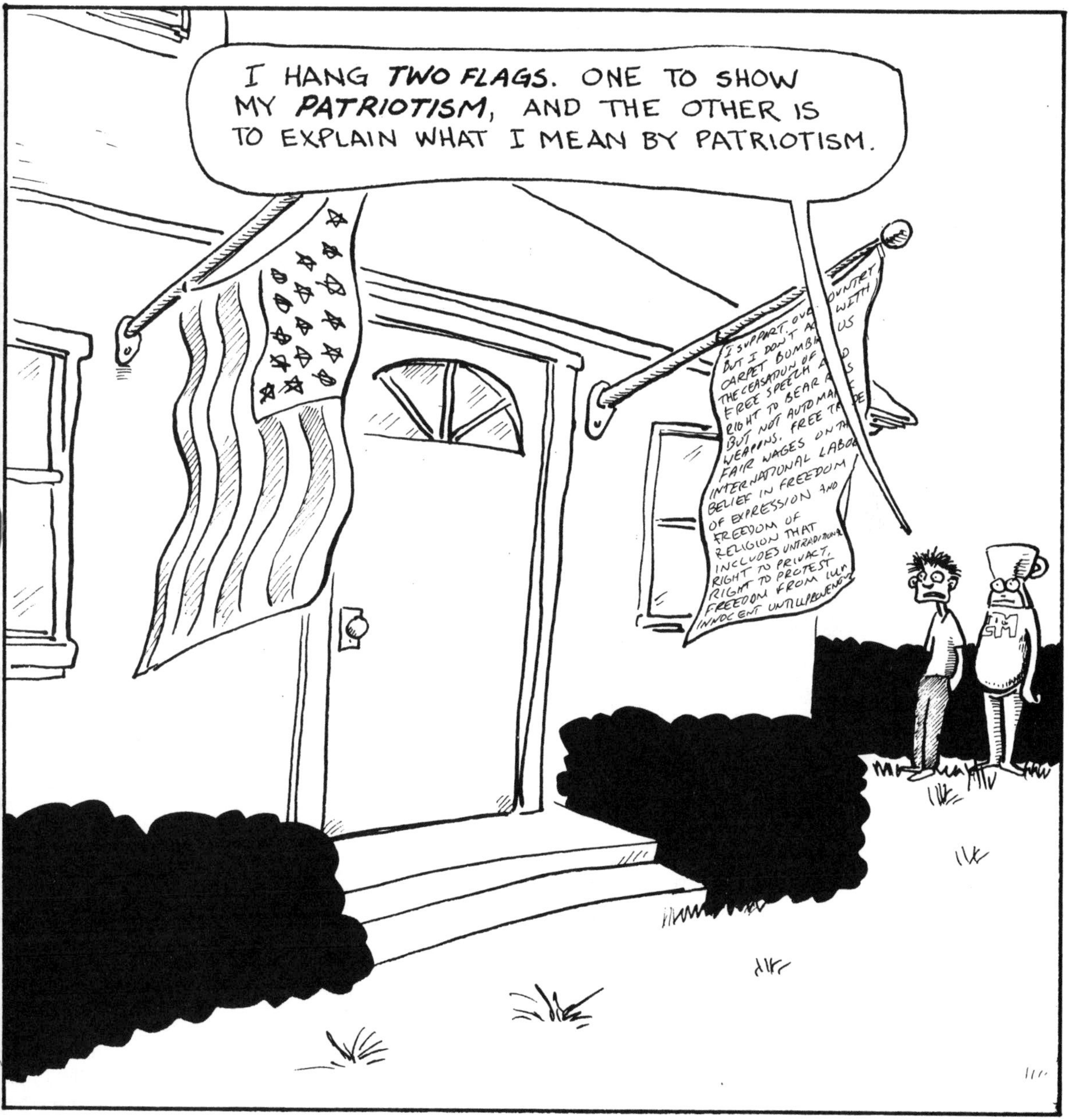
I HANG **TWO FLAGS**. ONE TO SHOW MY **PATRIOTISM**, AND THE OTHER IS TO EXPLAIN WHAT I MEAN BY PATRIOTISM.
I SUPPORT OV
BUT I DON'T A
CARPET BOMB
THE CEASATION OF
FREE SPEECH
RIGHT TO BEAR
BUT NOT AUTO MA
WEAPONS. FREE TR
FAIR WAGES ON TH
INTERNATIONAL LABO
BELIEF IN FREEDOM
OF EXPRESSION AND
FREEDOM OF
RELIGION THAT
INCLUDES UNTRADITIONAL
RIGHT TO PRIVACY,
RIGHT TO PROTEST
FREEDOM FROM
INNOCENT UNTIL

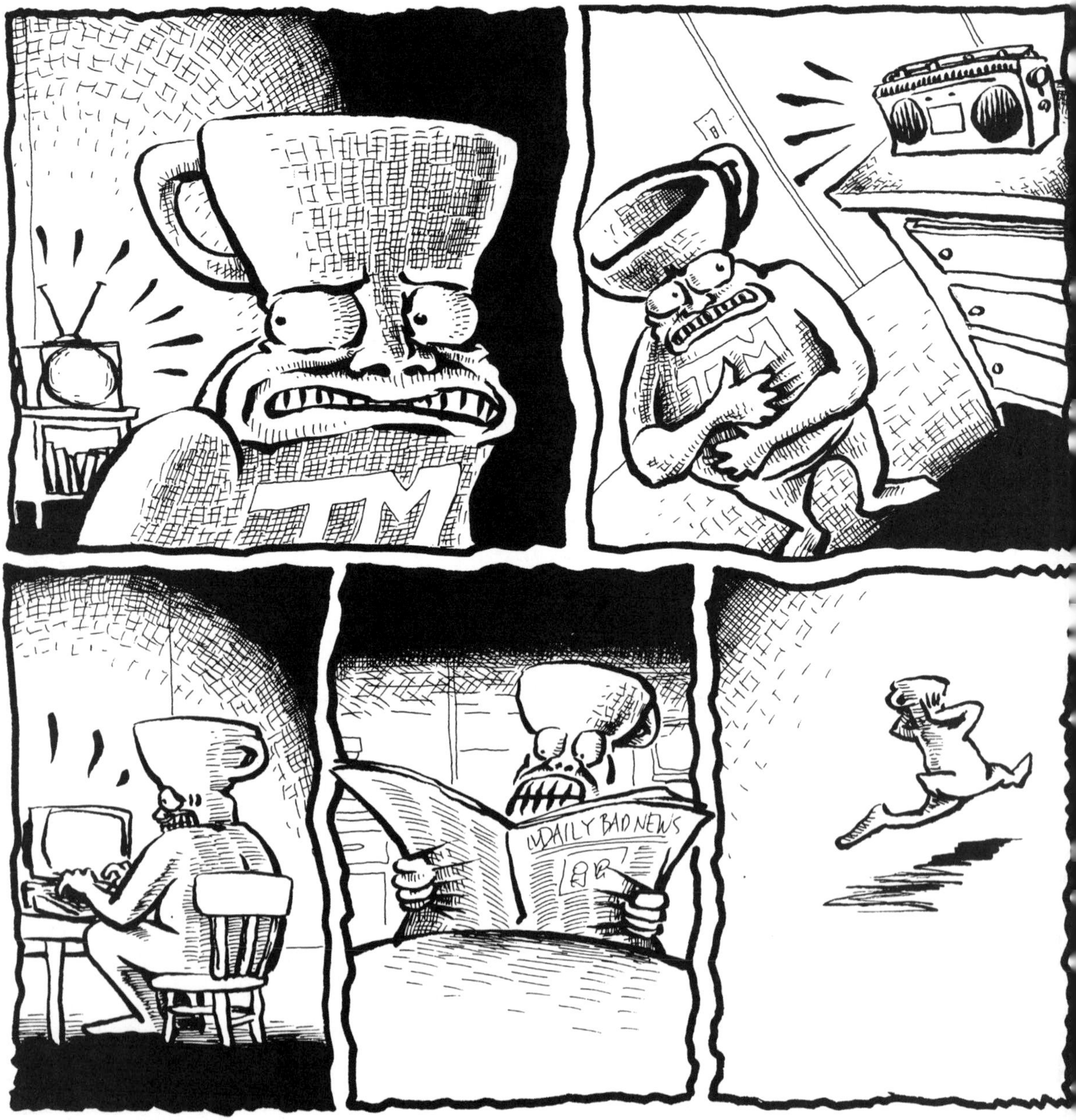
TM
TM
DAILY BAD NEWS

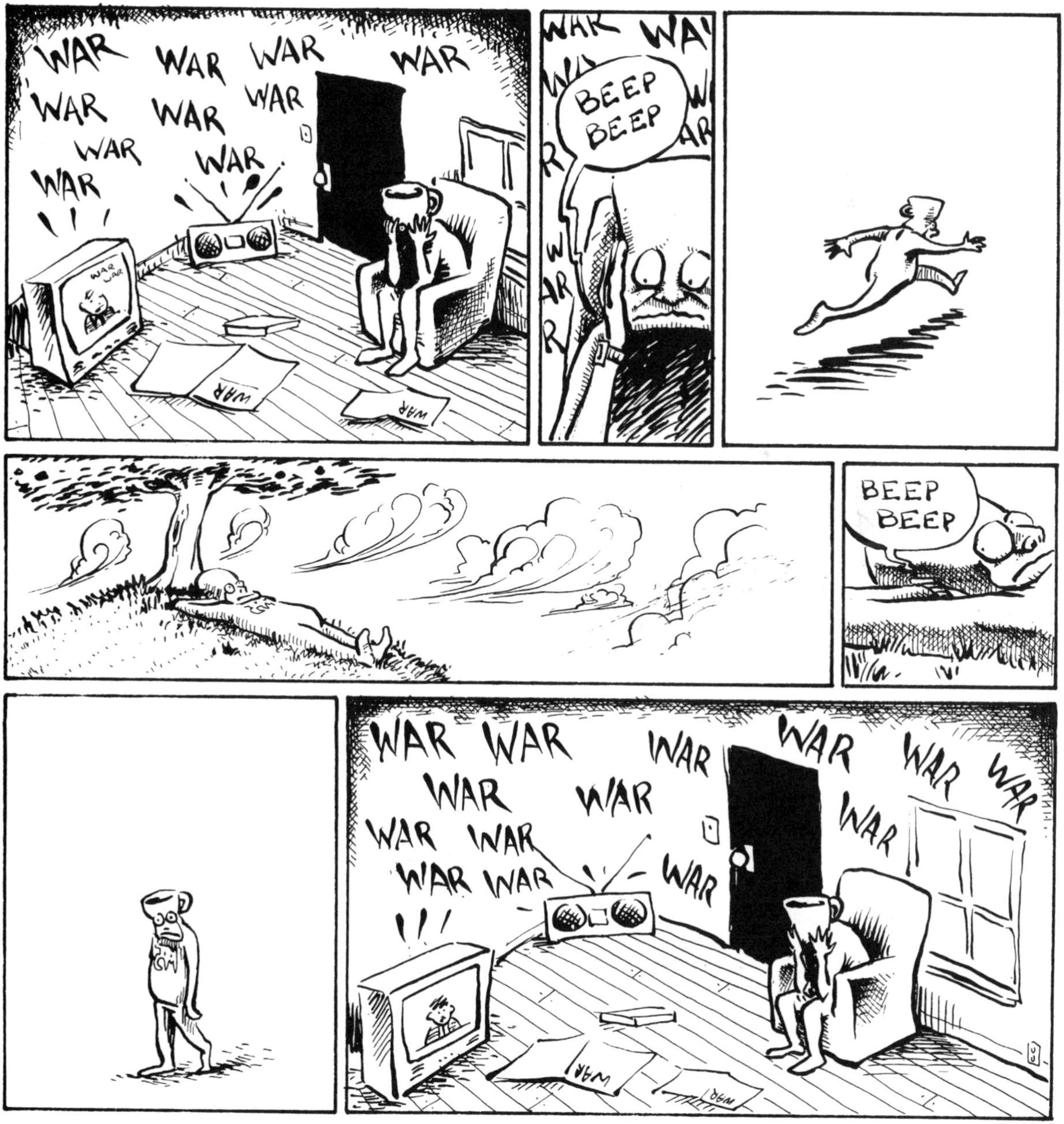
WAR WAR WAR WAR
WAR WAR WAR
WAR WAR WAR
WAR WAR
WAR
WAR
BEEP BEEP
BEEP BEEP
WAR WAR WAR WAR WAR WAR
WAR WAR WAR
WAR WAR WAR
WAR WAR WAR
WAR
WAR

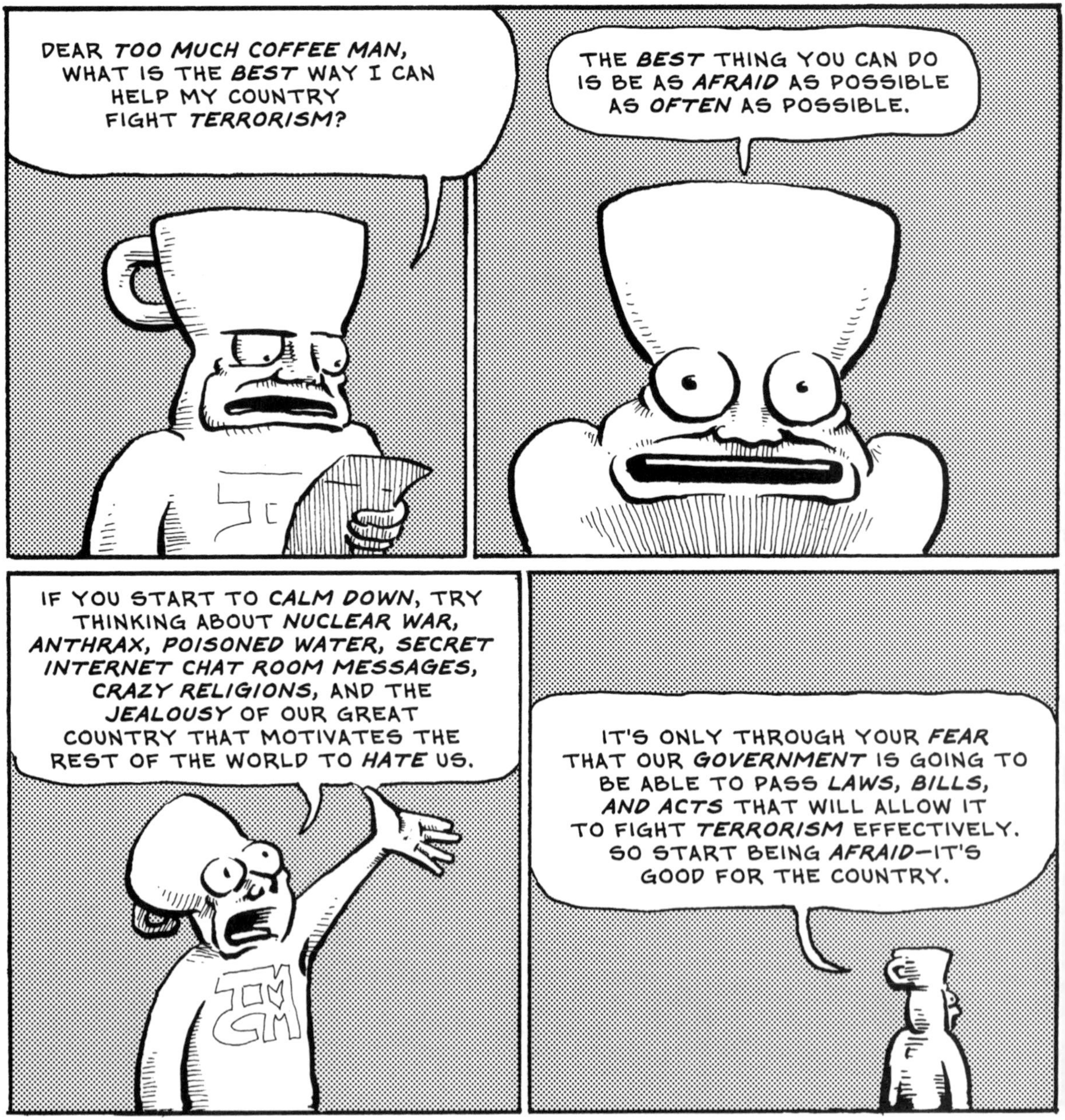
DEAR TOO MUCH COFFEE MAN, WHAT IS THE BEST WAY I CAN HELP MY COUNTRY FIGHT TERRORISM?
THE BEST THING YOU CAN DO IS BE AS AFRAID AS POSSIBLE AS OFTEN AS POSSIBLE.
IF YOU START TO CALM DOWN, TRY THINKING ABOUT NUCLEAR WAR, ANTHRAX, POISONED WATER, SECRET INTERNET CHAT ROOM MESSAGES, CRAZY RELIGIONS, AND THE JEALOUSY OF OUR GREAT COUNTRY THAT MOTIVATES THE REST OF THE WORLD TO HATE US.
IT'S ONLY THROUGH YOUR FEAR THAT OUR GOVERNMENT IS GOING TO BE ABLE TO PASS LAWS, BILLS, AND ACTS THAT WILL ALLOW IT TO FIGHT TERRORISM EFFECTIVELY. SO START BEING AFRAID—IT'S GOOD FOR THE COUNTRY.

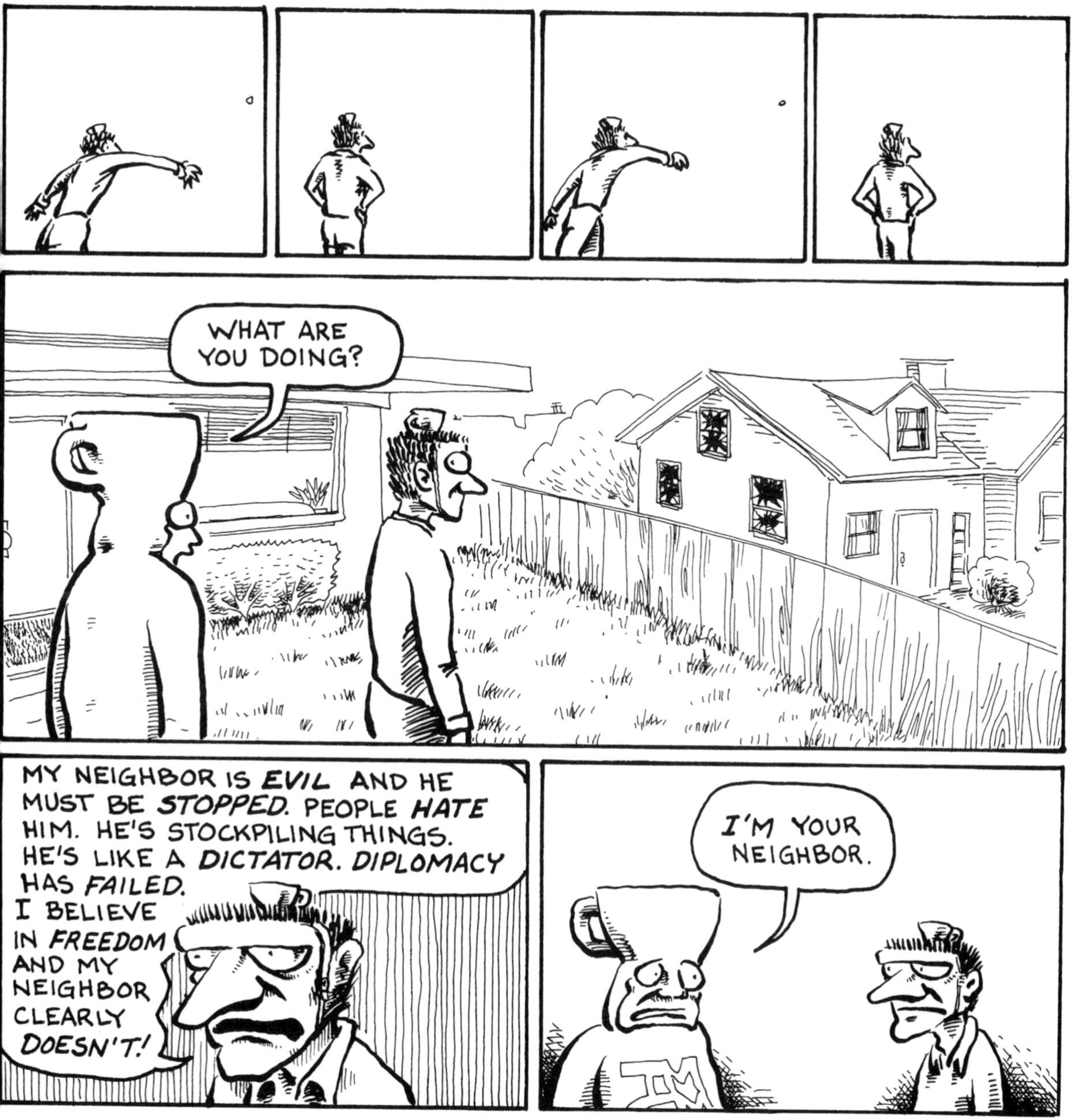
WHAT ARE YOU DOING?
MY NEIGHBOR IS EVIL AND HE MUST BE STOPPED. PEOPLE HATE HIM. HE'S STOCKPILING THINGS. HE'S LIKE A DICTATOR. DIPLOMACY HAS FAILED. I BELIEVE IN FREEDOM AND MY NEIGHBOR CLEARLY DOESN'T!
I'M YOUR NEIGHBOR.

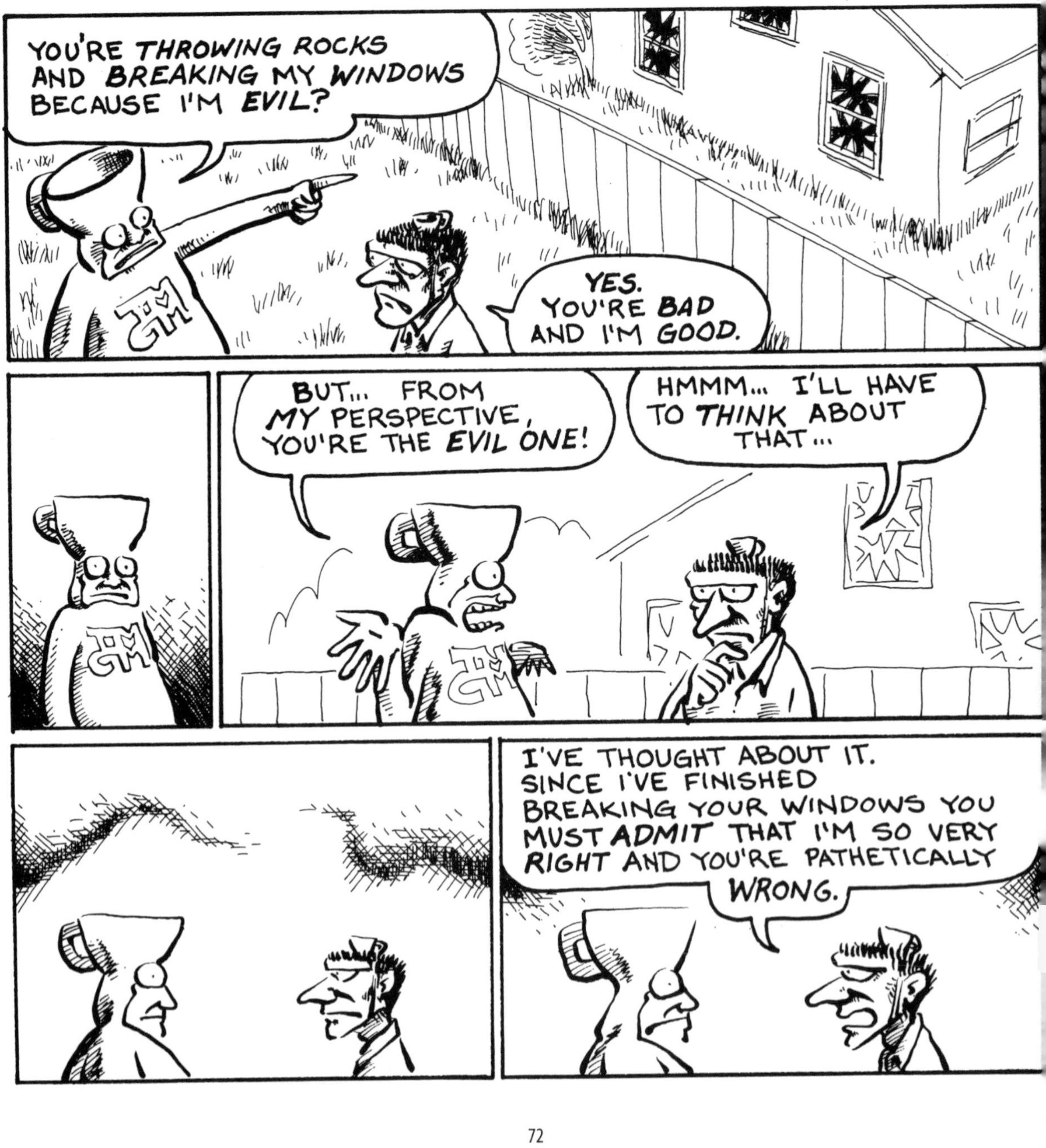
YOU'RE THROWING ROCKS AND BREAKING MY WINDOWS BECAUSE I'M EVIL?
YES. YOU'RE BAD AND I'M GOOD.
BUT... FROM MY PERSPECTIVE, YOU'RE THE EVIL ONE!
HMMM... I'LL HAVE TO THINK ABOUT THAT...
I'VE THOUGHT ABOUT IT. SINCE I'VE FINISHED BREAKING YOUR WINDOWS YOU MUST ADMIT THAT I'M SO VERY RIGHT AND YOU'RE PATHETICALLY WRONG.

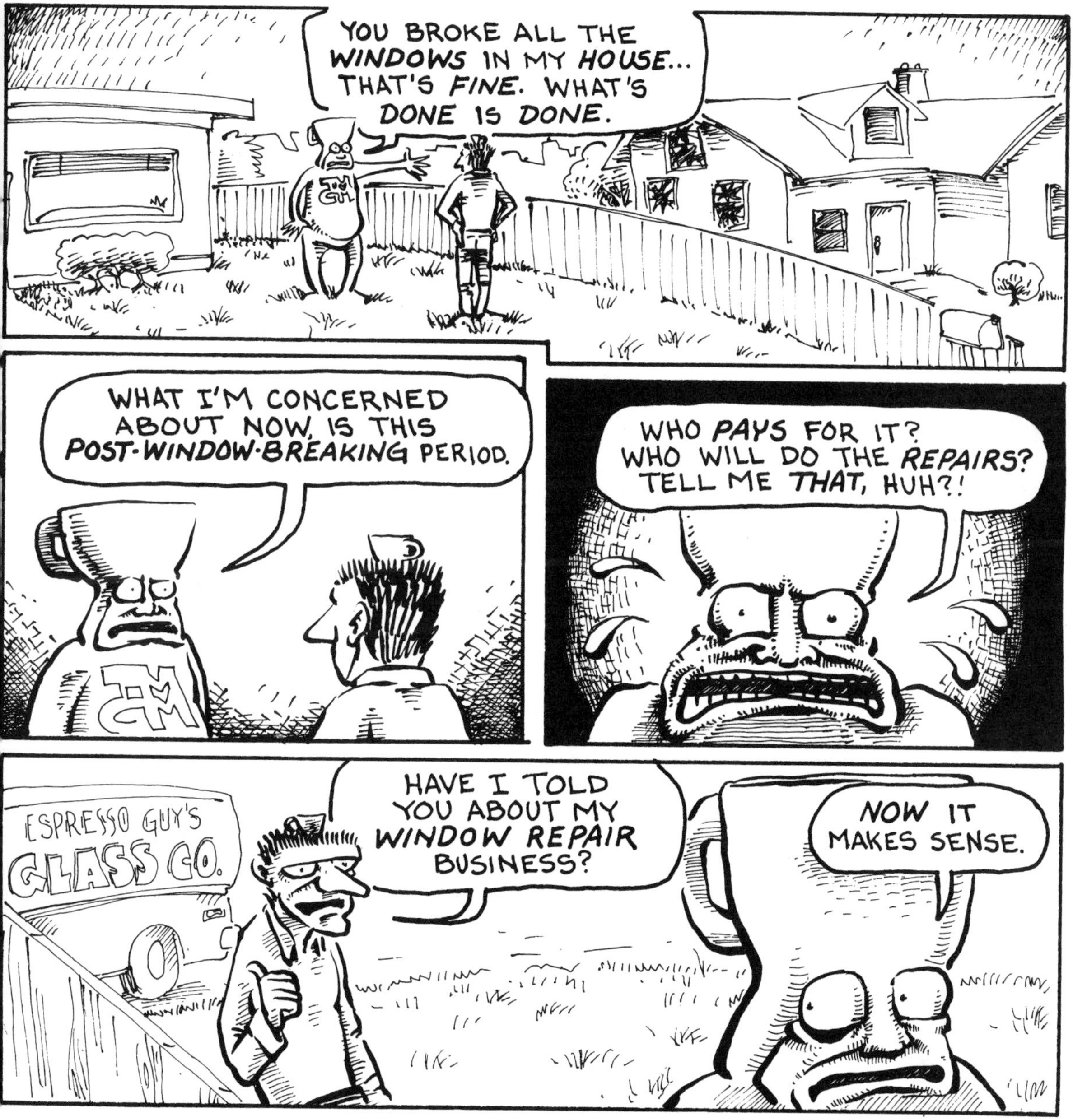
YOU BROKE ALL THE WINDOWS IN MY HOUSE... THAT'S FINE. WHAT'S DONE IS DONE.
WHAT I'M CONCERNED ABOUT NOW, IS THIS POST-WINDOW-BREAKING PERIOD.
WHO PAYS FOR IT? WHO WILL DO THE REPAIRS? TELL ME THAT, HUH?!
ESPRESSO GUY'S GLASS CO.
HAVE I TOLD YOU ABOUT MY WINDOW REPAIR BUSINESS?
NOW IT MAKES SENSE.

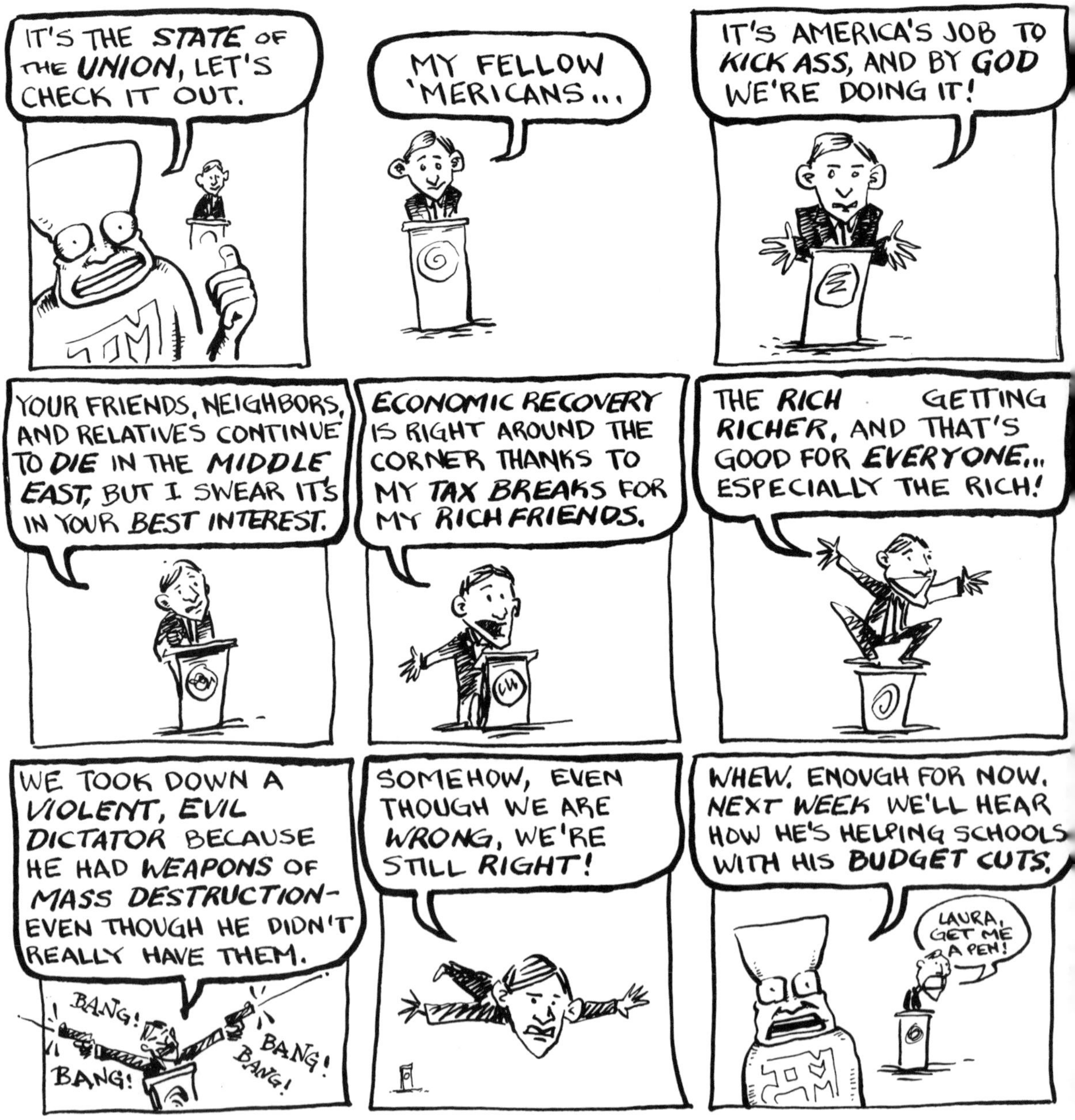
IT'S THE STATE OF THE UNION, LET'S CHECK IT OUT.
MY FELLOW 'MERICANS...
IT'S AMERICA'S JOB TO KICK ASS, AND BY GOD WE'RE DOING IT!
YOUR FRIENDS, NEIGHBORS, AND RELATIVES CONTINUE TO DIE IN THE MIDDLE EAST, BUT I SWEAR IT'S IN YOUR BEST INTEREST.
ECONOMIC RECOVERY IS RIGHT AROUND THE CORNER THANKS TO MY TAX BREAKS FOR MY RICH FRIENDS.
THE RICH GETTING RICHER, AND THAT'S GOOD FOR EVERYONE... ESPECIALLY THE RICH!
WE TOOK DOWN A VIOLENT, EVIL DICTATOR BECAUSE HE HAD WEAPONS OF MASS DESTRUCTION- EVEN THOUGH HE DIDN'T REALLY HAVE THEM.
BANG!
BANG!
BANG!
BANG!
SOMEHOW, EVEN THOUGH WE ARE WRONG, WE'RE STILL RIGHT!
WHEW. ENOUGH FOR NOW. NEXT WEEK WE'LL HEAR HOW HE'S HELPING SCHOOLS WITH HIS BUDGET CUTS.
LAURA, GET ME A PEN!

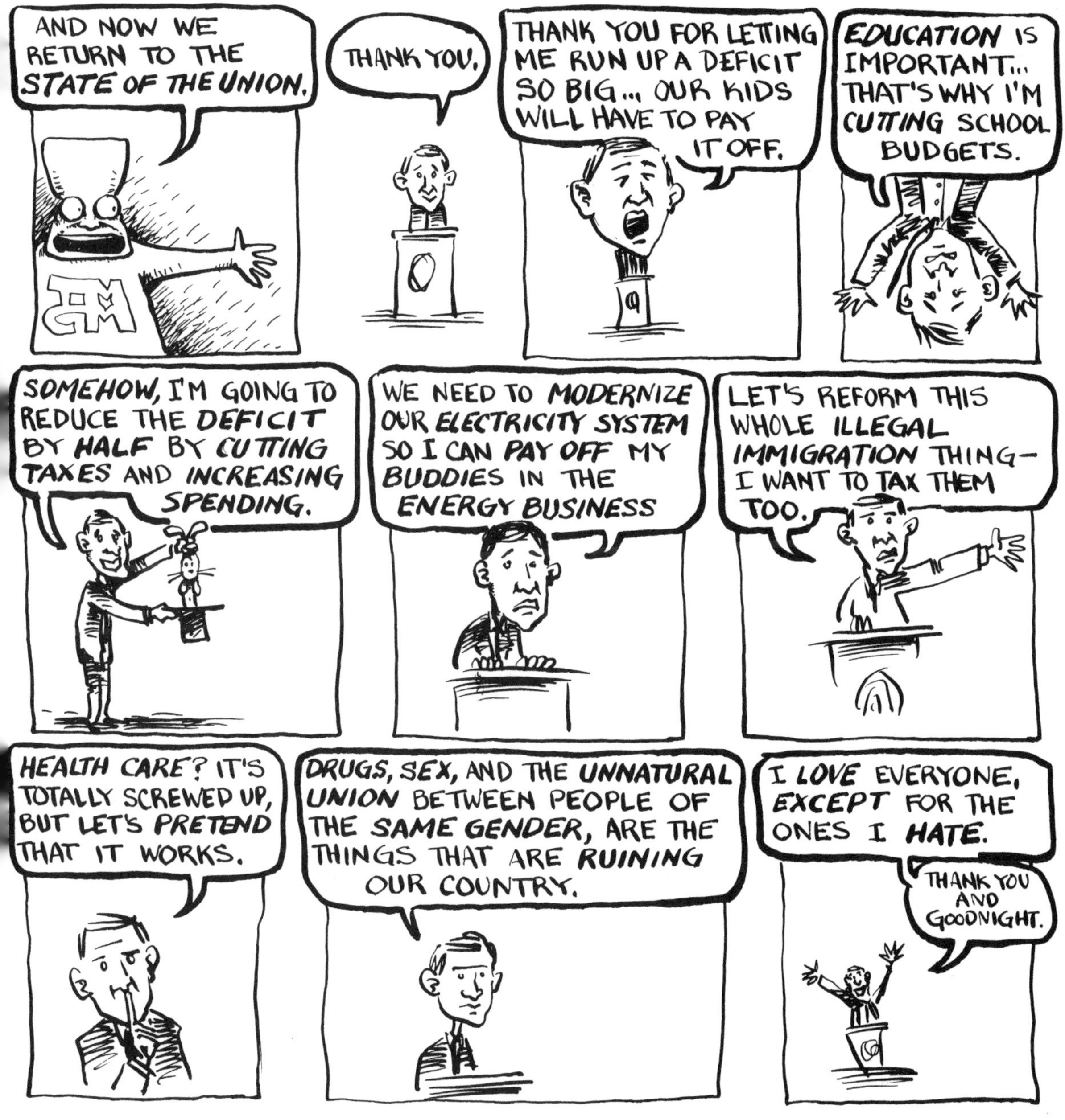
AND NOW WE RETURN TO THE STATE OF THE UNION.
THANK YOU.
THANK YOU FOR LETTING ME RUN UP A DEFICIT SO BIG... OUR KIDS WILL HAVE TO PAY IT OFF.
EDUCATION IS IMPORTANT... THAT'S WHY I'M CUTTING SCHOOL BUDGETS.
SOMEHOW, I'M GOING TO REDUCE THE DEFICIT BY HALF BY CUTTING TAXES AND INCREASING SPENDING.
WE NEED TO MODERNIZE OUR ELECTRICITY SYSTEM SO I CAN PAY OFF MY BUDDIES IN THE ENERGY BUSINESS
LET'S REFORM THIS WHOLE ILLEGAL IMMIGRATION THING- I WANT TO TAX THEM TOO.
HEALTH CARE? IT'S TOTALLY SCREWED UP, BUT LET'S PRETEND THAT IT WORKS.
DRUGS, SEX, AND THE UNNATURAL UNION BETWEEN PEOPLE OF THE SAME GENDER, ARE THE THINGS THAT ARE RUINING OUR COUNTRY.
I LOVE EVERYONE, EXCEPT FOR THE ONES I HATE.
THANK YOU AND GOODNIGHT.

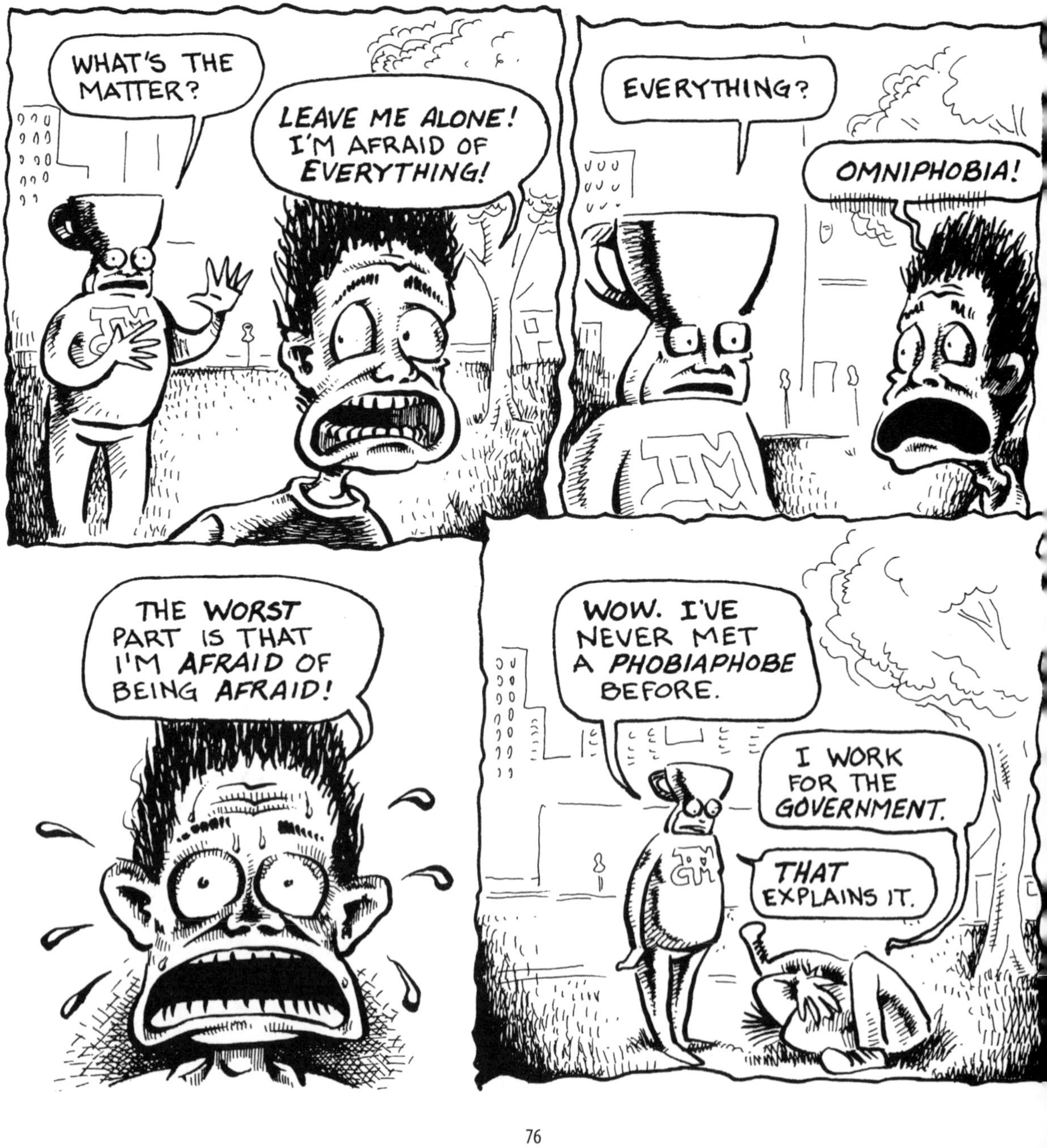
WHAT'S THE MATTER?
LEAVE ME ALONE! I'M AFRAID OF EVERYTHING!
EVERYTHING?
OMNIPHOBIA!
THE WORST PART IS THAT I'M AFRAID OF BEING AFRAID!
WOW. I'VE NEVER MET A PHOBIAPHOBE BEFORE.
I WORK FOR THE GOVERNMENT.
THAT EXPLAINS IT.

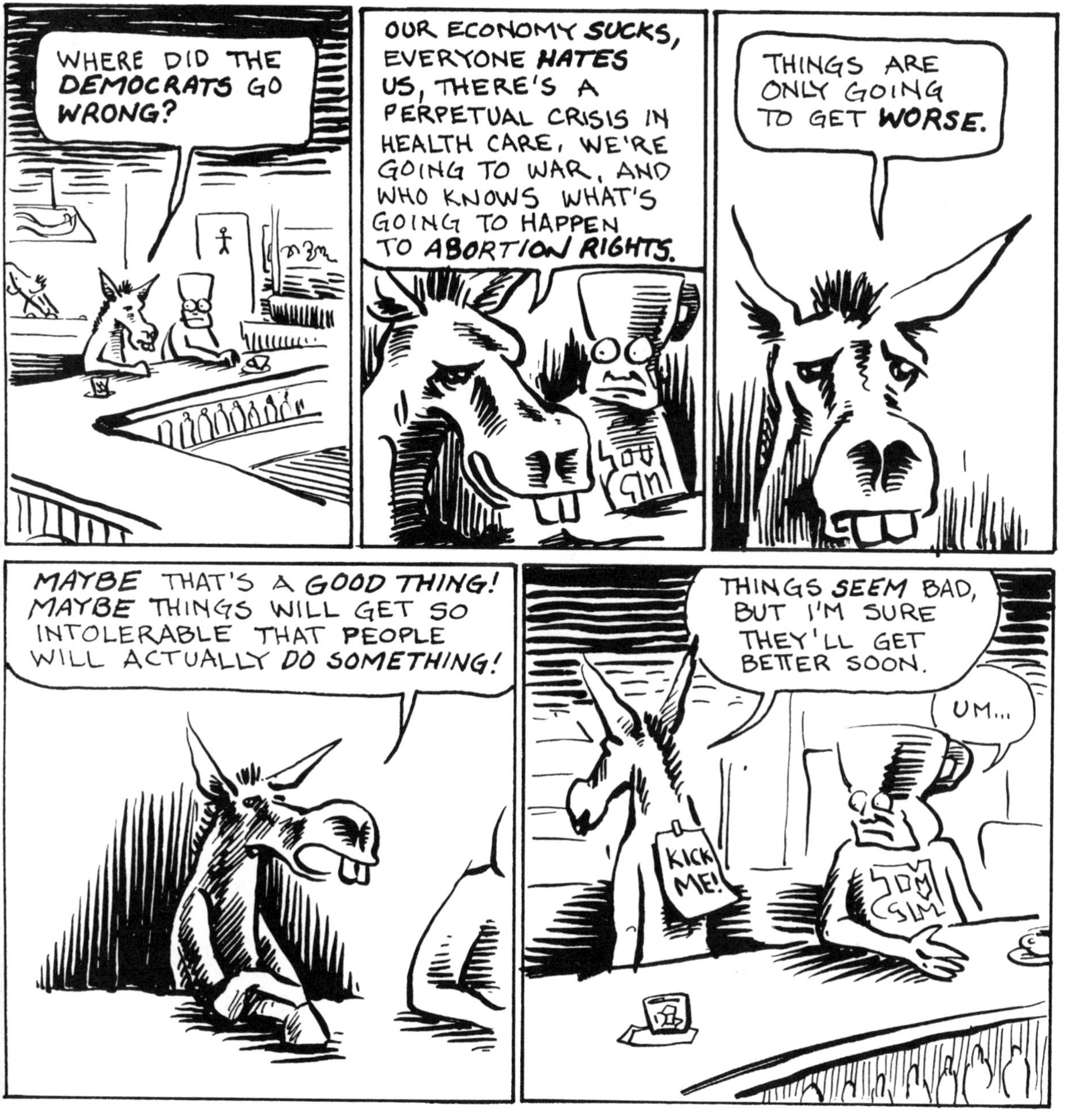
WHERE DID THE DEMOCRATS GO WRONG?
OUR ECONOMY SUCKS, EVERYONE HATES US, THERE'S A PERPETUAL CRISIS IN HEALTH CARE, WE'RE GOING TO WAR, AND WHO KNOWS WHAT'S GOING TO HAPPEN TO ABORTION RIGHTS.
THINGS ARE ONLY GOING TO GET WORSE.
MAYBE THAT'S A GOOD THING! MAYBE THINGS WILL GET SO INTOLERABLE THAT PEOPLE WILL ACTUALLY DO SOMETHING!
THINGS SEEM BAD, BUT I'M SURE THEY'LL GET BETTER SOON.
UM...
KICK ME!

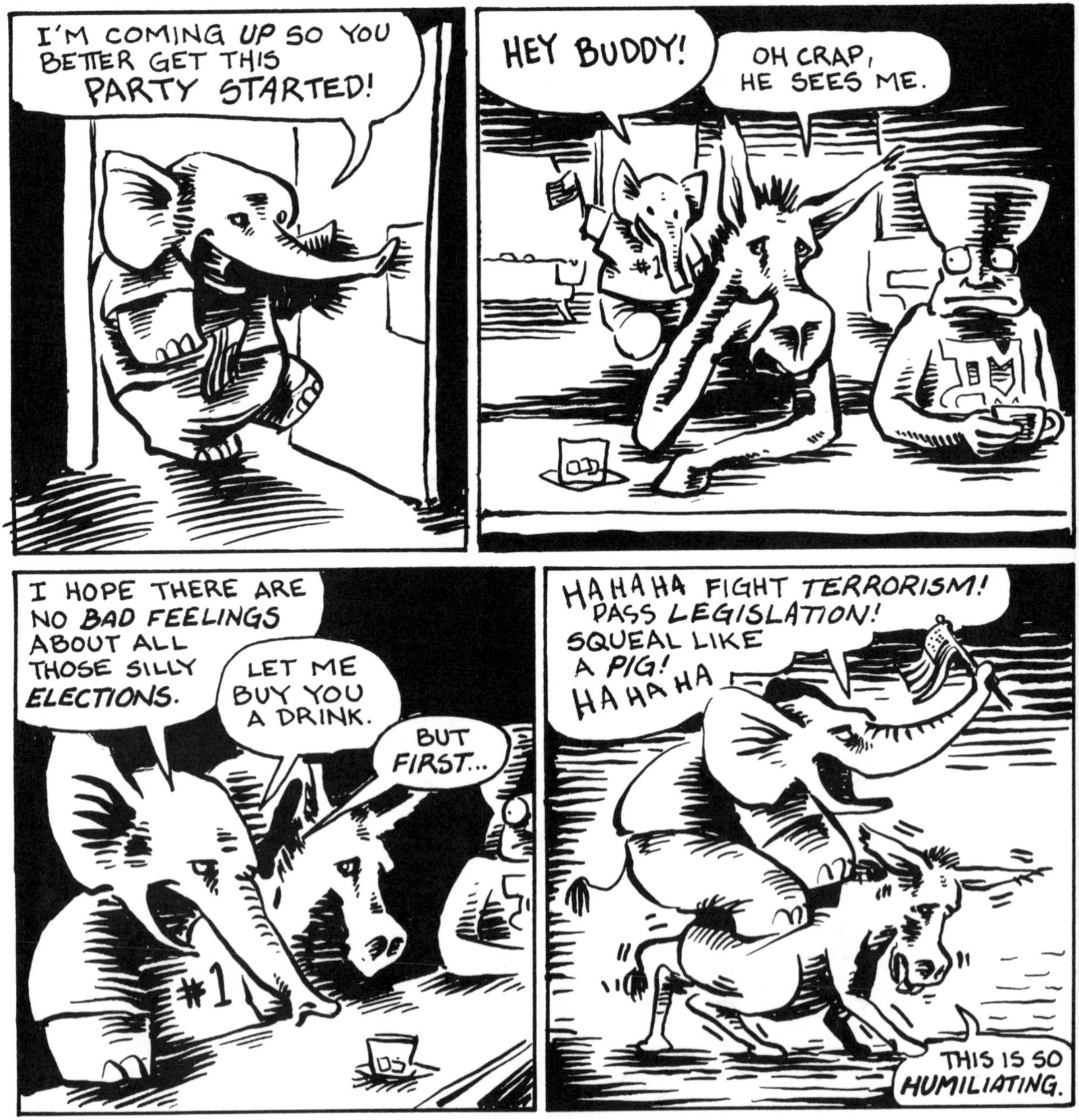
I'M COMING UP SO YOU BETTER GET THIS PARTY STARTED!
HEY BUDDY!
OH CRAP, HE SEES ME.
I HOPE THERE ARE NO BAD FEELINGS ABOUT ALL THOSE SILLY ELECTIONS.
LET ME BUY YOU A DRINK.
BUT FIRST...
HA HA HA FIGHT TERRORISM! PASS LEGISLATION! SQUEAL LIKE A PIG! HA HA HA
THIS IS SO HUMILIATING.

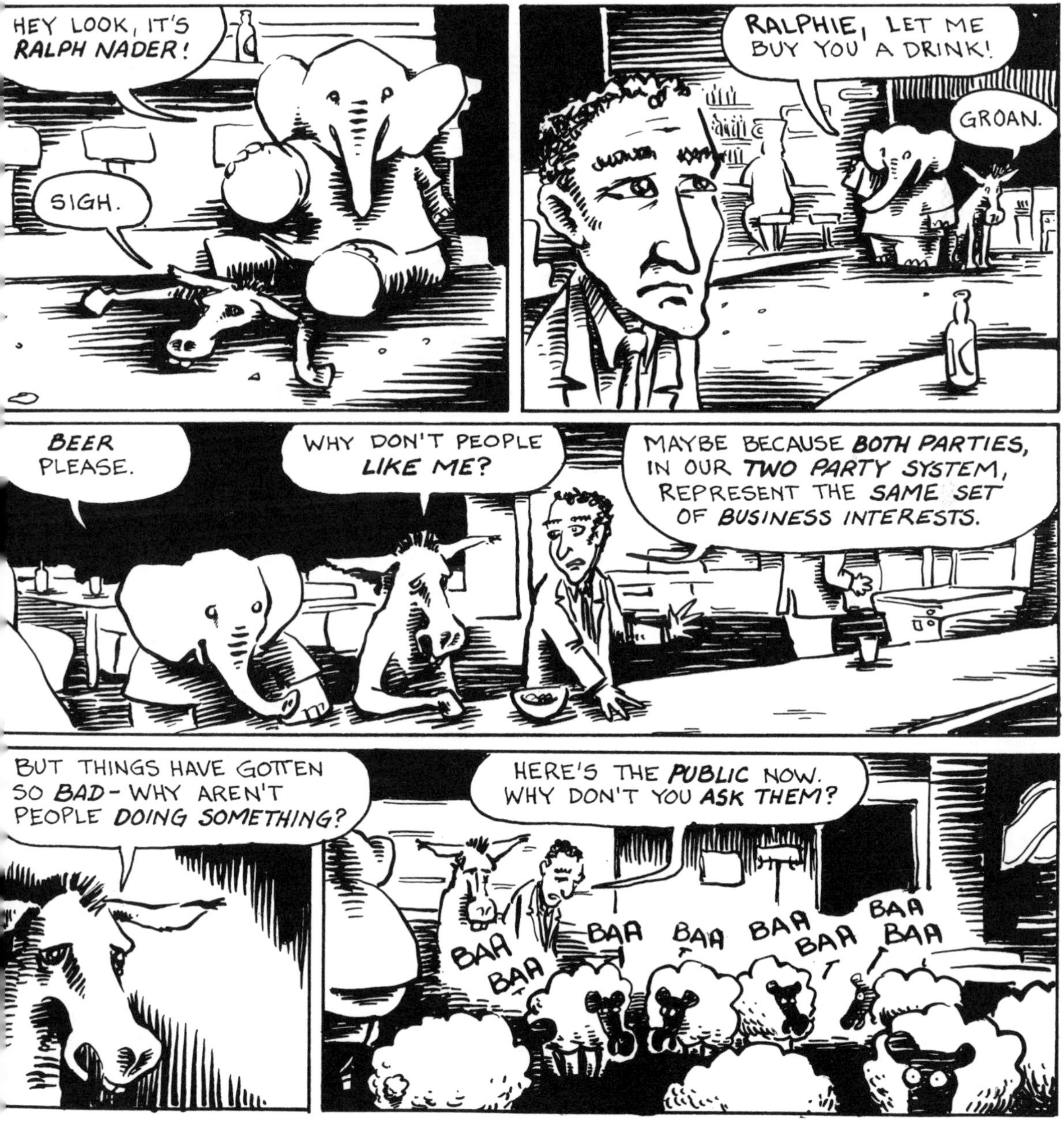

HEY LOOK, IT'S RALPH NADER!
SIGH.
RALPHIE, LET ME BUY YOU A DRINK!
GROAN.
BEER PLEASE.
WHY DON'T PEOPLE LIKE ME?
MAYBE BECAUSE BOTH PARTIES, IN OUR TWO PARTY SYSTEM, REPRESENT THE SAME SET OF BUSINESS INTERESTS.
BUT THINGS HAVE GOTTEN SO BAD - WHY AREN'T PEOPLE DOING SOMETHING?
HERE'S THE PUBLIC NOW. WHY DON'T YOU ASK THEM?
BAA BAA BAA BAA BAA BAA BAA BAA

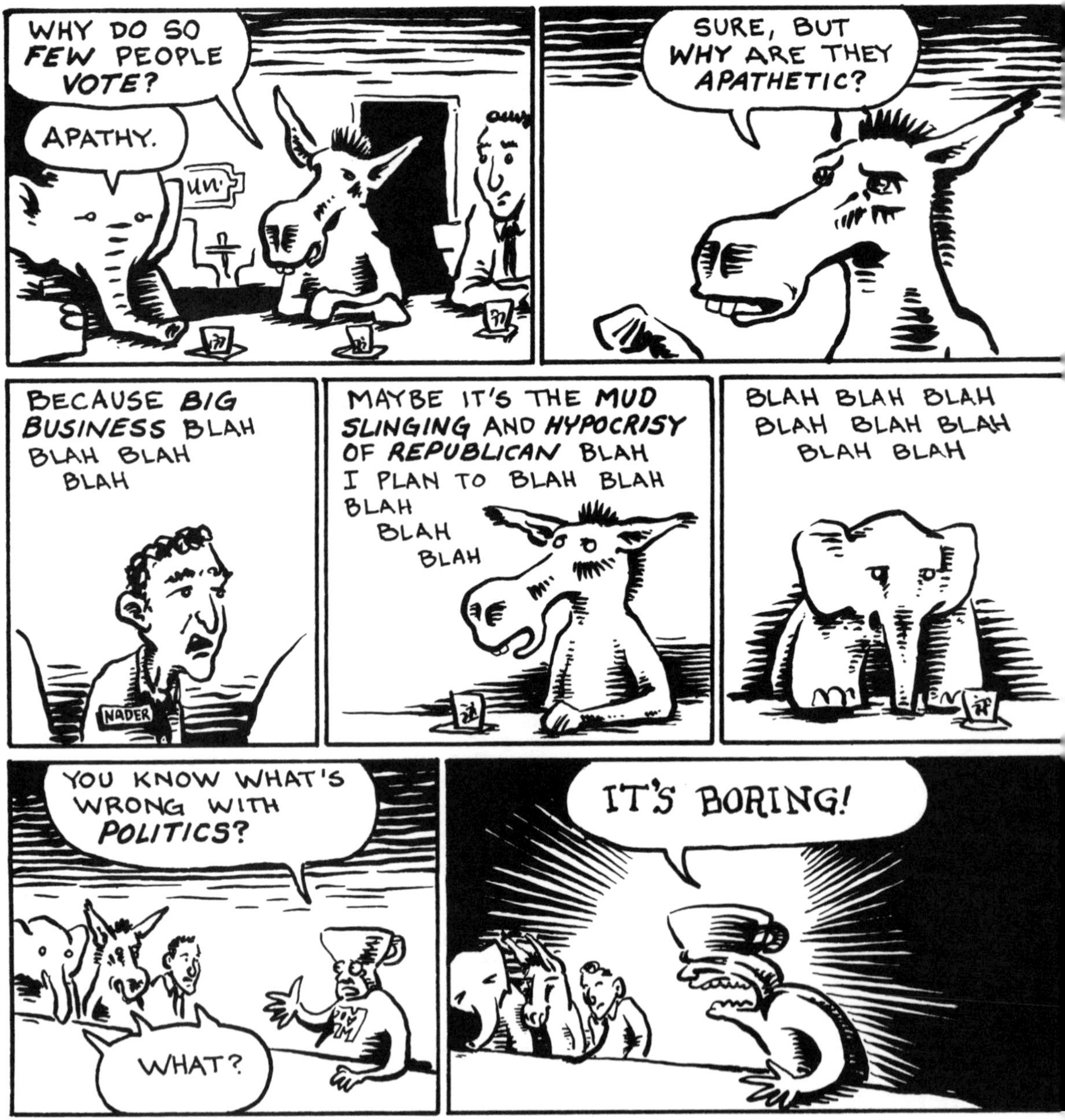
WHY DO SO FEW PEOPLE VOTE?
APATHY.
SURE, BUT WHY ARE THEY APATHETIC?
BECAUSE BIG BUSINESS BLAH BLAH BLAH BLAH
NADER
MAYBE IT'S THE MUD SLINGING AND HYPOCRISY OF REPUBLICAN BLAH I PLAN TO BLAH BLAH BLAH BLAH BLAH
BLAH BLAH BLAH BLAH BLAH BLAH BLAH BLAH
YOU KNOW WHAT'S WRONG WITH POLITICS?
WHAT?
IT'S BORING!

CHAPTER THREE

DON'T STOP BELIEVING

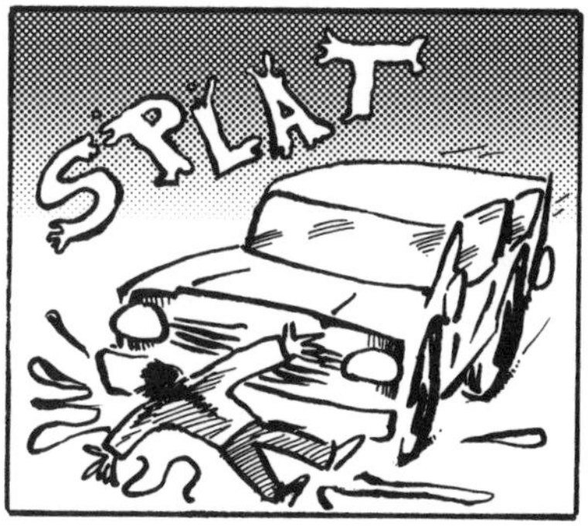
SPLAT

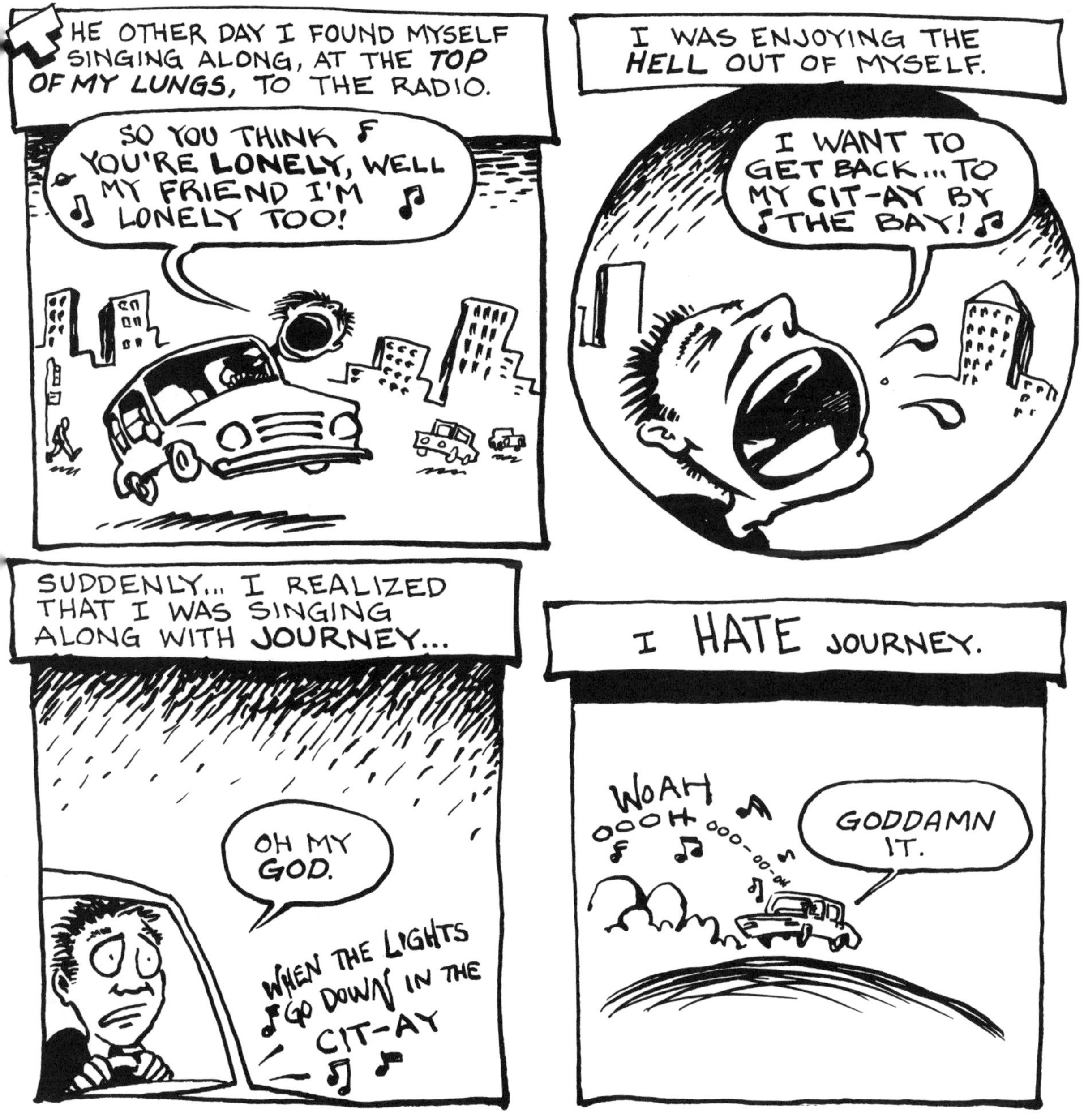
THE OTHER DAY I FOUND MYSELF SINGING ALONG, AT THE TOP OF MY LUNGS, TO THE RADIO.
SO YOU THINK YOU'RE LONELY, WELL MY FRIEND I'M LONELY TOO!
I WAS ENJOYING THE HELL OUT OF MYSELF.
I WANT TO GET BACK... TO MY CIT-AY BY THE BAY!
SUDDENLY... I REALIZED THAT I WAS SINGING ALONG WITH JOURNEY...
OH MY GOD.
WHEN THE LIGHTS GO DOWN IN THE CIT-AY
I HATE JOURNEY.
WOAH OOOH OOO-OO-OO-OH
GODDAMN IT.

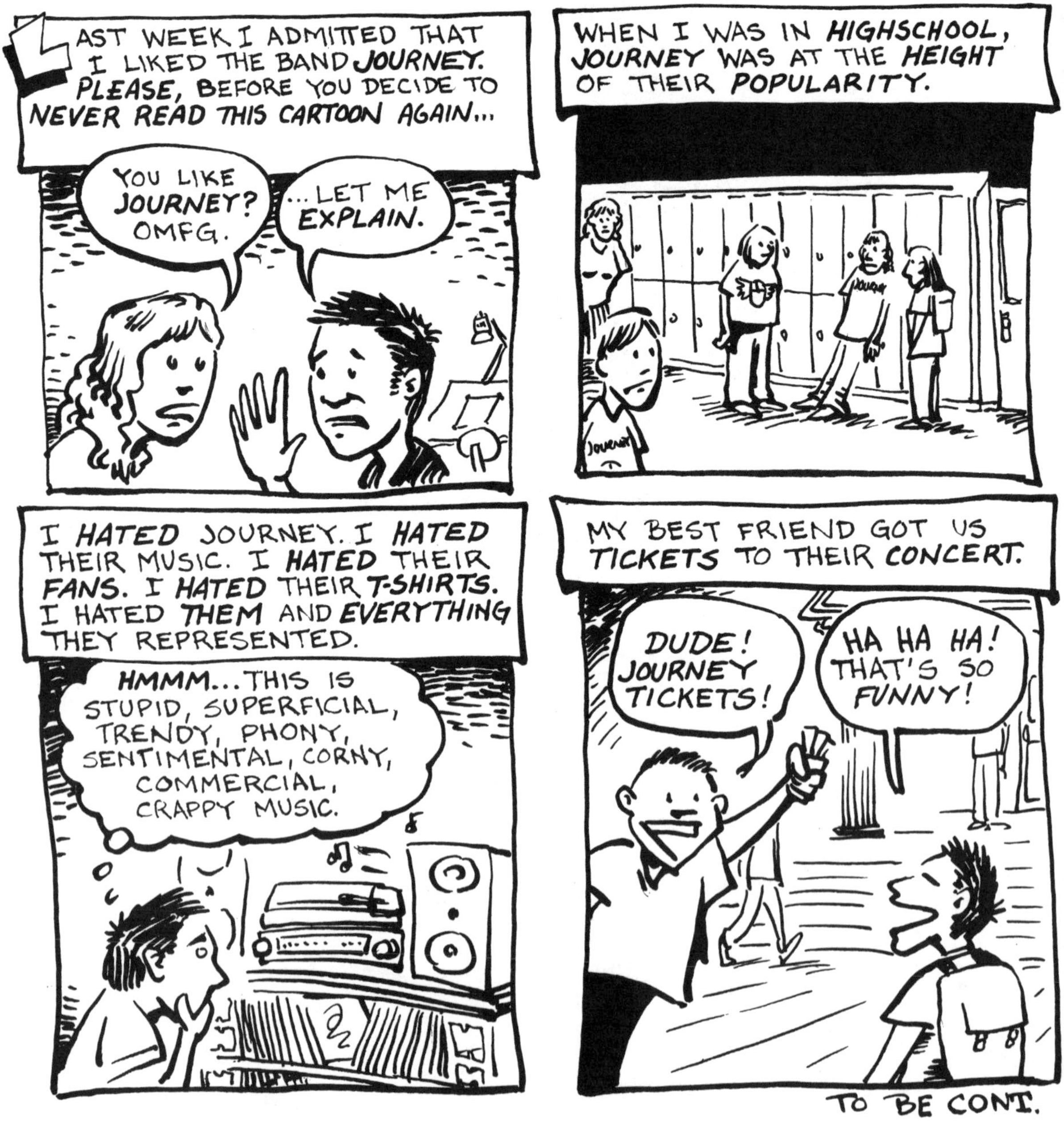
LAST WEEK I ADMITTED THAT I LIKED THE BAND JOURNEY. PLEASE, BEFORE YOU DECIDE TO NEVER READ THIS CARTOON AGAIN...
YOU LIKE JOURNEY? OMFG.
...LET ME EXPLAIN.
WHEN I WAS IN HIGHSCHOOL, JOURNEY WAS AT THE HEIGHT OF THEIR POPULARITY.
I HATED JOURNEY. I HATED THEIR MUSIC. I HATED THEIR FANS. I HATED THEIR T-SHIRTS. I HATED THEM AND EVERYTHING THEY REPRESENTED.
HMMM... THIS IS STUPID, SUPERFICIAL, TRENDY, PHONY, SENTIMENTAL, CORNY, COMMERCIAL, CRAPPY MUSIC.
MY BEST FRIEND GOT US TICKETS TO THEIR CONCERT.
DUDE! JOURNEY TICKETS!
HA HA HA! THAT'S SO FUNNY!
TO BE CONT.

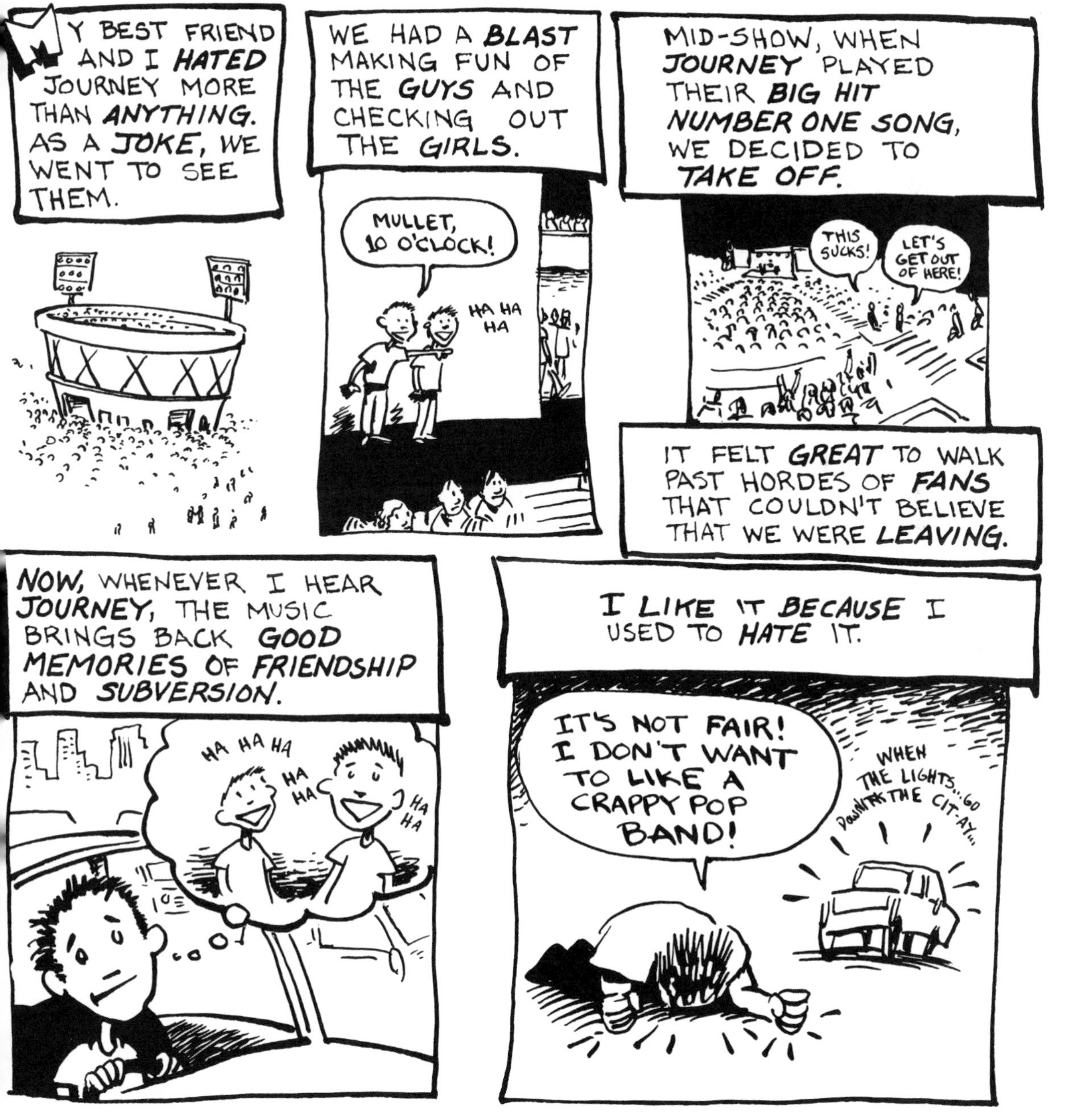
MY BEST FRIEND AND I HATED JOURNEY MORE THAN ANYTHING. AS A JOKE, WE WENT TO SEE THEM.
WE HAD A BLAST MAKING FUN OF THE GUYS AND CHECKING OUT THE GIRLS.
MULLET, 10 O'CLOCK!
HA HA HA
MID-SHOW, WHEN JOURNEY PLAYED THEIR BIG HIT NUMBER ONE SONG, WE DECIDED TO TAKE OFF.
THIS SUCKS!
LET'S GET OUT OF HERE!
IT FELT GREAT TO WALK PAST HORDES OF FANS THAT COULDN'T BELIEVE THAT WE WERE LEAVING.
NOW, WHENEVER I HEAR JOURNEY, THE MUSIC BRINGS BACK GOOD MEMORIES OF FRIENDSHIP AND SUBVERSION.
HA HA HA
HA HA
HA HA
I LIKE IT BECAUSE I USED TO HATE IT.
IT'S NOT FAIR! I DON'T WANT TO LIKE A CRAPPY POP BAND!
WHEN THE LIGHTS...GO DOWN IN THE CIT-AY...

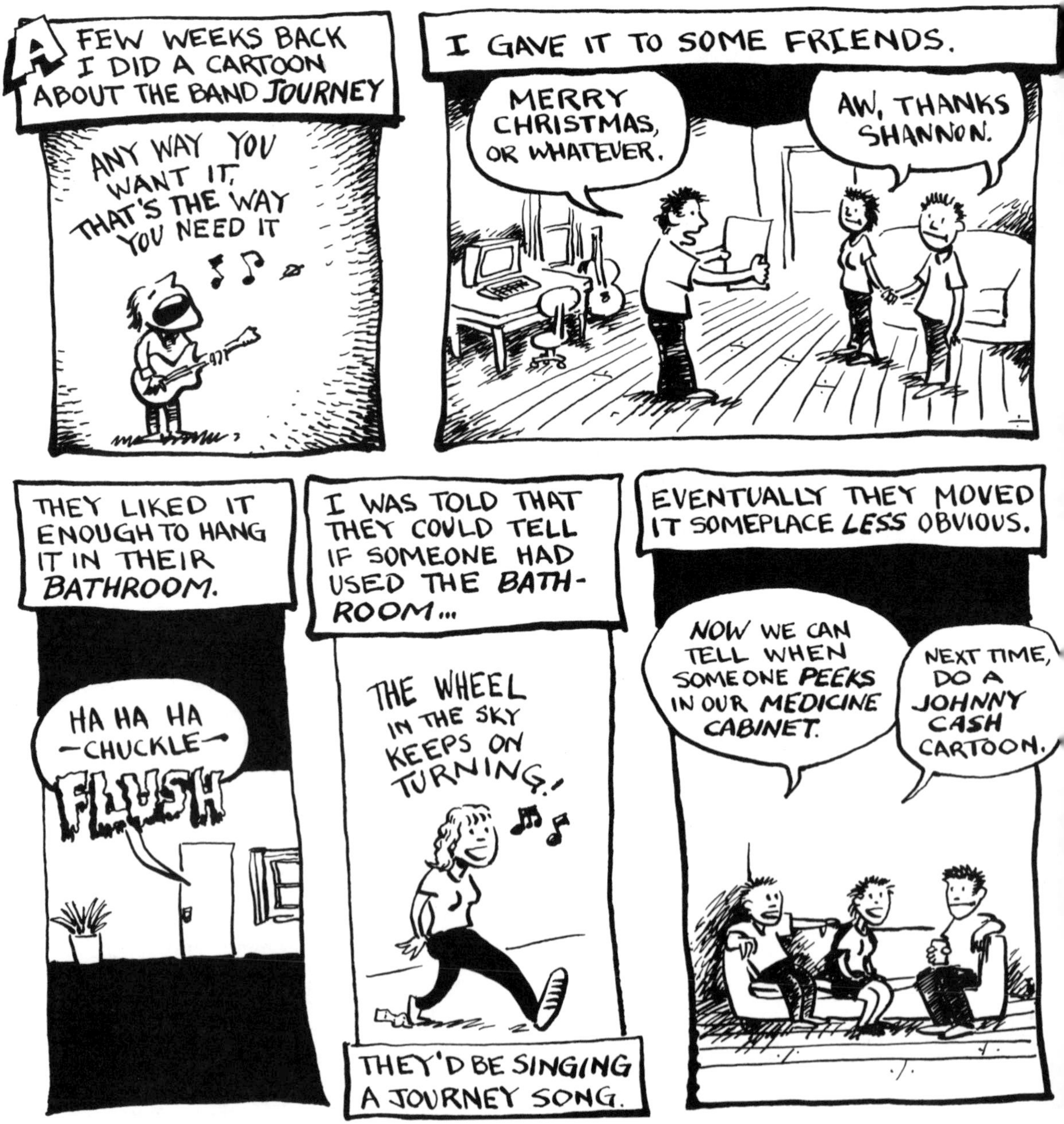
A FEW WEEKS BACK I DID A CARTOON ABOUT THE BAND JOURNEY
ANY WAY YOU WANT IT, THAT'S THE WAY YOU NEED IT
I GAVE IT TO SOME FRIENDS.
MERRY CHRISTMAS, OR WHATEVER.
AW, THANKS SHANNON.
THEY LIKED IT ENOUGH TO HANG IT IN THEIR BATHROOM.
HA HA HA -CHUCKLE-
FLUSH
I WAS TOLD THAT THEY COULD TELL IF SOMEONE HAD USED THE BATH-ROOM...
THE WHEEL IN THE SKY KEEPS ON TURNING!
THEY'D BE SINGING A JOURNEY SONG.
EVENTUALLY THEY MOVED IT SOMEPLACE LESS OBVIOUS.
NOW WE CAN TELL WHEN SOMEONE PEEKS IN OUR MEDICINE CABINET.
NEXT TIME, DO A JOHNNY CASH CARTOON.

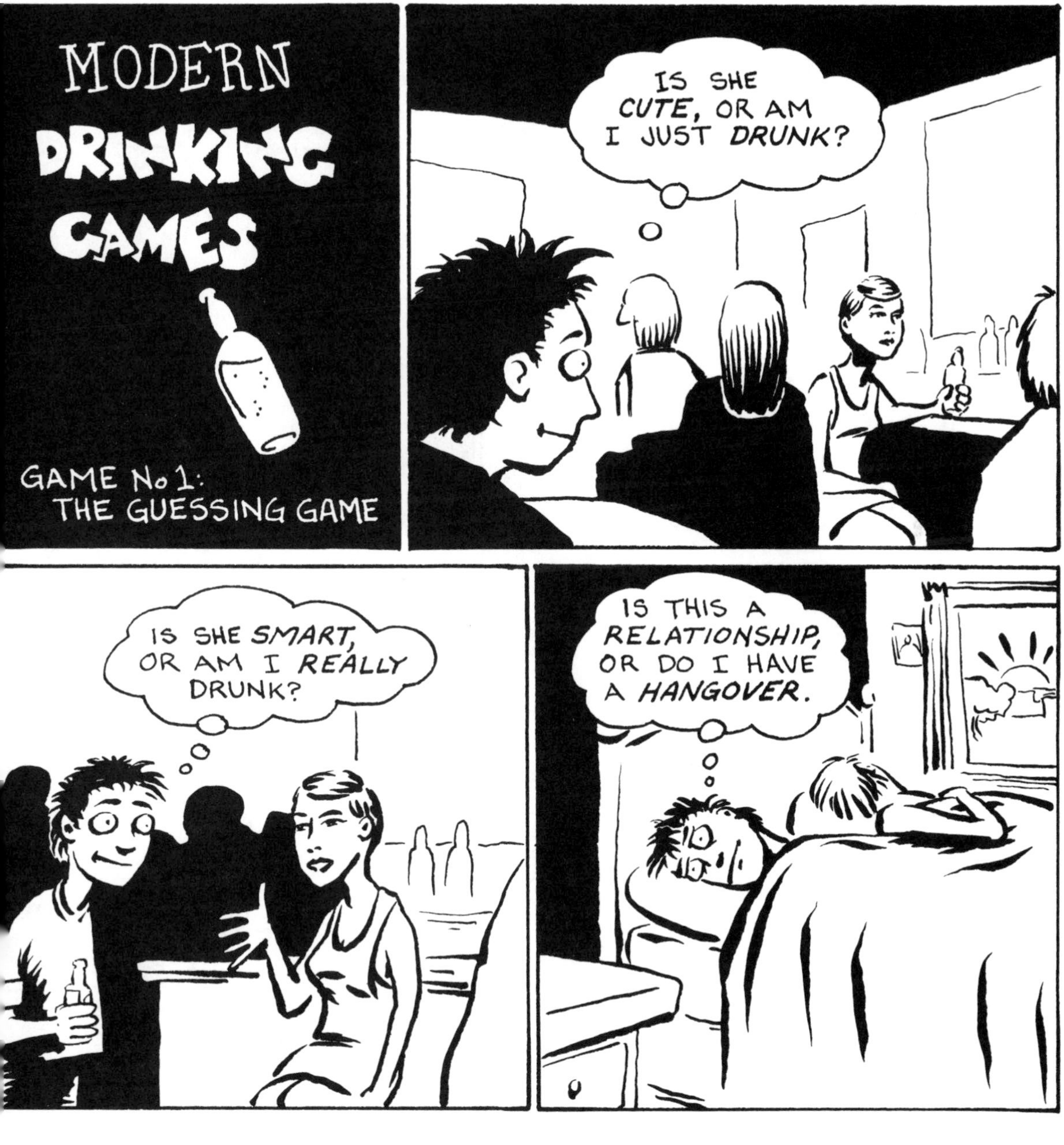
MODERN DRINKING GAMES
GAME No 1: THE GUESSING GAME
IS SHE CUTE, OR AM I JUST DRUNK?
IS SHE SMART, OR AM I REALLY DRUNK?
IS THIS A RELATIONSHIP, OR DO I HAVE A HANGOVER.

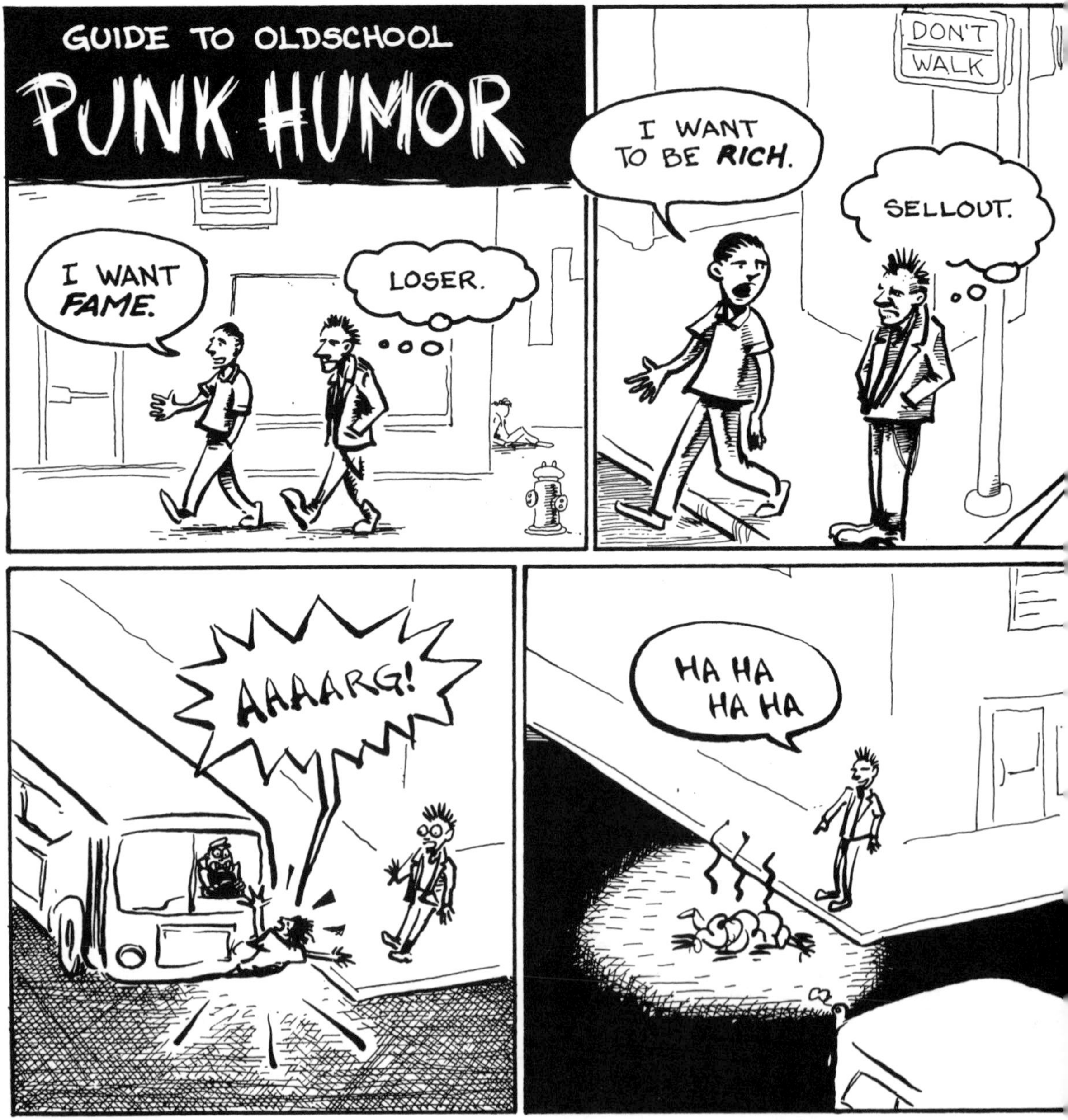
GUIDE TO OLDSCHOOL
PUNK HUMOR
I WANT FAME.
LOSER.
DON'T WALK
I WANT TO BE RICH.
SELLOUT.
AAAARG!
HA HA HA HA

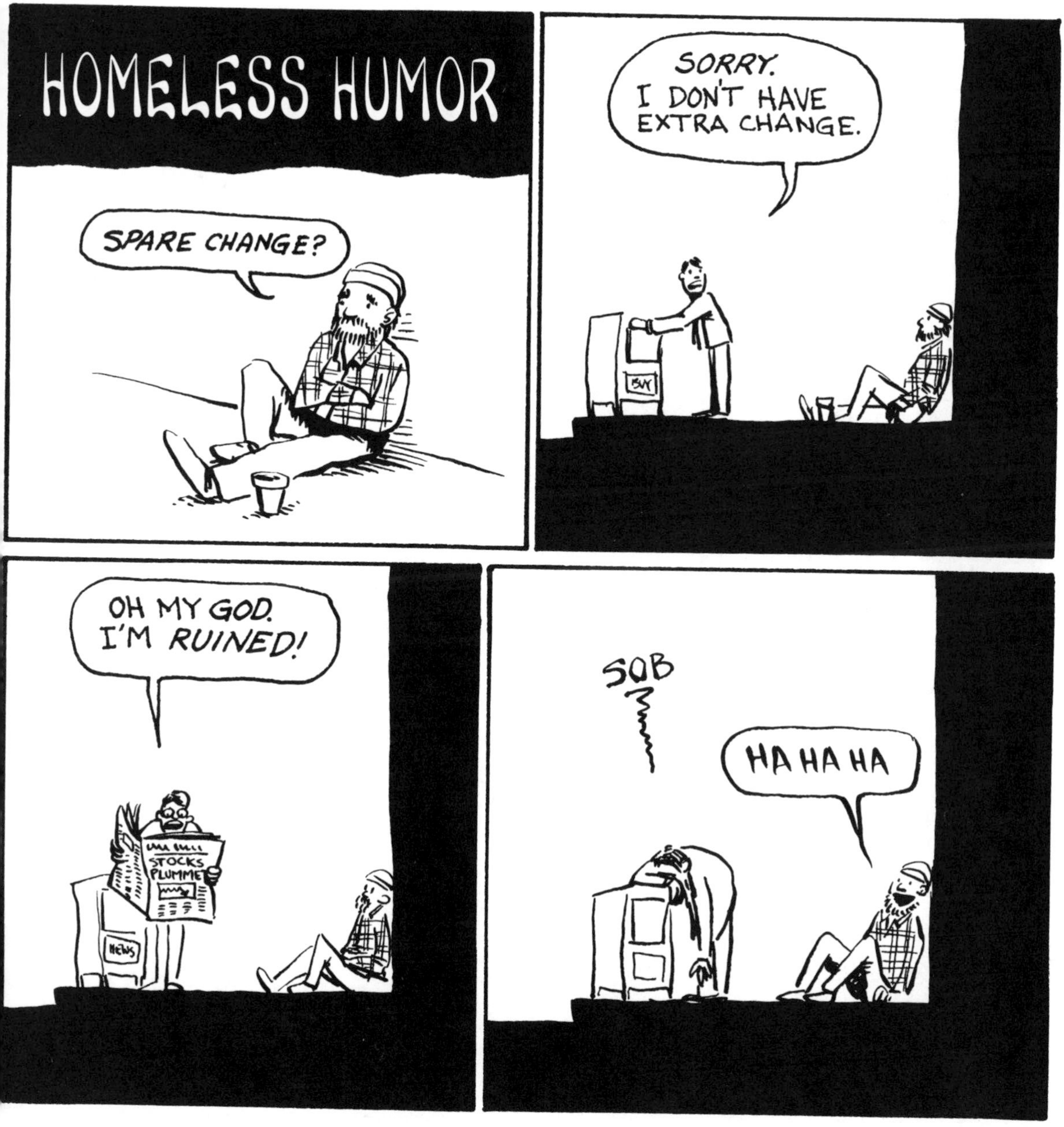
HOMELESS HUMOR
SPARE CHANGE?
SORRY. I DON'T HAVE EXTRA CHANGE.
BUY
OH MY GOD. I'M RUINED!
STOCKS PLUMMET
NEWS
SOB
HA HA HA

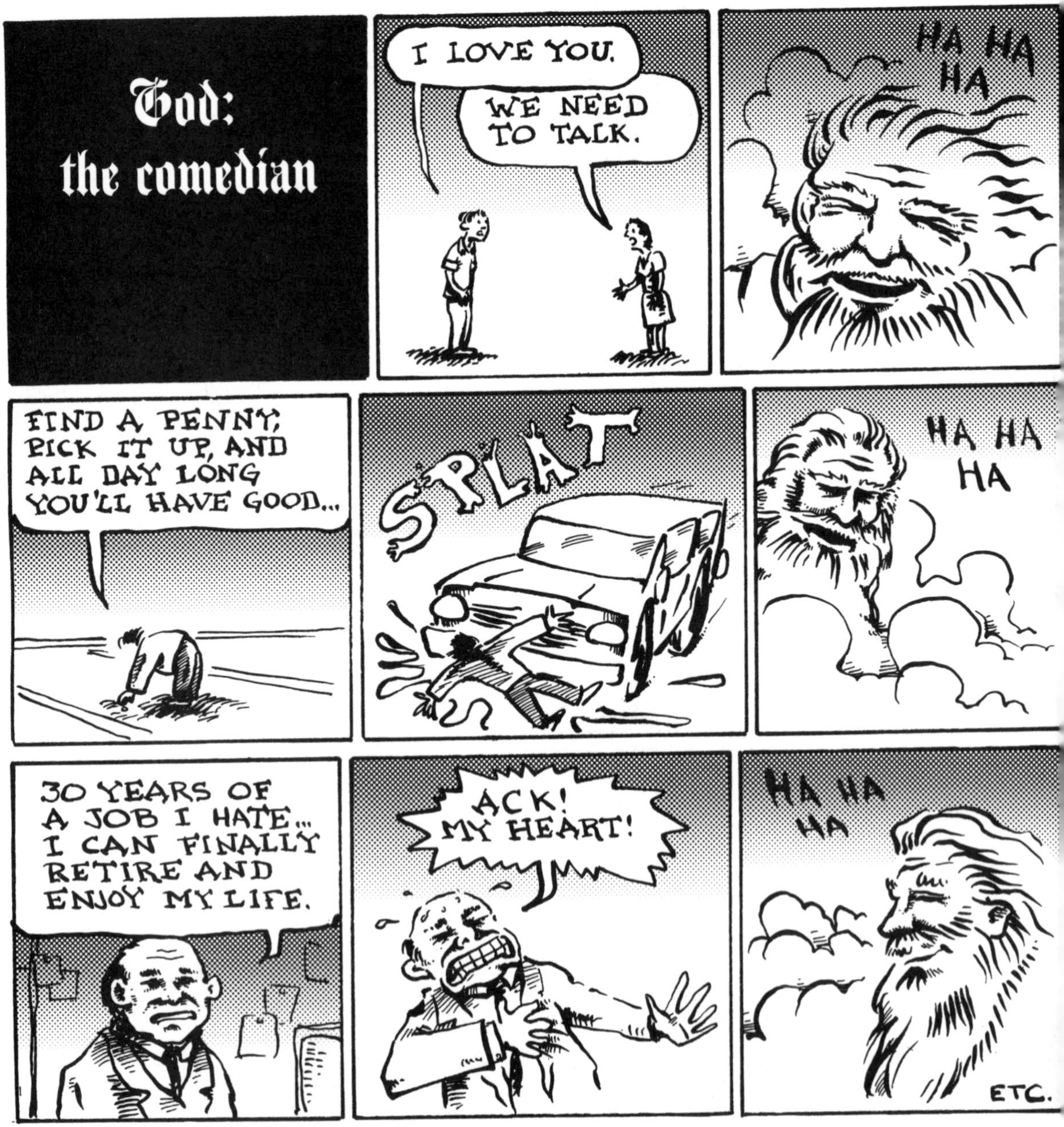
God:
the comedian
I LOVE YOU.
WE NEED TO TALK.
HA HA HA
FIND A PENNY, PICK IT UP, AND ALL DAY LONG YOU'LL HAVE GOOD...
SPLAT
HA HA HA
30 YEARS OF A JOB I HATE... I CAN FINALLY RETIRE AND ENJOY MY LIFE.
ACK! MY HEART!
HA HA HA
ETC.

HERE'S THE CHURCH,

HERE'S THE STEEPLE,

OPEN THE DOORS, WHERE ARE THE PEOPLE?

ACROSS THE STREET,

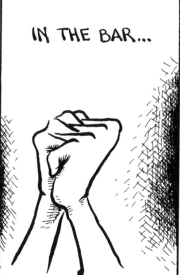

IN THE BAR...

OPEN THE DOORS...

AND THERE THEY ARE!

LIFE:

PLAY, PLAY, PLAY, PLAY, PLAY, PLAY, PLAY, PLAY, PLAY, PLAY,
PLAY, PLAY, PLAY, PLAY, PLAY, PLAY, PLAY, PLAY, PLAY, PLAY,
PLAY, PLAY, PLAY, PLAY, PLAY, PLAY, PLAY, PLAY, PLAY, PLAY,
PLAY, SCHOOL, PLAY, SCHOOL, PLAY, SCHOOL, PLAY, SCHOOL,
SCHOOL, SCHOOL, SCHOOL, SCHOOL, SCHOOL, SCHOOL, SCHOOL,
SCHOOL, SCHOOL, SCHOOL, SCHOOL, SCHOOL, SCHOOL, SCHOOL,
SCHOOL, SCHOOL, SCHOOL, SCHOOL, SCHOOL, SCHOOL, SCHOOL,
FIRST LOVE, BRIEF HAPPINESS, BREAK UP, REGRET, SCHOOL,
SCHOOL, SCHOOL, SCHOOL, SCHOOL, SCHOOL, SCHOOL, SCHOOL,
SCHOOL, SCHOOL, SCHOOL, SCHOOL, SCHOOL, SCHOOL, SCHOOL,
PLAY, WORK, PLAY, WORK, PLAY, WORK, PLAY, WORK,
IDEALISM, EFFORT, REJECTION, FAILURE, WORK, EFFORT, FAILURE,
COMPROMISE, WORK, WORK, WORK, WORK, WORK, WORK, PLAY,
COMMITMENT, WORK, WORK, WORK, WORK, WORK, WORK, PLAY,
WORK, WORK, WORK, WORK, WORK, WORK, WORK, WORK, PLAY,
WORK, WORK, WORK, WORK, WORK, WORK, WORK, WORK, PLAY,
WORK, WORK, WORK, WORK, WORK, WORK, WORK, WORK, PLAY,
WORK, WORK, WORK, WORK, WORK, WORK, WORK, WORK, PLAY,
WORK, WORK, WORK, WORK, WORK, WORK, WORK, WORK, PLAY,
WORK, WORK, WORK, WORK, WORK, WORK, WORK, WORK, PLAY,
WORK, WORK, WORK, WORK, WORK, WORK, WORK, WORK, PLAY,
WORK, WORK, WORK, WORK, WORK, WORK, WORK, WORK, PLAY,
WORK, WORK, WORK, WORK, WORK, WORK, WORK, WORK, PLAY,
WORK, WORK, WORK, WORK, WORK, WORK, WORK, WORK, PLAY,
WORK, WORK, WORK, WORK, WORK, WORK, WORK, WORK, PLAY,
WORK, WORK, WORK, WORK, WORK, WORK, WORK, WORK, PLAY,
WORK, WORK, WORK, WORK, WORK, WORK, WORK, WORK, PLAY,
WORK, WORK, WORK, WORK, WORK, WORK, WORK, WORK, PLAY,
RETIRE, PLAY, DIE.

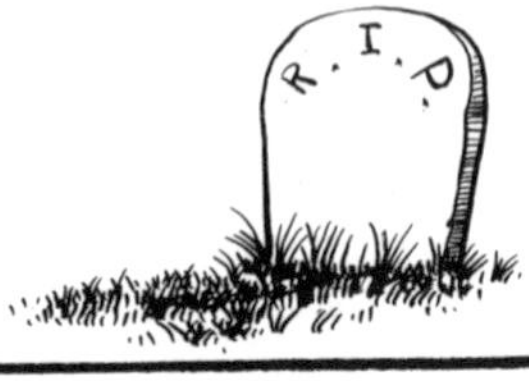
R.I.P.

TOO MUCH COFFEE MAN

BY SHANNON WHEELER

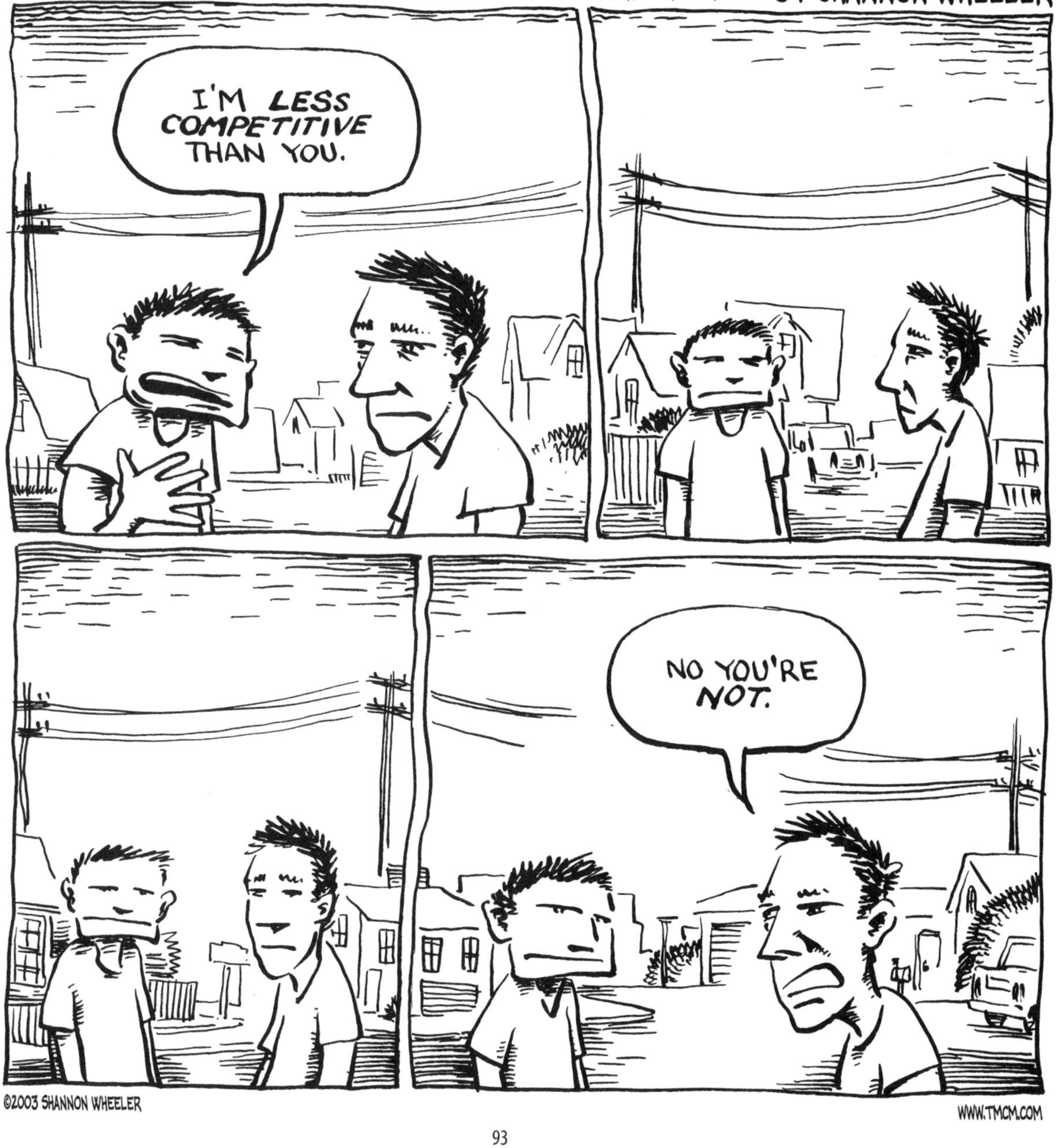
I'M *LESS* COMPETITIVE THAN YOU.
NO YOU'RE *NOT.*

WWW.TMCM.COM

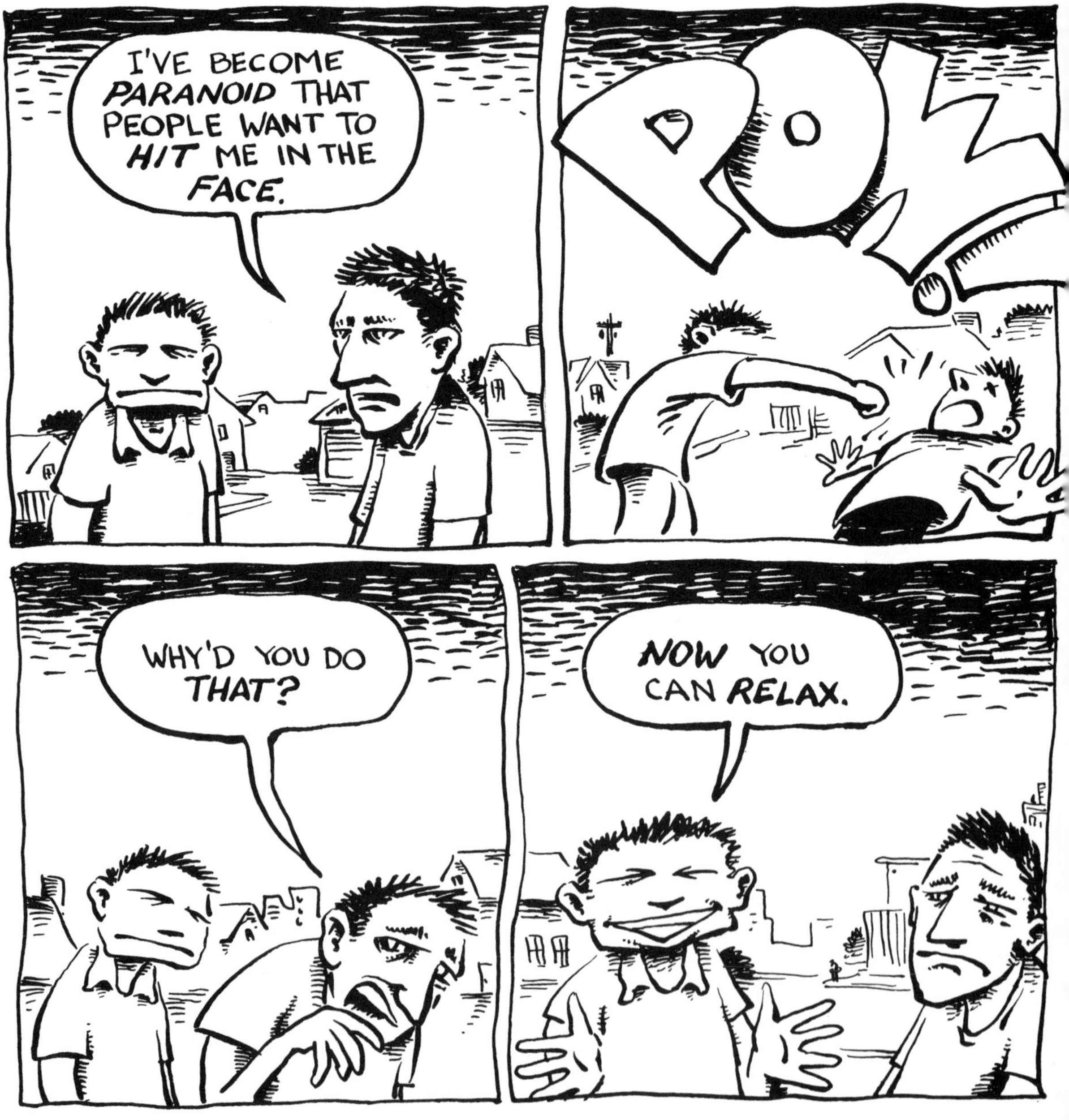
I'VE BECOME PARANOID THAT PEOPLE WANT TO HIT ME IN THE FACE.
POW
WHY'D YOU DO THAT?
NOW YOU CAN RELAX.

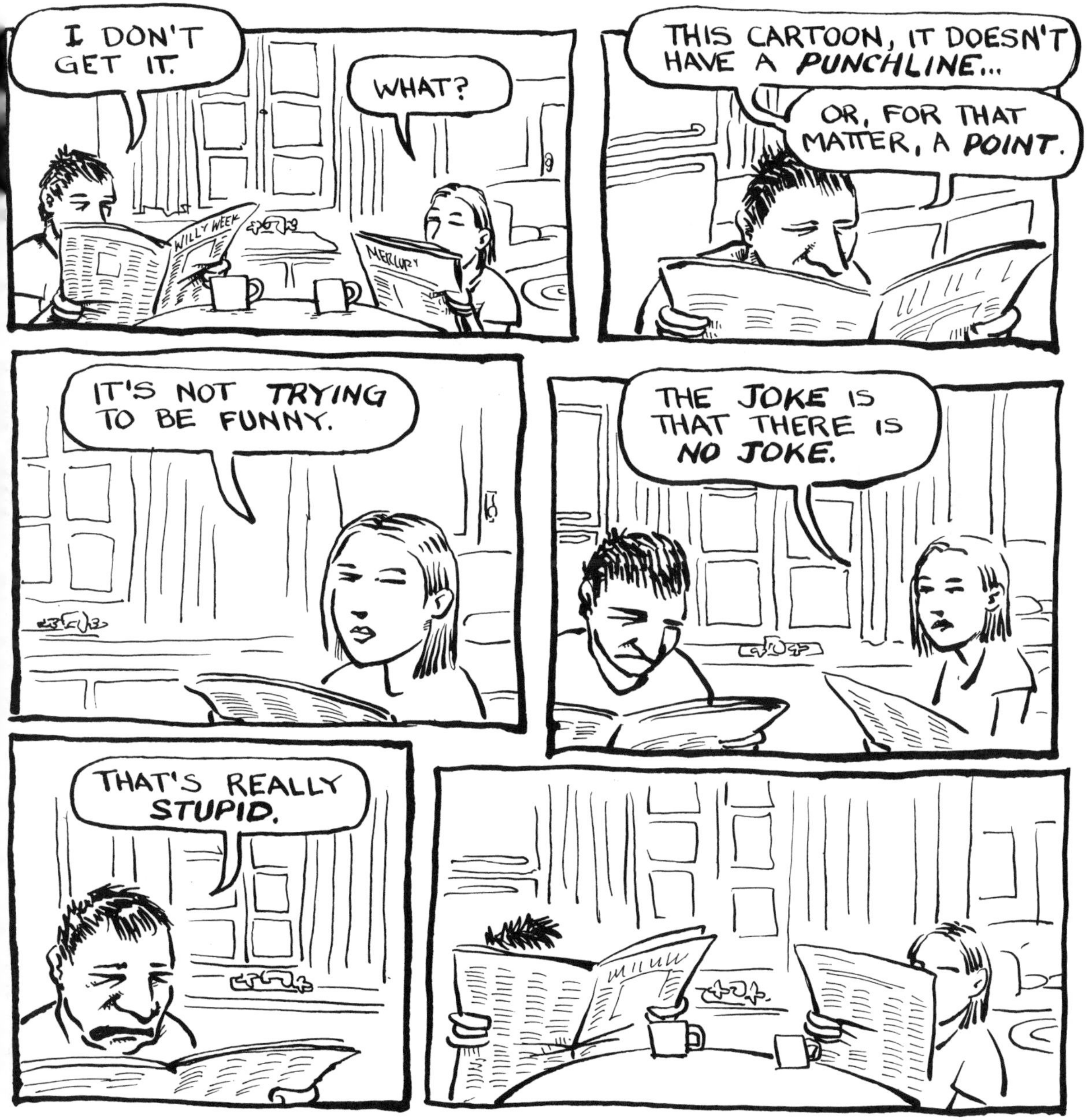
I DON'T GET IT.
WHAT?
WILLY WEEK
MERCURY
THIS CARTOON, IT DOESN'T HAVE A PUNCHLINE...
OR, FOR THAT MATTER, A POINT.
IT'S NOT TRYING TO BE FUNNY.
THE JOKE IS THAT THERE IS NO JOKE.
THAT'S REALLY STUPID.

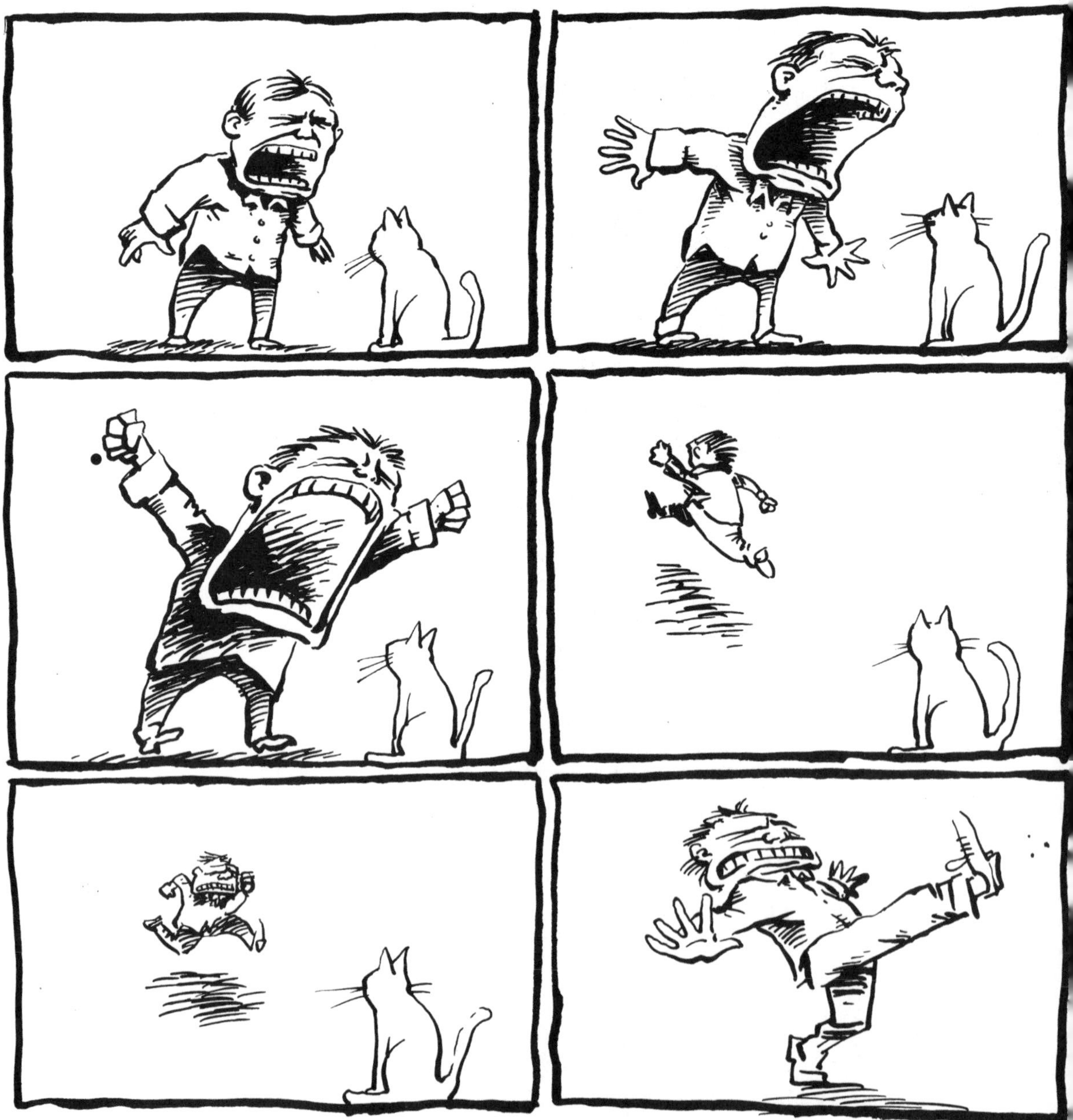

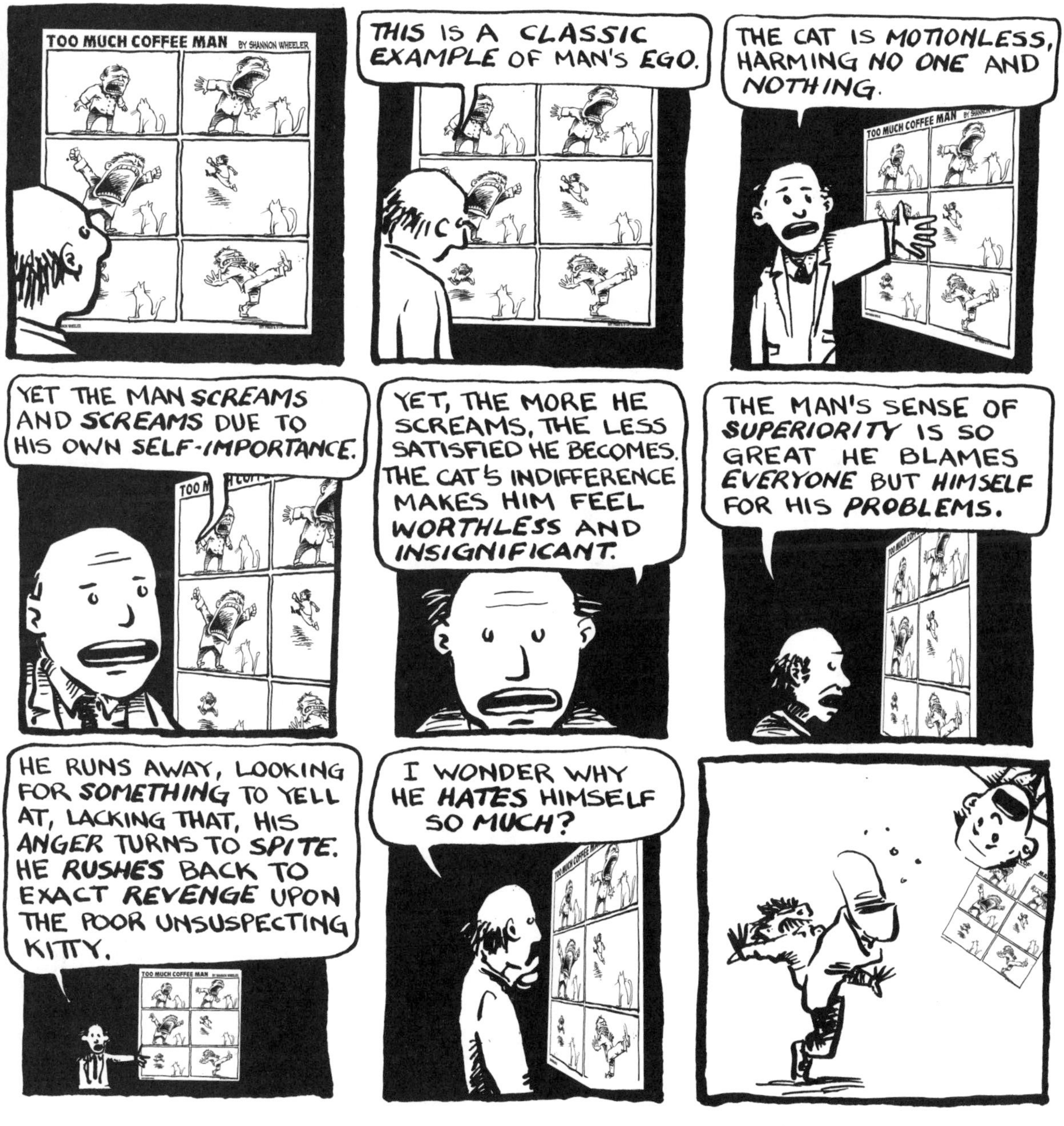
TOO MUCH COFFEE MAN BY SHANNON WHEELER
THIS IS A CLASSIC EXAMPLE OF MAN'S EGO.
THE CAT IS MOTIONLESS, HARMING NO ONE AND NOTHING.
YET THE MAN SCREAMS AND SCREAMS DUE TO HIS OWN SELF-IMPORTANCE.
YET, THE MORE HE SCREAMS, THE LESS SATISFIED HE BECOMES. THE CAT'S INDIFFERENCE MAKES HIM FEEL WORTHLESS AND INSIGNIFICANT.
THE MAN'S SENSE OF SUPERIORITY IS SO GREAT HE BLAMES EVERYONE BUT HIMSELF FOR HIS PROBLEMS.
HE RUNS AWAY, LOOKING FOR SOMETHING TO YELL AT, LACKING THAT, HIS ANGER TURNS TO SPITE. HE RUSHES BACK TO EXACT REVENGE UPON THE POOR UNSUSPECTING KITTY.
I WONDER WHY HE HATES HIMSELF SO MUCH?

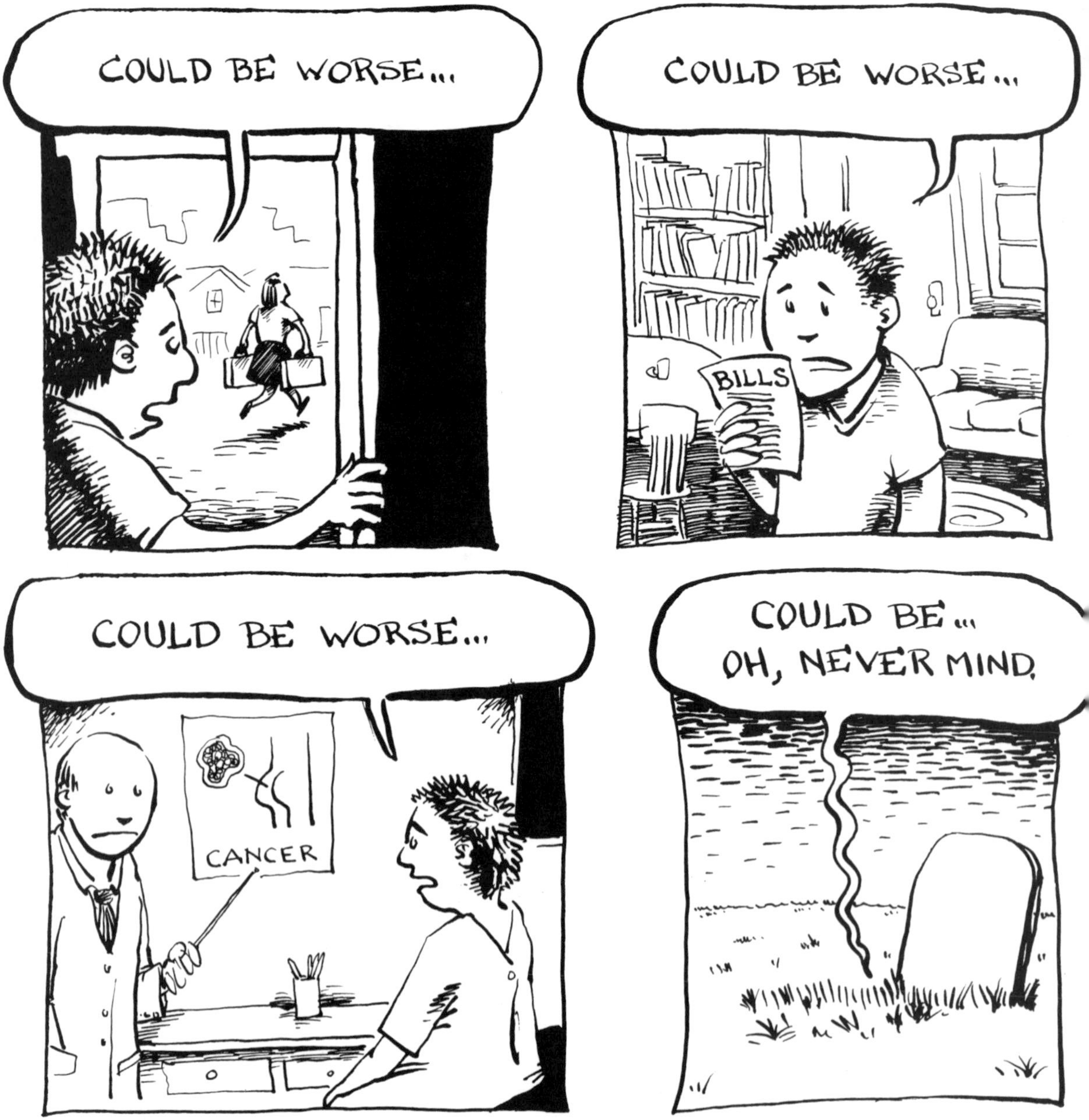
COULD BE WORSE...
COULD BE WORSE...
BILLS
COULD BE WORSE...
CANCER
COULD BE... OH, NEVER MIND.

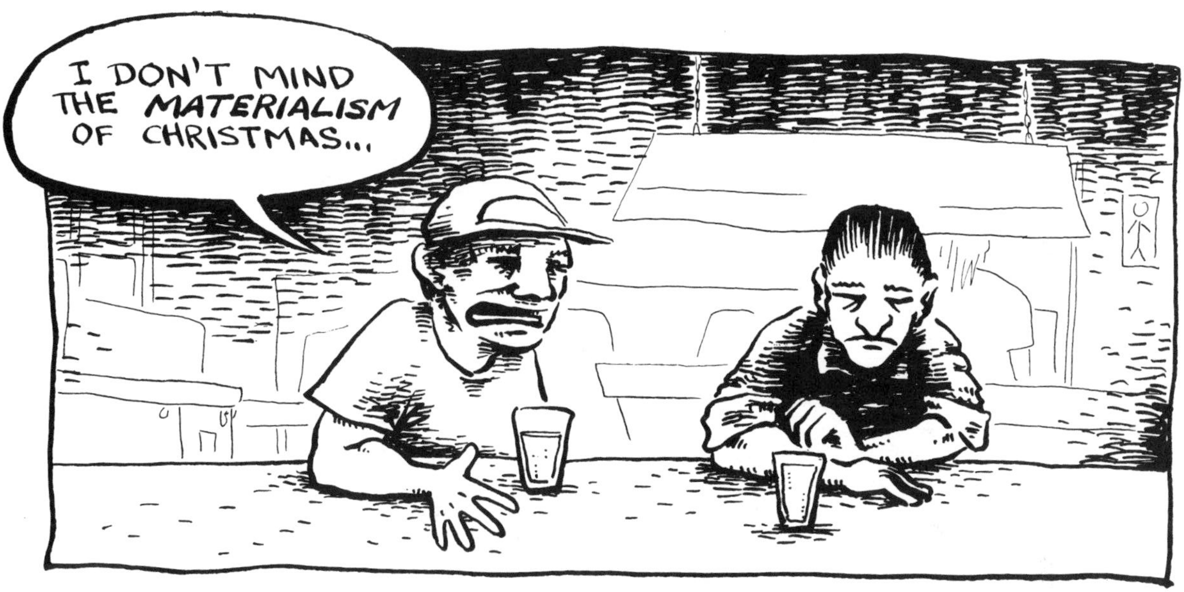
I DON'T MIND THE MATERIALISM OF CHRISTMAS...

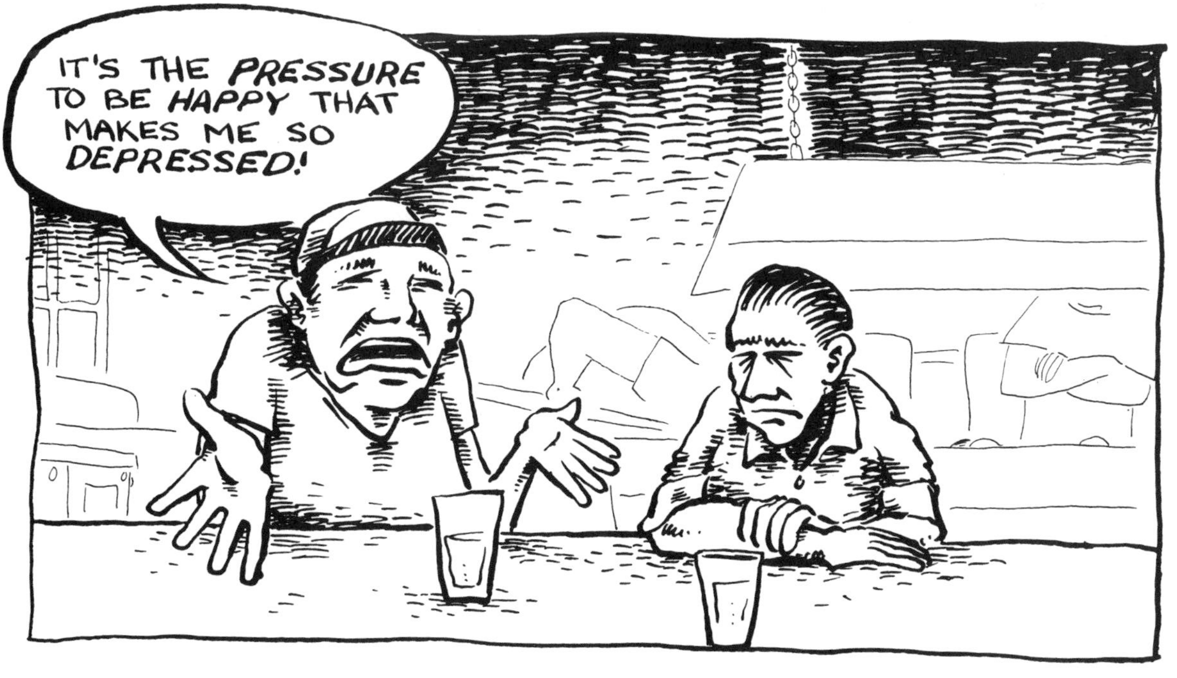
IT'S THE PRESSURE TO BE HAPPY THAT MAKES ME SO DEPRESSED!

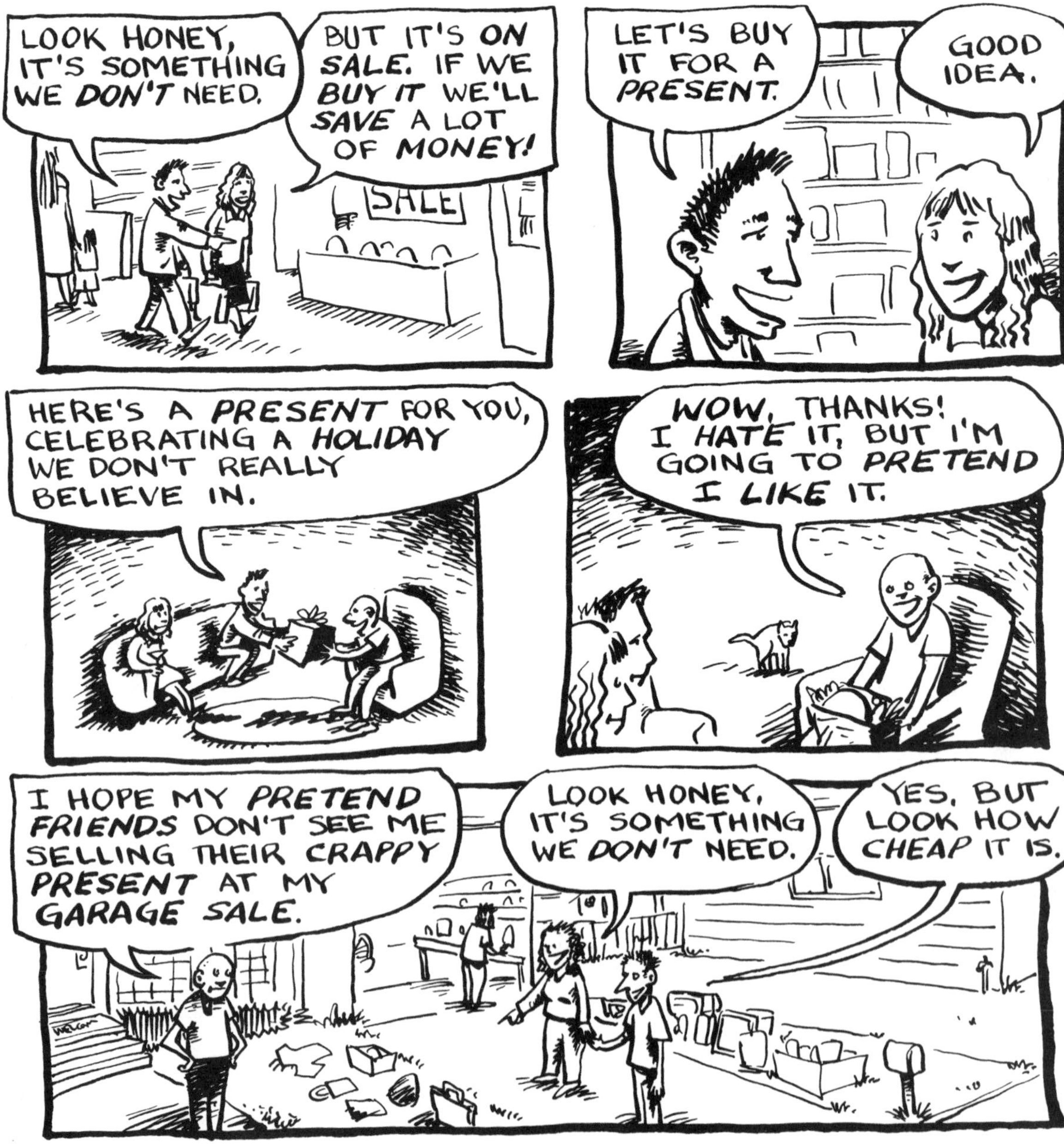
LOOK HONEY, IT'S SOMETHING WE DON'T NEED.
BUT IT'S ON SALE. IF WE BUY IT WE'LL SAVE A LOT OF MONEY!
SALE
LET'S BUY IT FOR A PRESENT.
GOOD IDEA.
HERE'S A PRESENT FOR YOU, CELEBRATING A HOLIDAY WE DON'T REALLY BELIEVE IN.
WOW, THANKS! I HATE IT, BUT I'M GOING TO PRETEND I LIKE IT.
I HOPE MY PRETEND FRIENDS DON'T SEE ME SELLING THEIR CRAPPY PRESENT AT MY GARAGE SALE.
LOOK HONEY, IT'S SOMETHING WE DON'T NEED.
YES, BUT LOOK HOW CHEAP IT IS.

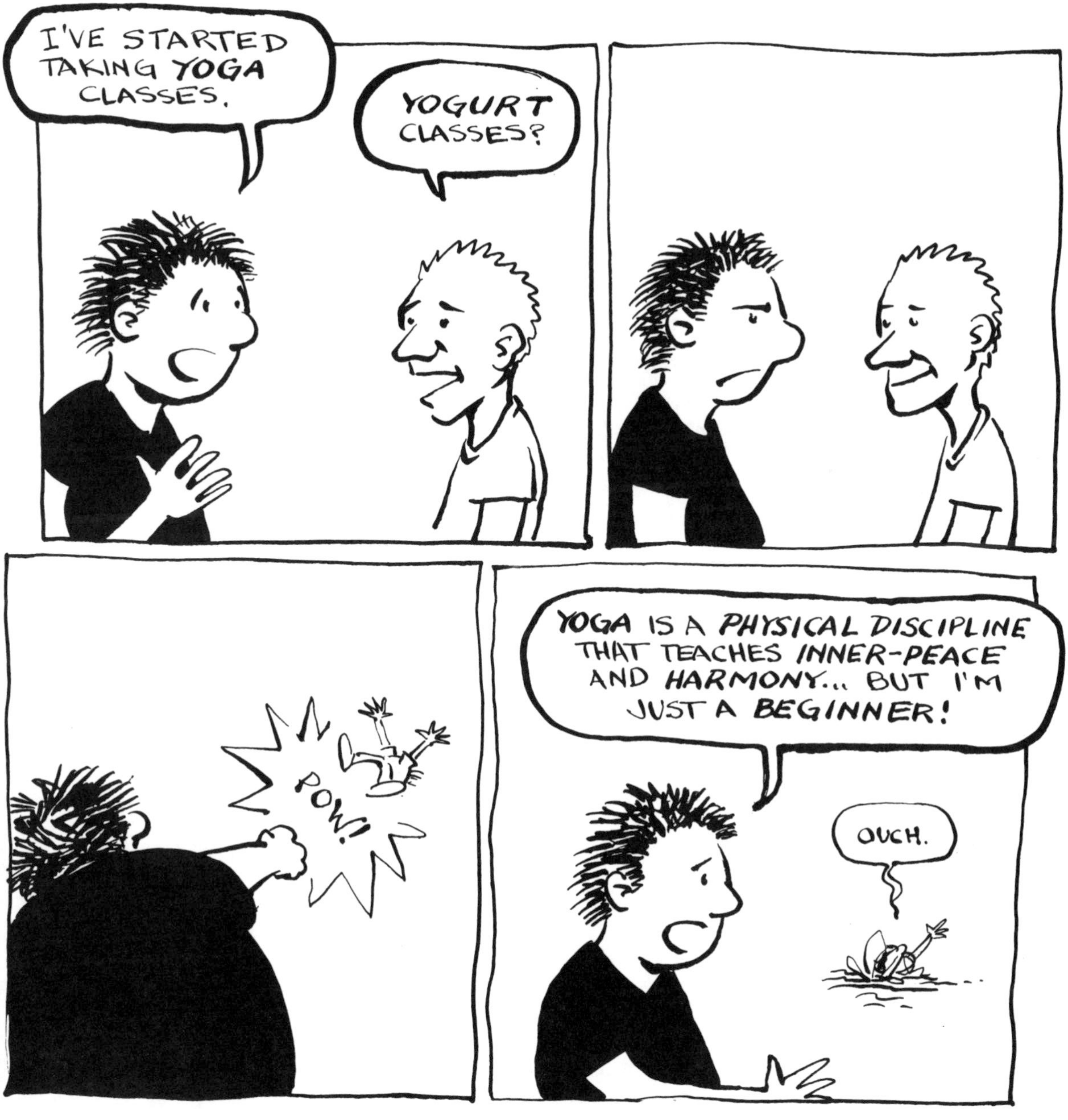
I'VE STARTED TAKING YOGA CLASSES.
YOGURT CLASSES?
POW!
YOGA IS A PHYSICAL DISCIPLINE THAT TEACHES INNER-PEACE AND HARMONY... BUT I'M JUST A BEGINNER!
OUCH.

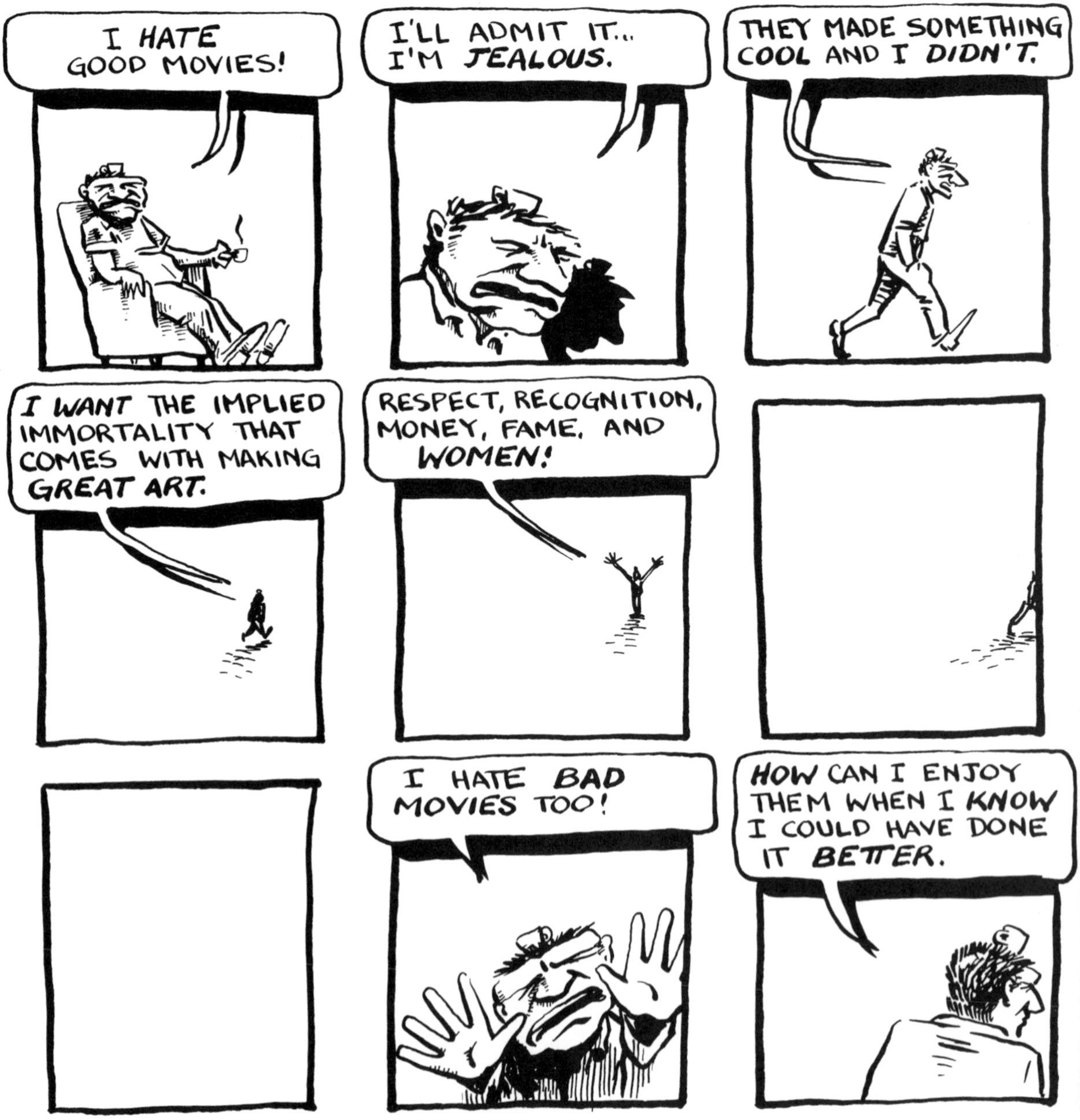
I HATE GOOD MOVIES!
I'LL ADMIT IT... I'M JEALOUS.
THEY MADE SOMETHING COOL AND I DIDN'T.
I WANT THE IMPLIED IMMORTALITY THAT COMES WITH MAKING GREAT ART.
RESPECT, RECOGNITION, MONEY, FAME, AND WOMEN!
I HATE BAD MOVIES TOO!
HOW CAN I ENJOY THEM WHEN I KNOW I COULD HAVE DONE IT BETTER.

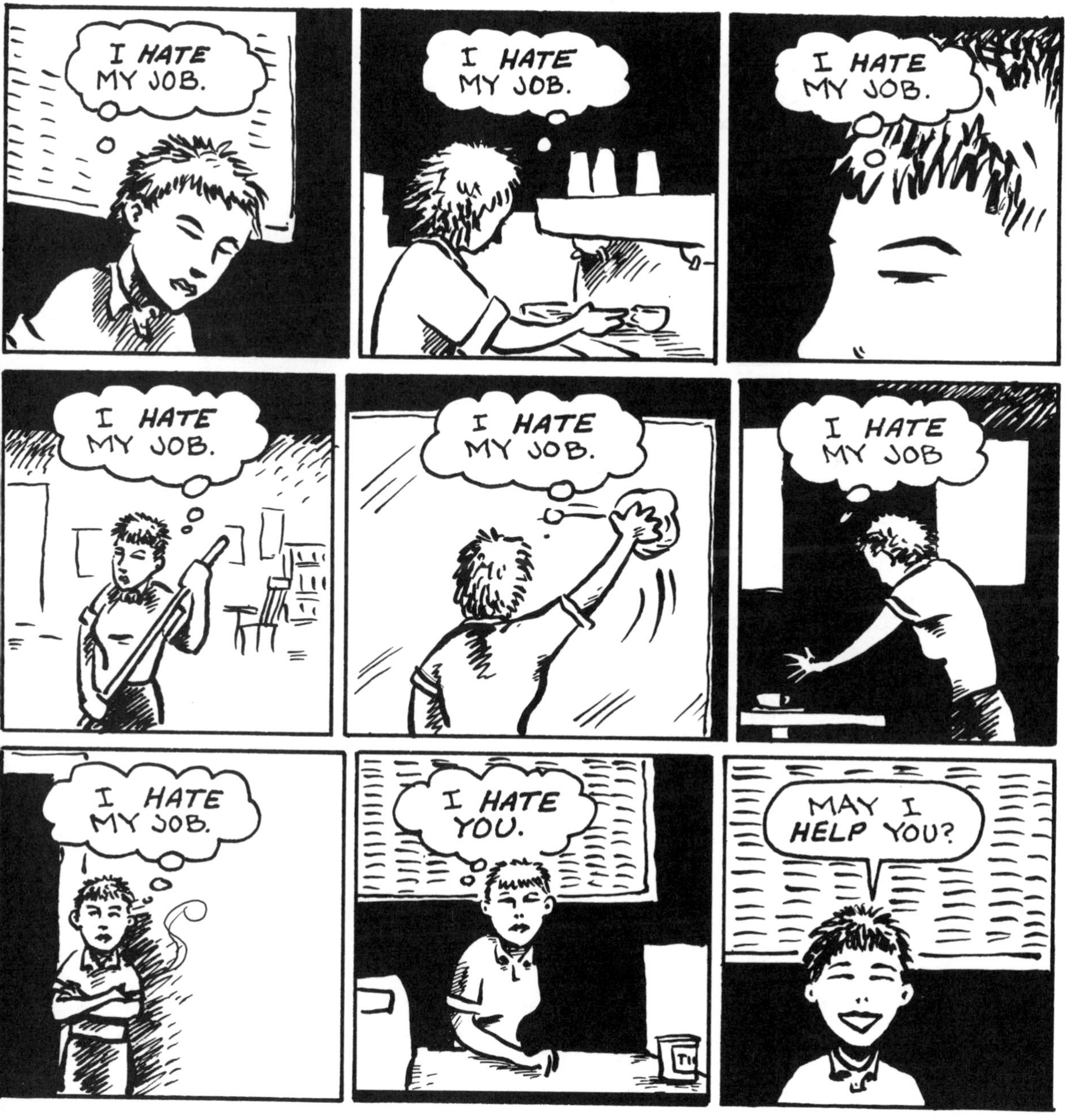
I HATE MY JOB.
I HATE MY JOB.
I HATE MY JOB.
I HATE MY JOB.
I HATE MY JOB.
I HATE MY JOB
I HATE MY JOB.
I HATE YOU.
MAY I HELP YOU?

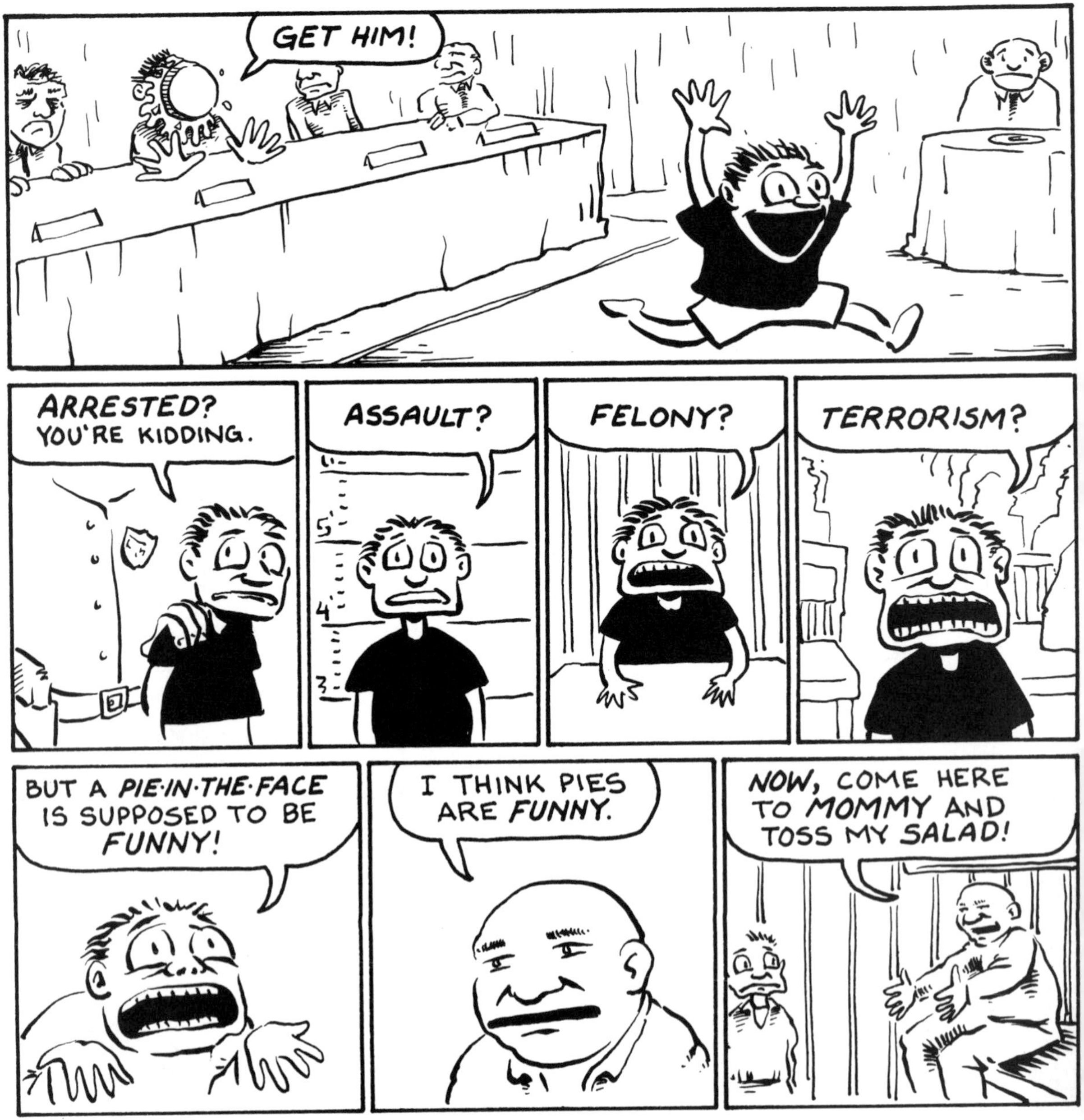
GET HIM!
ARRESTED? YOU'RE KIDDING.
ASSAULT?
FELONY?
TERRORISM?
BUT A PIE·IN·THE·FACE IS SUPPOSED TO BE FUNNY!
I THINK PIES ARE FUNNY.
NOW, COME HERE TO MOMMY AND TOSS MY SALAD!

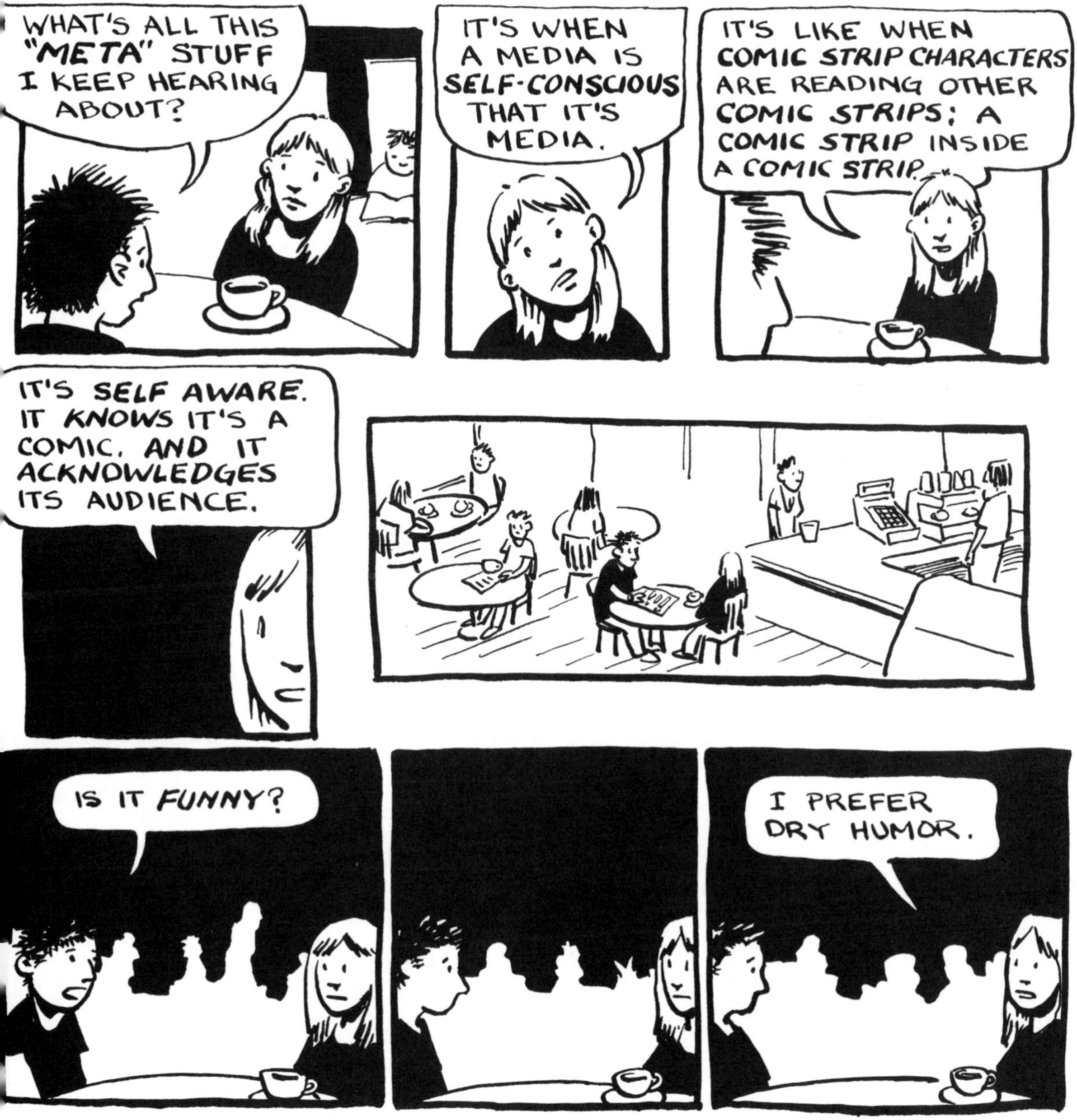
WHAT'S ALL THIS "META" STUFF I KEEP HEARING ABOUT?
IT'S WHEN A MEDIA IS SELF-CONSCIOUS THAT IT'S MEDIA.
IT'S LIKE WHEN COMIC STRIP CHARACTERS ARE READING OTHER COMIC STRIPS; A COMIC STRIP INSIDE A COMIC STRIP.
IT'S SELF AWARE. IT KNOWS IT'S A COMIC. AND IT ACKNOWLEDGES ITS AUDIENCE.
IS IT FUNNY?
I PREFER DRY HUMOR.

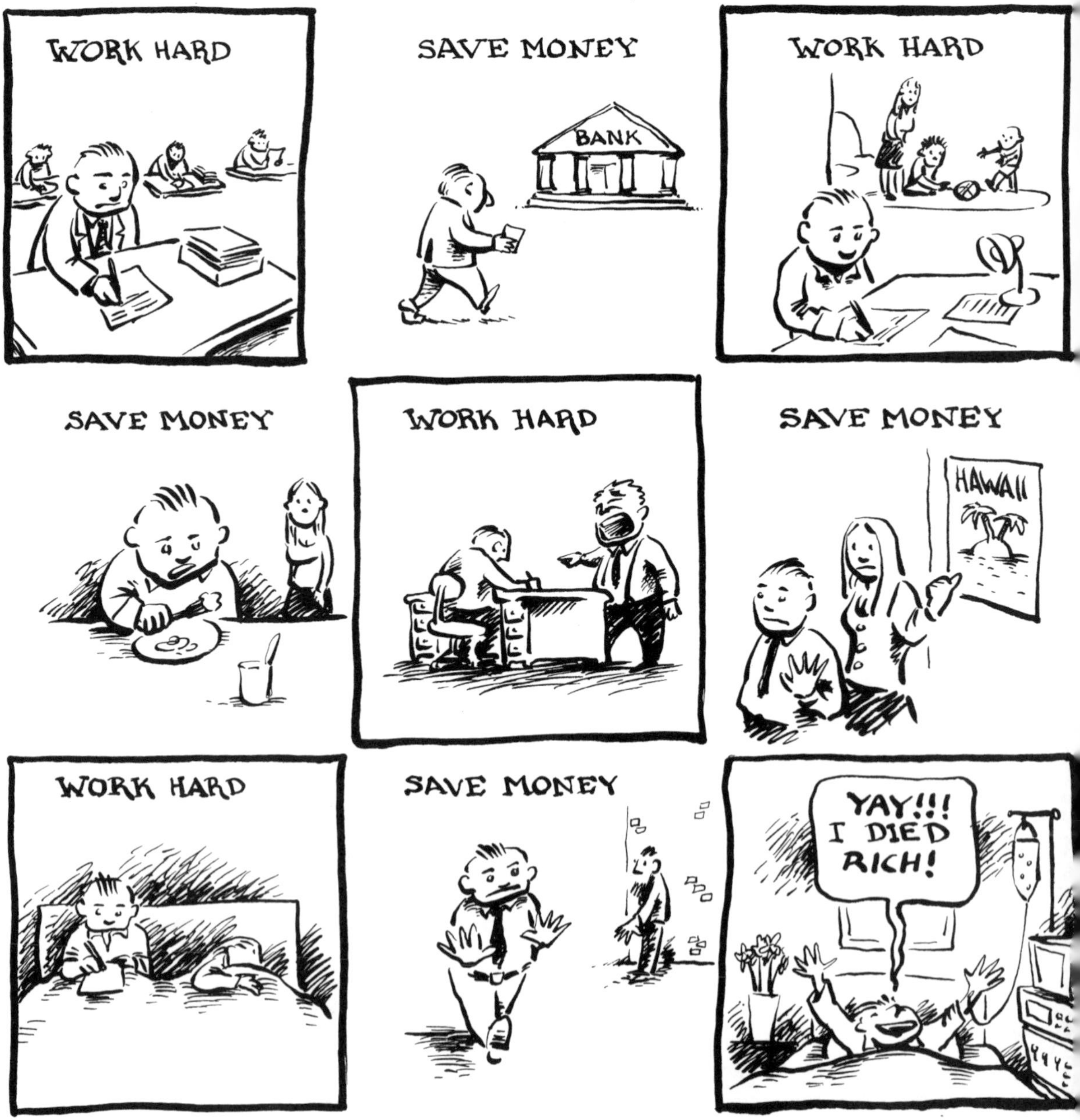
WORK HARD
SAVE MONEY
BANK
WORK HARD
SAVE MONEY
WORK HARD
SAVE MONEY
HAWAII
WORK HARD
SAVE MONEY
YAY!!! I DIED RICH!

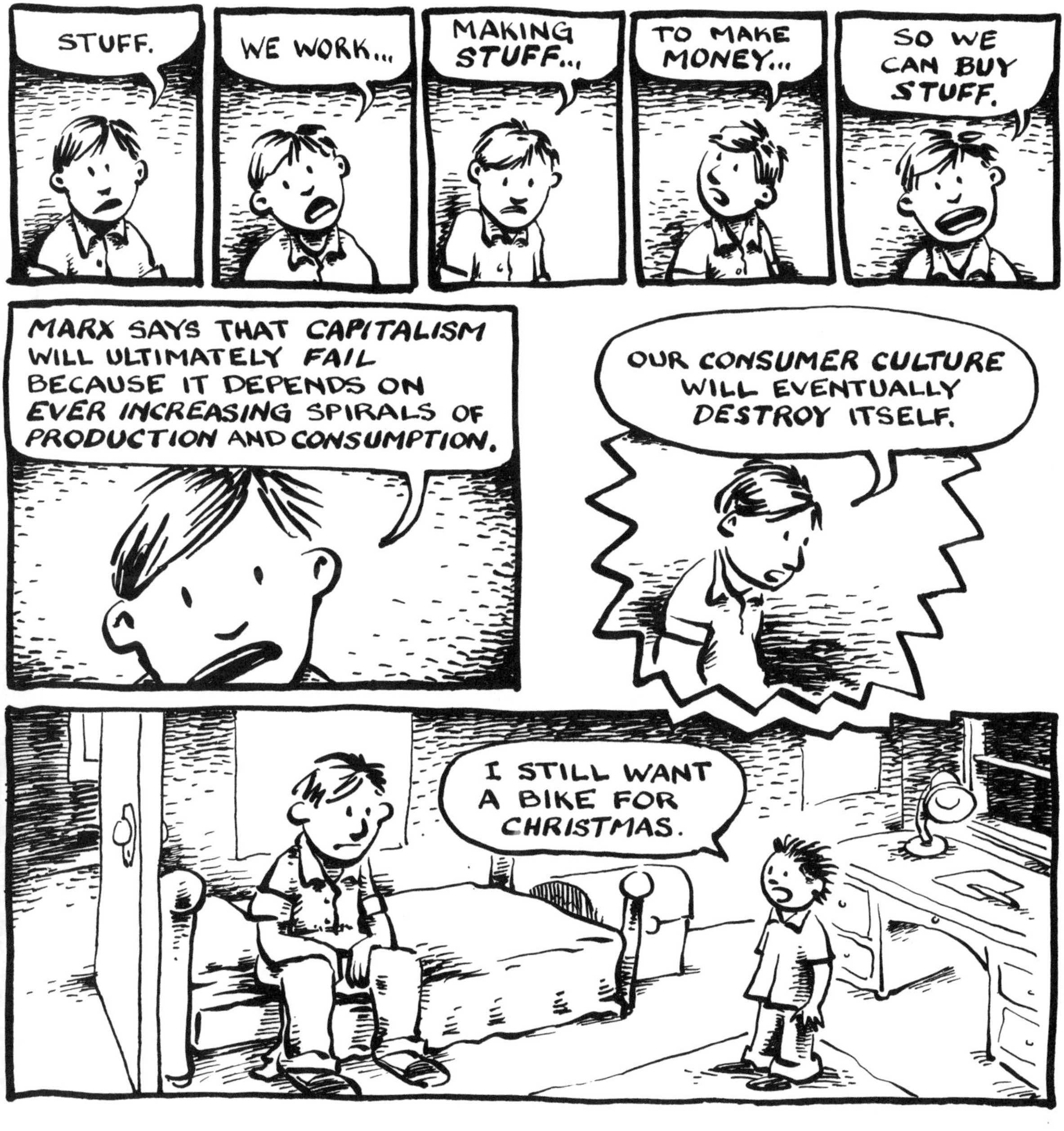
STUFF.
WE WORK...
MAKING STUFF...
TO MAKE MONEY...
SO WE CAN BUY STUFF.
MARX SAYS THAT CAPITALISM WILL ULTIMATELY FAIL BECAUSE IT DEPENDS ON EVER INCREASING SPIRALS OF PRODUCTION AND CONSUMPTION.
OUR CONSUMER CULTURE WILL EVENTUALLY DESTROY ITSELF.
I STILL WANT A BIKE FOR CHRISTMAS.

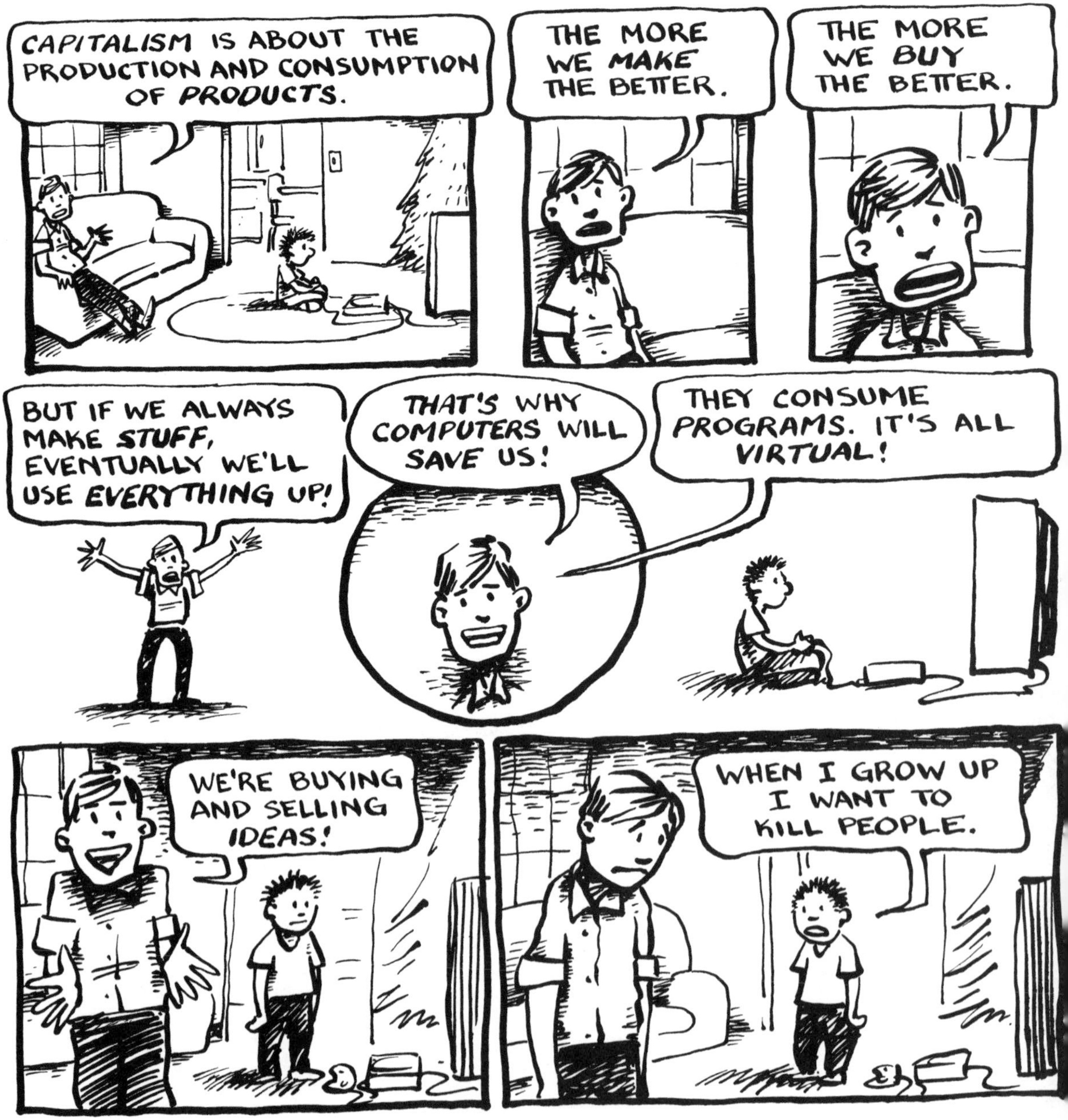
CAPITALISM IS ABOUT THE PRODUCTION AND CONSUMPTION OF PRODUCTS.
THE MORE WE MAKE THE BETTER.
THE MORE WE BUY THE BETTER.
BUT IF WE ALWAYS MAKE STUFF, EVENTUALLY WE'LL USE EVERYTHING UP!
THAT'S WHY COMPUTERS WILL SAVE US!
THEY CONSUME PROGRAMS. IT'S ALL VIRTUAL!
WE'RE BUYING AND SELLING IDEAS!
WHEN I GROW UP I WANT TO KILL PEOPLE.

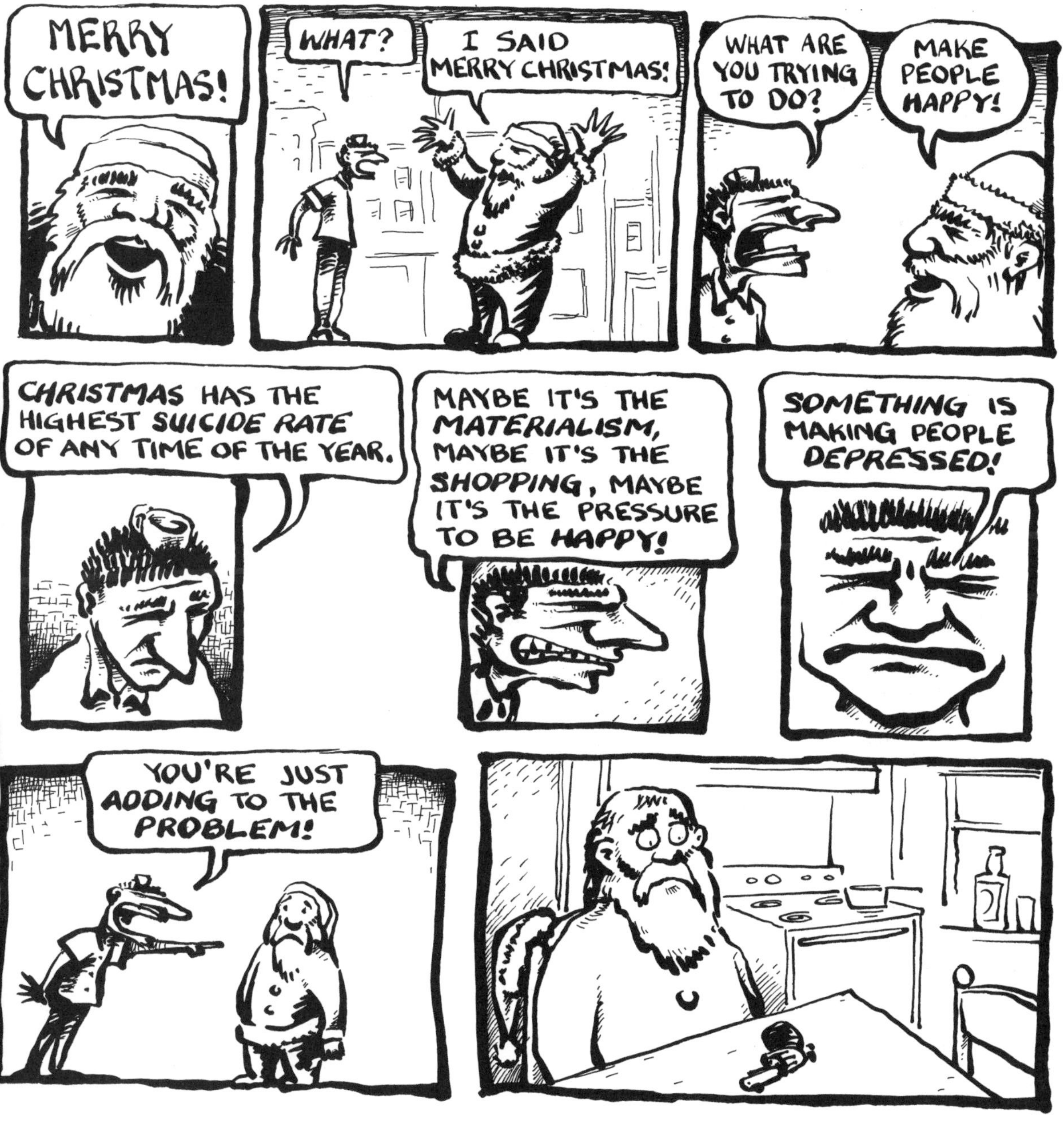
MERRY CHRISTMAS!
WHAT?
I SAID MERRY CHRISTMAS!
WHAT ARE YOU TRYING TO DO?
MAKE PEOPLE HAPPY!
CHRISTMAS HAS THE HIGHEST SUICIDE RATE OF ANY TIME OF THE YEAR.
MAYBE IT'S THE MATERIALISM, MAYBE IT'S THE SHOPPING, MAYBE IT'S THE PRESSURE TO BE HAPPY!
SOMETHING IS MAKING PEOPLE DEPRESSED!
YOU'RE JUST ADDING TO THE PROBLEM!

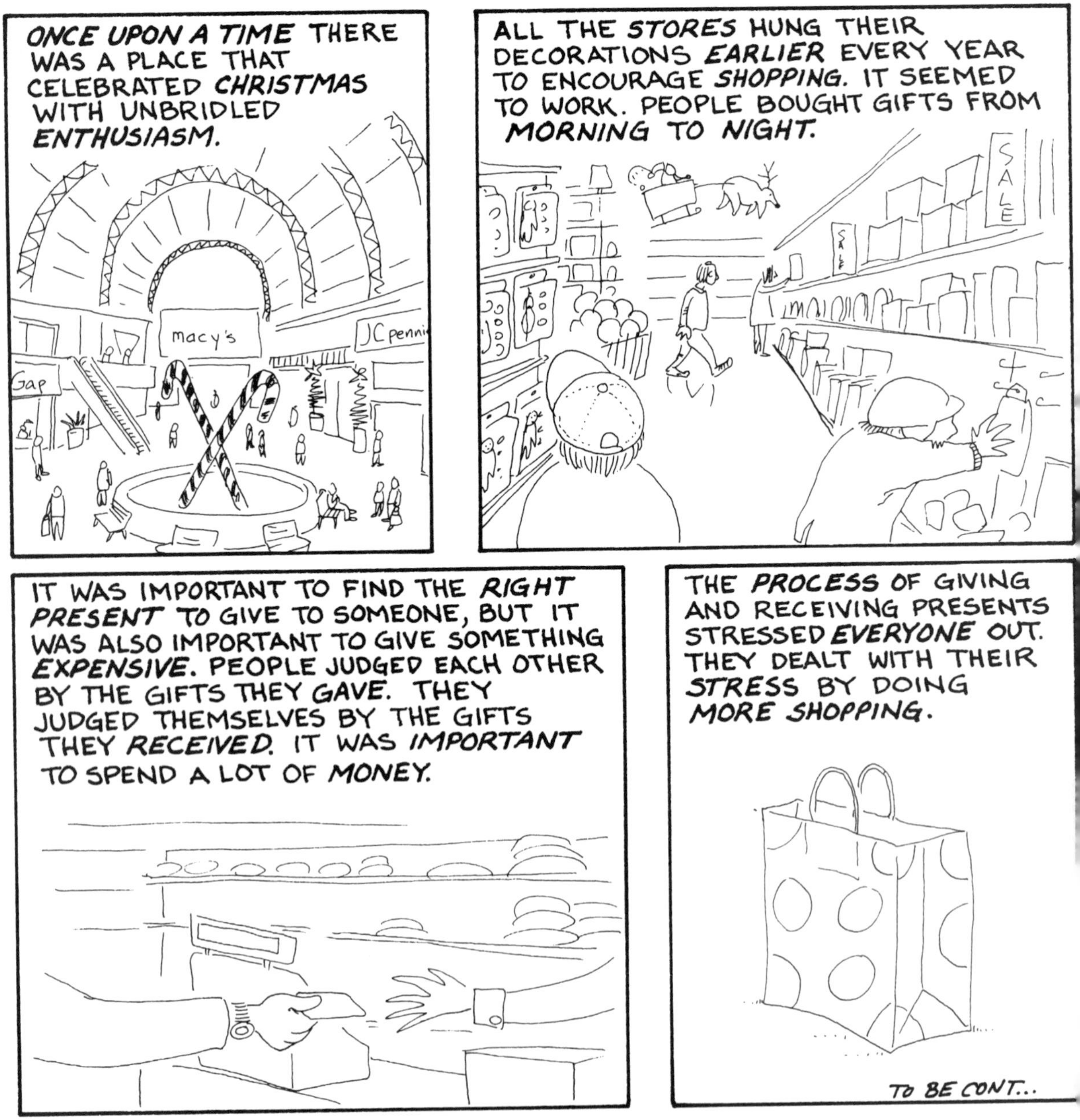
ONCE UPON A TIME THERE WAS A PLACE THAT CELEBRATED CHRISTMAS WITH UNBRIDLED ENTHUSIASM.
macy's
JC penni
Gap
ALL THE STORES HUNG THEIR DECORATIONS EARLIER EVERY YEAR TO ENCOURAGE SHOPPING. IT SEEMED TO WORK. PEOPLE BOUGHT GIFTS FROM MORNING TO NIGHT.
SALE
SALE
IT WAS IMPORTANT TO FIND THE RIGHT PRESENT TO GIVE TO SOMEONE, BUT IT WAS ALSO IMPORTANT TO GIVE SOMETHING EXPENSIVE. PEOPLE JUDGED EACH OTHER BY THE GIFTS THEY GAVE. THEY JUDGED THEMSELVES BY THE GIFTS THEY RECEIVED. IT WAS IMPORTANT TO SPEND A LOT OF MONEY.
THE PROCESS OF GIVING AND RECEIVING PRESENTS STRESSED EVERYONE OUT. THEY DEALT WITH THEIR STRESS BY DOING MORE SHOPPING.
TO BE CONT...

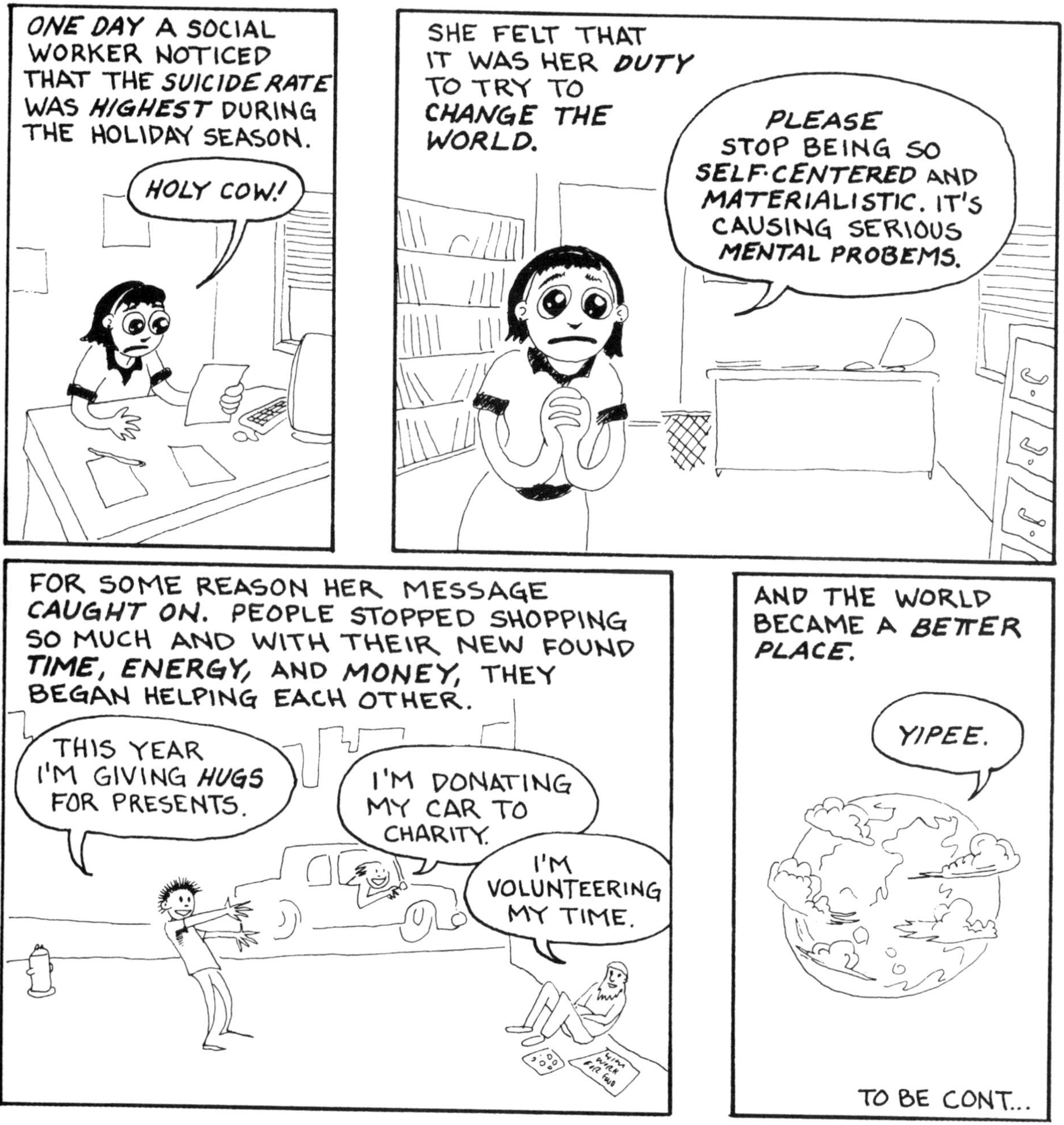
ONE DAY A SOCIAL WORKER NOTICED THAT THE SUICIDE RATE WAS HIGHEST DURING THE HOLIDAY SEASON.
HOLY COW!
SHE FELT THAT IT WAS HER DUTY TO TRY TO CHANGE THE WORLD.
PLEASE STOP BEING SO SELF-CENTERED AND MATERIALISTIC. IT'S CAUSING SERIOUS MENTAL PROBEMS.
FOR SOME REASON HER MESSAGE CAUGHT ON. PEOPLE STOPPED SHOPPING SO MUCH AND WITH THEIR NEW FOUND TIME, ENERGY, AND MONEY, THEY BEGAN HELPING EACH OTHER.
THIS YEAR I'M GIVING HUGS FOR PRESENTS.
I'M DONATING MY CAR TO CHARITY.
I'M VOLUNTEERING MY TIME.
AND THE WORLD BECAME A BETTER PLACE.
YIPEE.
TO BE CONT...

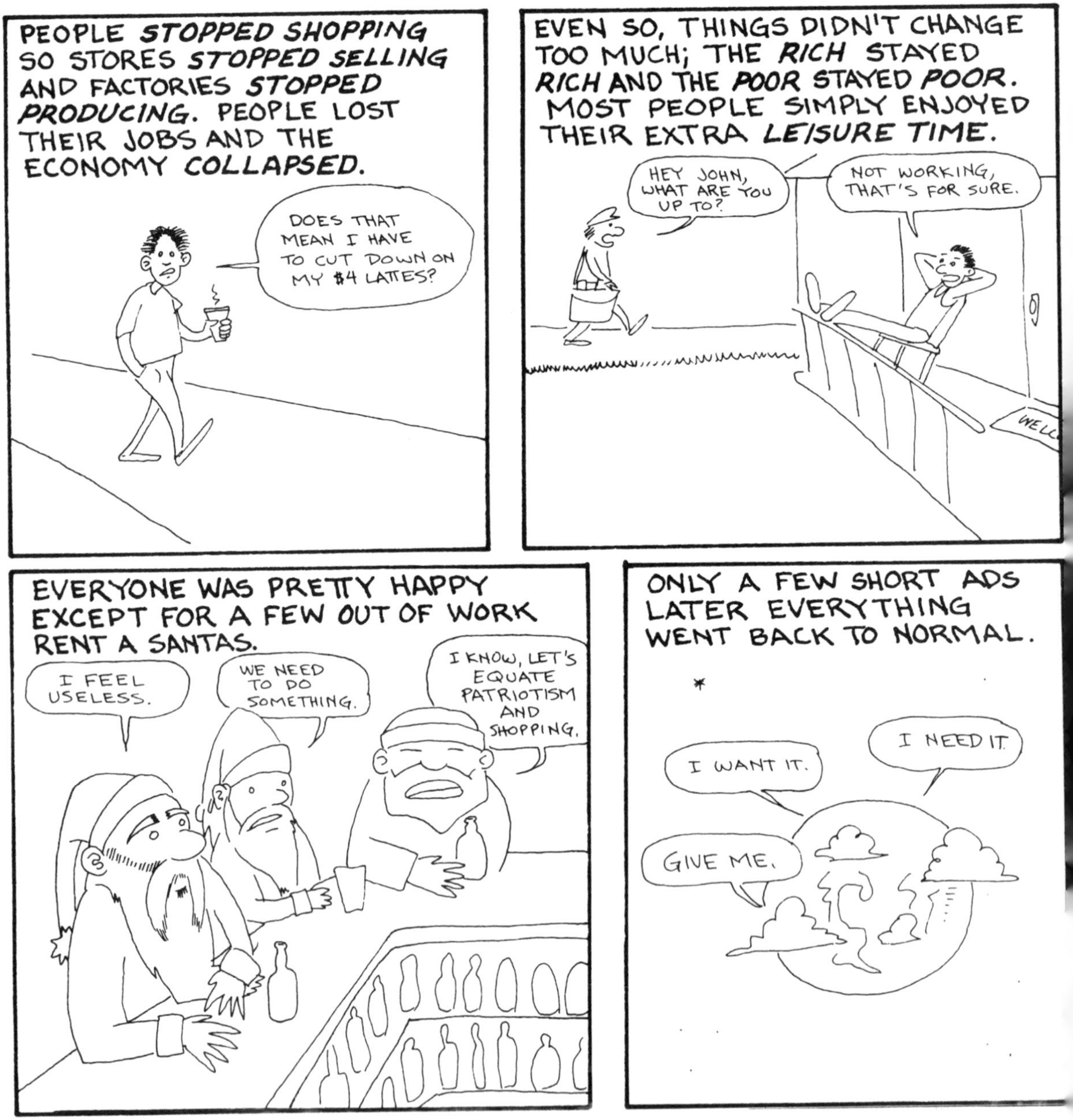
PEOPLE STOPPED SHOPPING SO STORES STOPPED SELLING AND FACTORIES STOPPED PRODUCING. PEOPLE LOST THEIR JOBS AND THE ECONOMY COLLAPSED.
DOES THAT MEAN I HAVE TO CUT DOWN ON MY $4 LATTES?
EVEN SO, THINGS DIDN'T CHANGE TOO MUCH; THE RICH STAYED RICH AND THE POOR STAYED POOR. MOST PEOPLE SIMPLY ENJOYED THEIR EXTRA LEISURE TIME.
HEY JOHN, WHAT ARE YOU UP TO?
NOT WORKING, THAT'S FOR SURE.
EVERYONE WAS PRETTY HAPPY EXCEPT FOR A FEW OUT OF WORK RENT A SANTAS.
I FEEL USELESS.
WE NEED TO DO SOMETHING.
I KNOW, LET'S EQUATE PATRIOTISM AND SHOPPING.
ONLY A FEW SHORT ADS LATER EVERYTHING WENT BACK TO NORMAL.
I WANT IT.
I NEED IT.
GIVE ME.

CHAPTER FOUR

GET HAPPY. BE HAPPY. LIVE HAPPY.

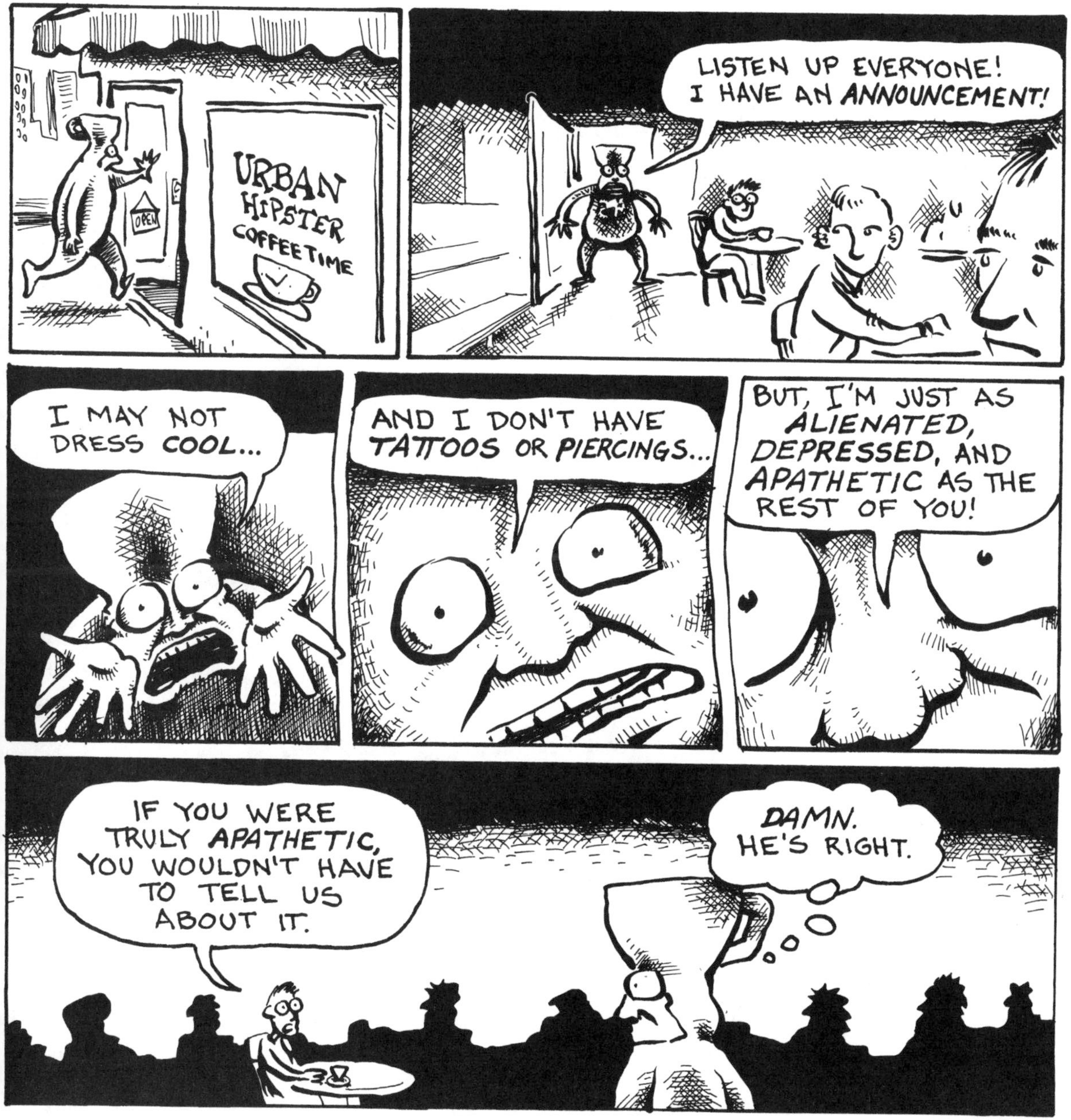
URBAN HIPSTER COFFEETIME
OPEN
LISTEN UP EVERYONE! I HAVE AN ANNOUNCEMENT!
I MAY NOT DRESS COOL...
AND I DON'T HAVE TATTOOS OR PIERCINGS...
BUT, I'M JUST AS ALIENATED, DEPRESSED, AND APATHETIC AS THE REST OF YOU!
IF YOU WERE TRULY APATHETIC, YOU WOULDN'T HAVE TO TELL US ABOUT IT.
DAMN. HE'S RIGHT.

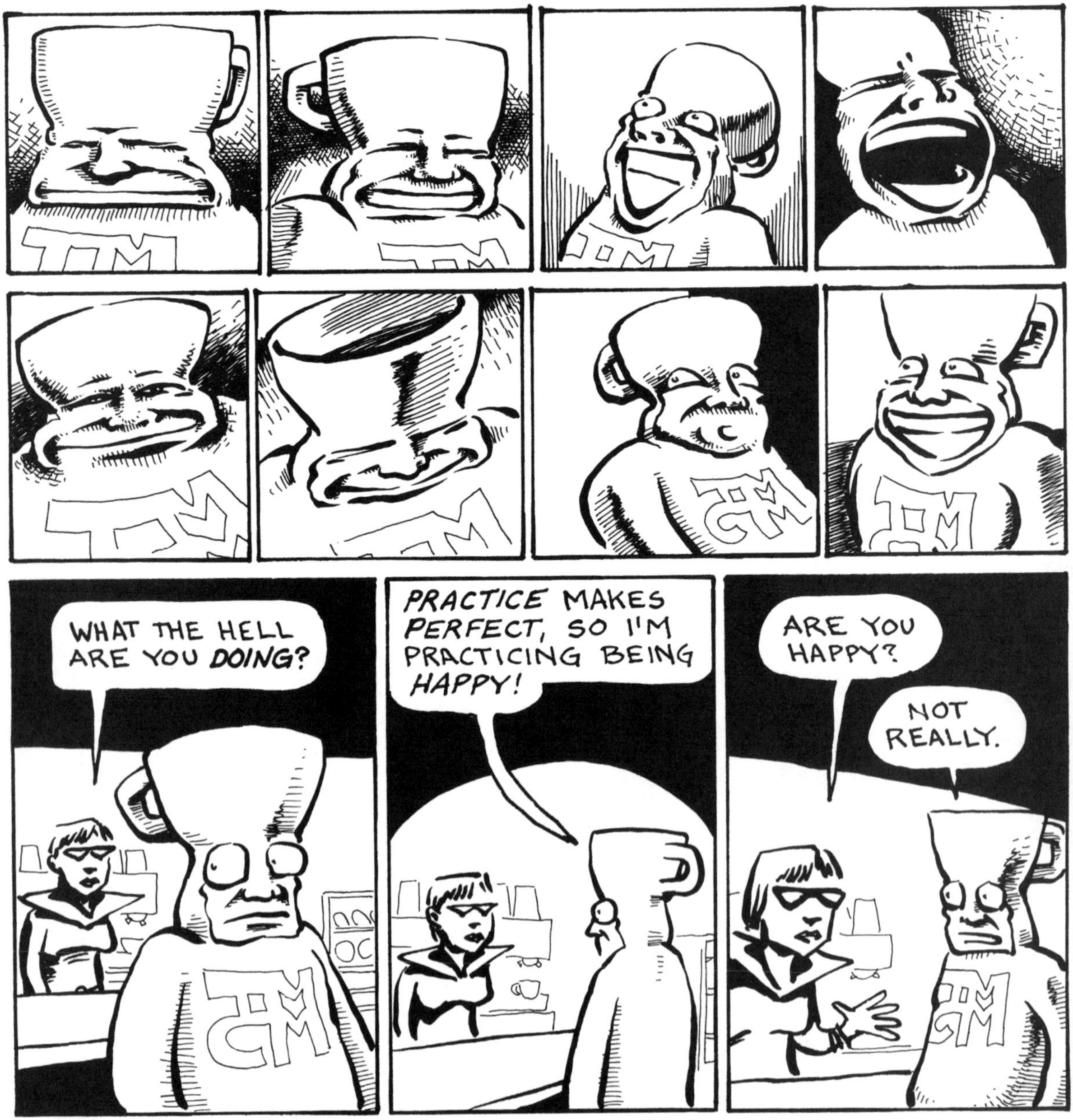

WHAT THE HELL ARE YOU DOING?
PRACTICE MAKES PERFECT, SO I'M PRACTICING BEING HAPPY!
ARE YOU HAPPY?
NOT REALLY.

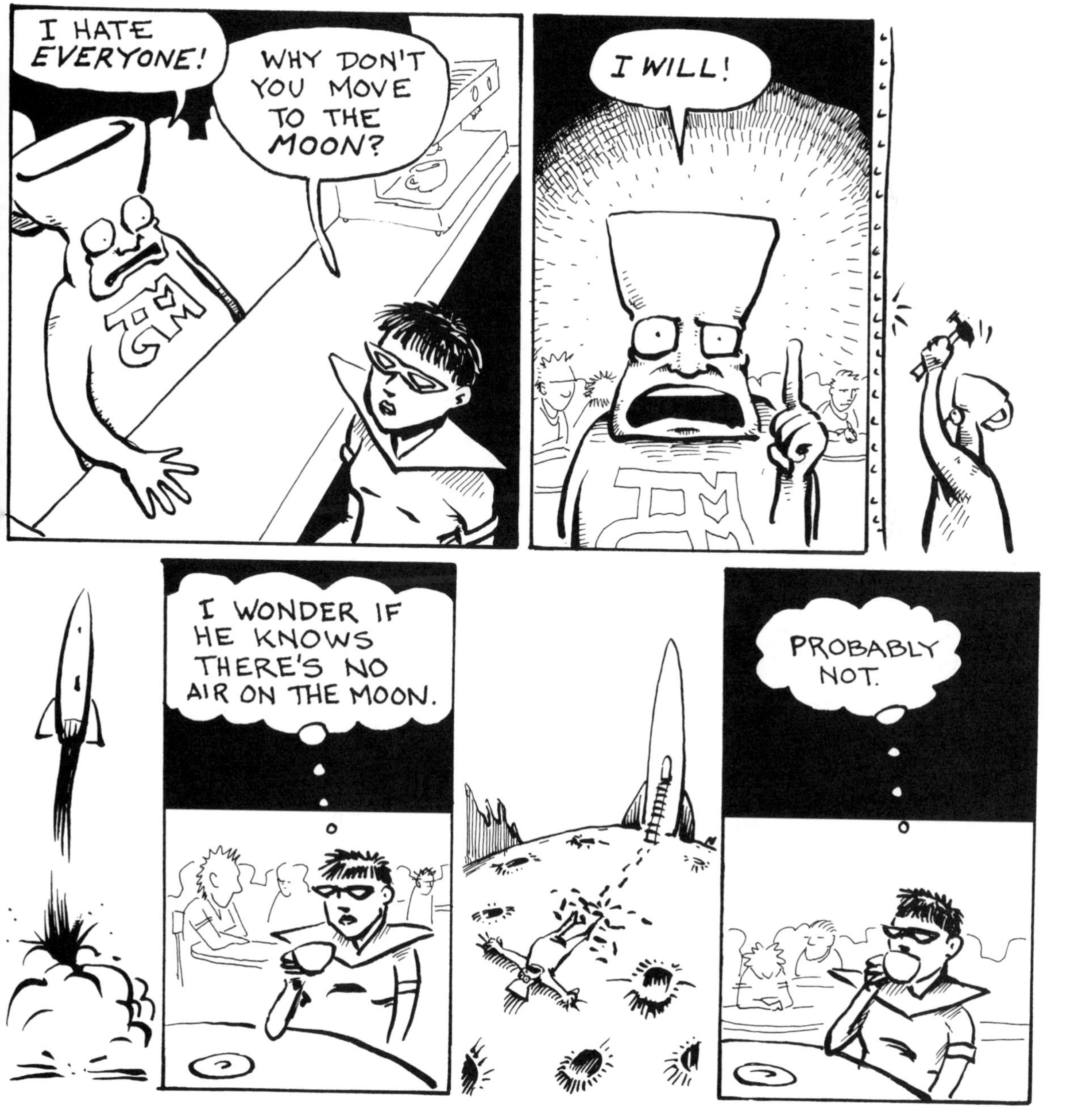
I HATE EVERYONE!
WHY DON'T YOU MOVE TO THE MOON?
I WILL!
I WONDER IF HE KNOWS THERE'S NO AIR ON THE MOON.
PROBABLY NOT.

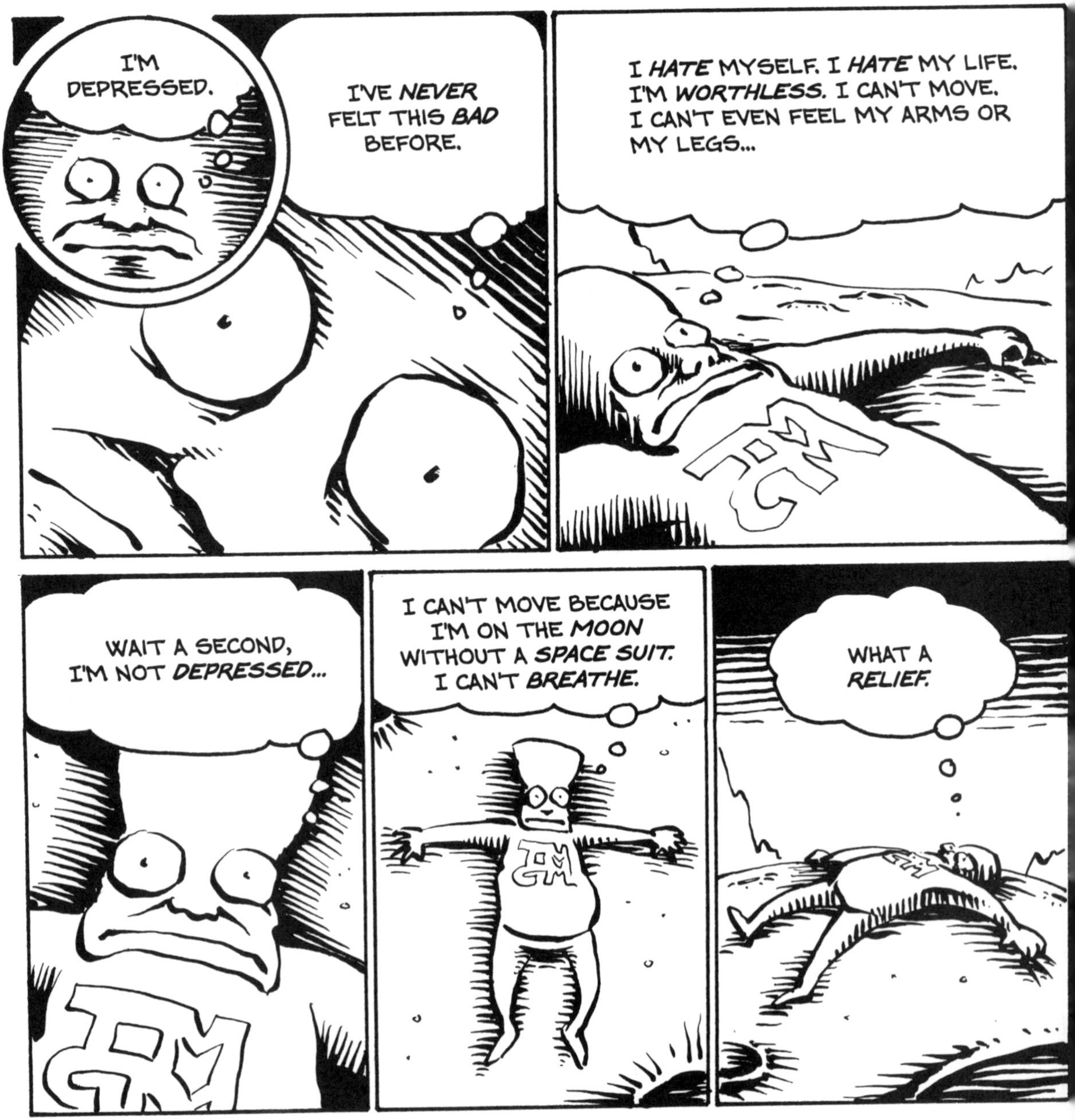
I'M DEPRESSED.
I'VE NEVER FELT THIS BAD BEFORE.
I HATE MYSELF. I HATE MY LIFE. I'M WORTHLESS. I CAN'T MOVE. I CAN'T EVEN FEEL MY ARMS OR MY LEGS...
WAIT A SECOND, I'M NOT DEPRESSED...
I CAN'T MOVE BECAUSE I'M ON THE MOON WITHOUT A SPACE SUIT. I CAN'T BREATHE.
WHAT A RELIEF.

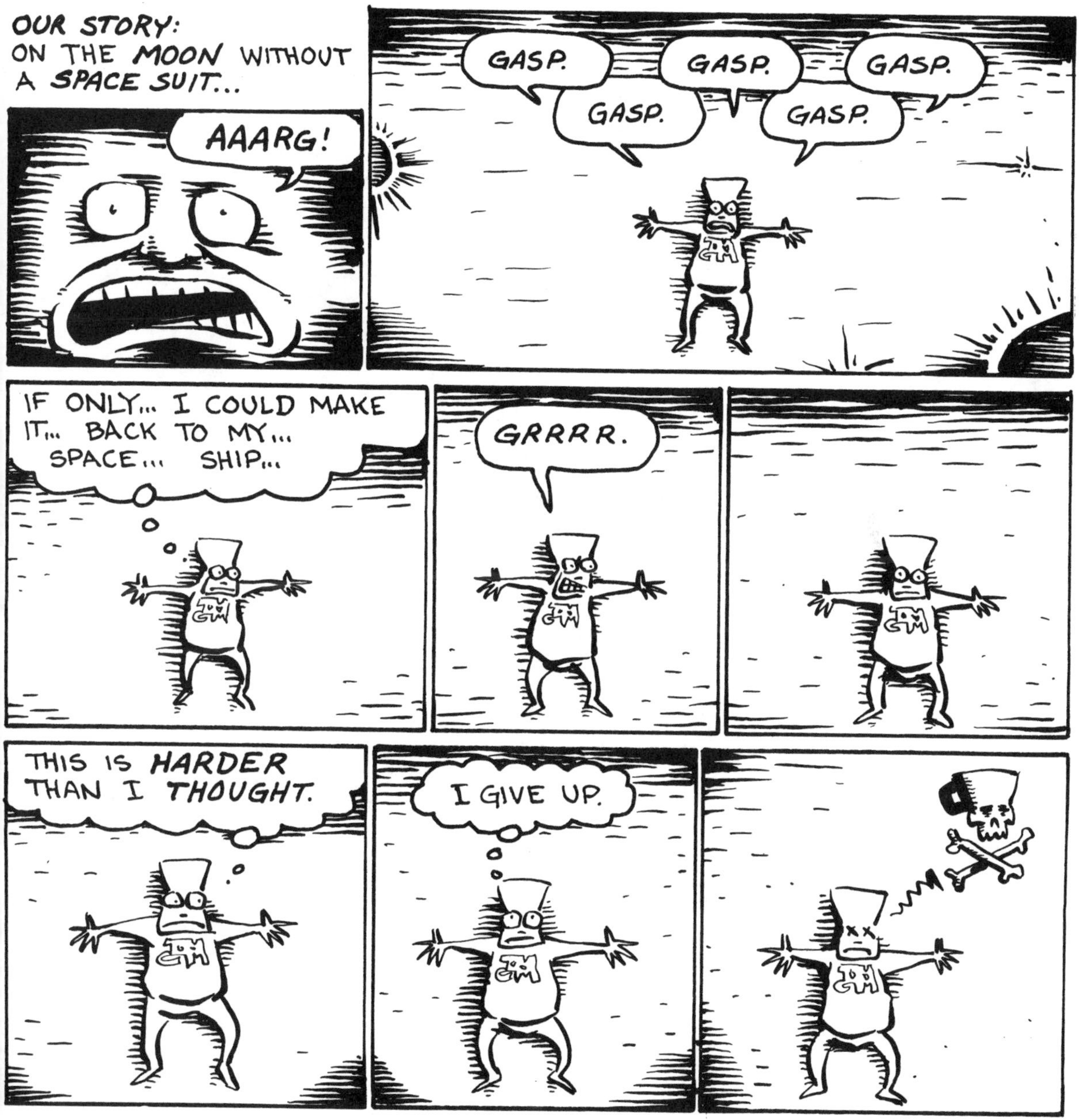
OUR STORY:
ON THE MOON WITHOUT A SPACE SUIT...
AAARG!
GASP.
GASP.
GASP.
GASP.
GASP.
IF ONLY... I COULD MAKE IT... BACK TO MY... SPACE... SHIP...
GRRRR.
THIS IS HARDER THAN I THOUGHT.
I GIVE UP.

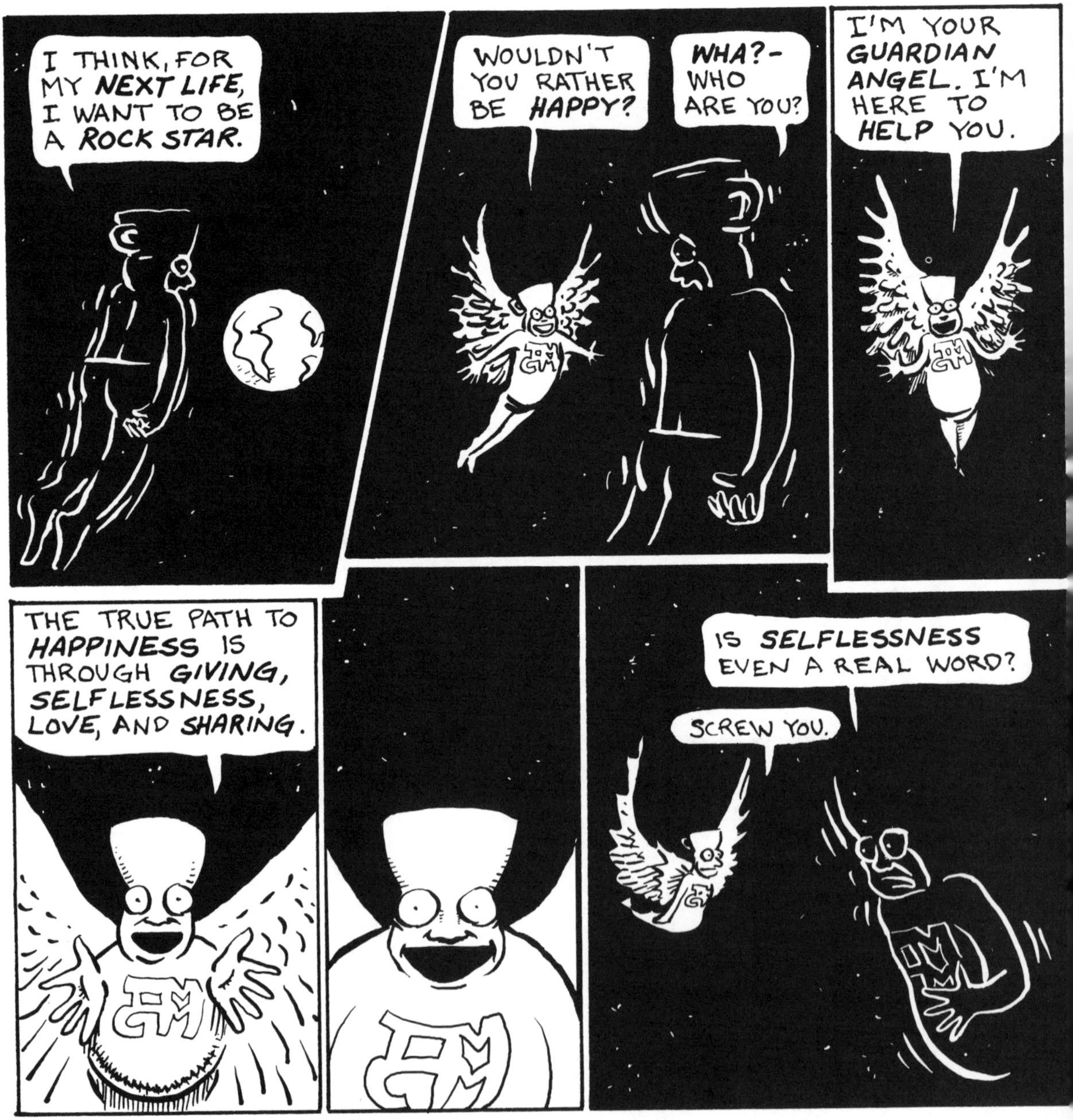
I THINK, FOR MY NEXT LIFE, I WANT TO BE A ROCK STAR.
WOULDN'T YOU RATHER BE HAPPY?
WHA?- WHO ARE YOU?
I'M YOUR GUARDIAN ANGEL. I'M HERE TO HELP YOU.
THE TRUE PATH TO HAPPINESS IS THROUGH GIVING, SELFLESSNESS, LOVE, AND SHARING.
IS SELFLESSNESS EVEN A REAL WORD?
SCREW YOU.

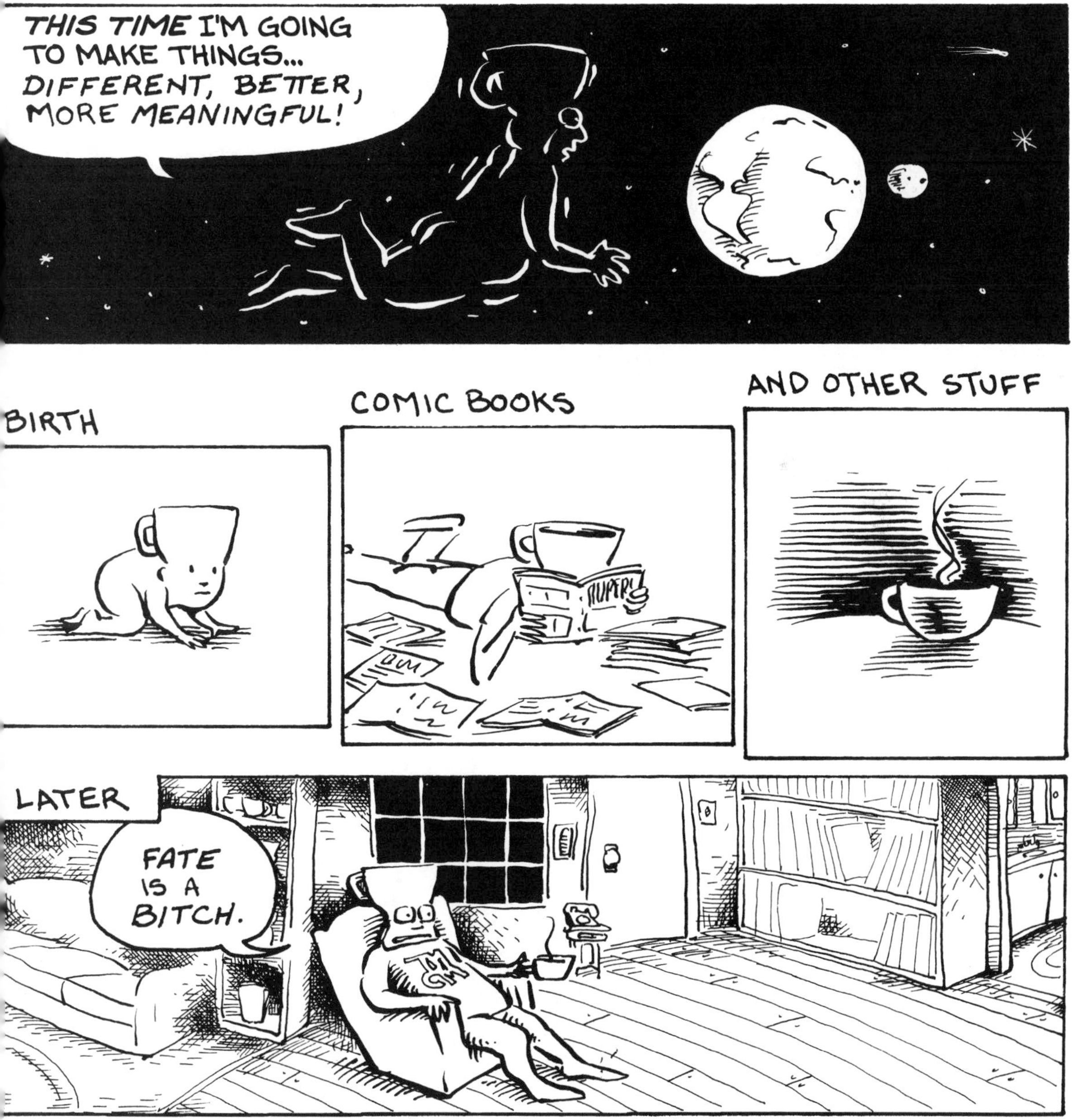
THIS TIME I'M GOING TO MAKE THINGS... DIFFERENT, BETTER, MORE MEANINGFUL!
BIRTH
COMIC BOOKS
SUPER!
AND OTHER STUFF
LATER
FATE IS A BITCH.

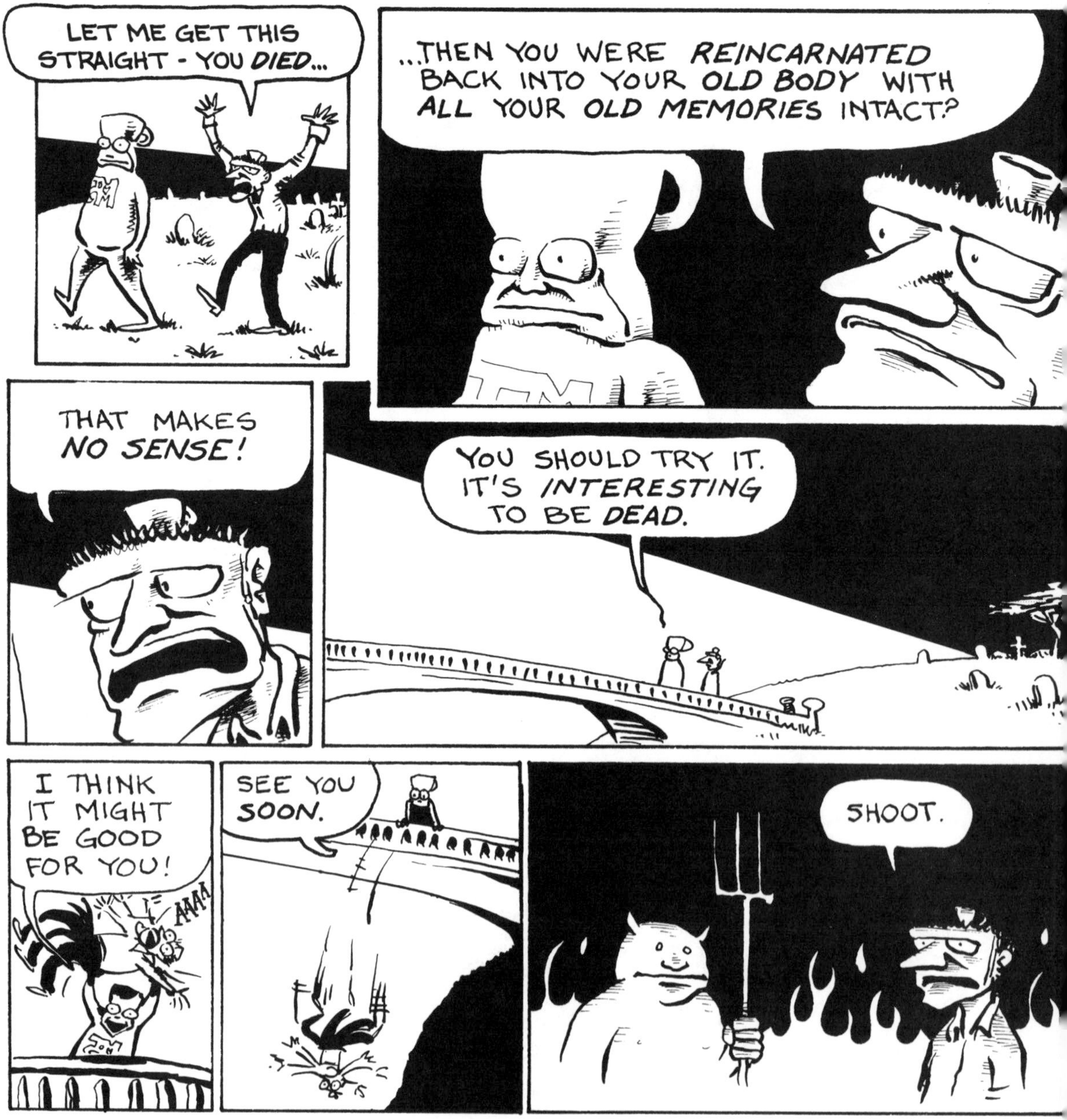
LET ME GET THIS STRAIGHT - YOU *DIED*...
...THEN YOU WERE *REINCARNATED* BACK INTO YOUR *OLD BODY* WITH *ALL* YOUR *OLD MEMORIES* INTACT?
THAT MAKES *NO SENSE*!
YOU SHOULD TRY IT. IT'S *INTERESTING* TO BE *DEAD*.
I THINK IT MIGHT BE GOOD FOR YOU!
AAA!
SEE YOU *SOON*.
SHOOT.

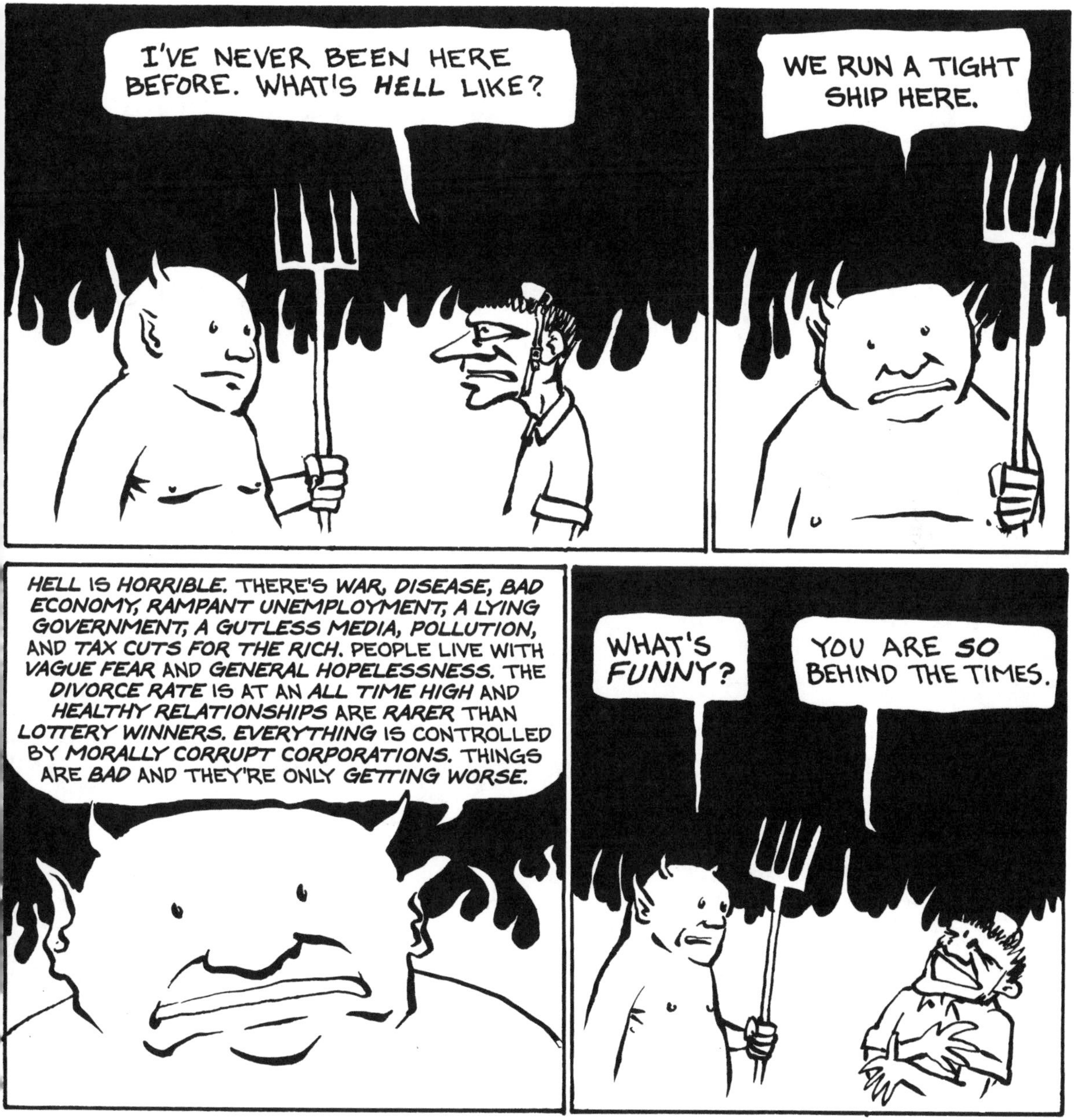
I'VE NEVER BEEN HERE BEFORE. WHAT'S HELL LIKE?
WE RUN A TIGHT SHIP HERE.
HELL IS HORRIBLE. THERE'S WAR, DISEASE, BAD ECONOMY, RAMPANT UNEMPLOYMENT, A LYING GOVERNMENT, A GUTLESS MEDIA, POLLUTION, AND TAX CUTS FOR THE RICH. PEOPLE LIVE WITH VAGUE FEAR AND GENERAL HOPELESSNESS. THE DIVORCE RATE IS AT AN ALL TIME HIGH AND HEALTHY RELATIONSHIPS ARE RARER THAN LOTTERY WINNERS. EVERYTHING IS CONTROLLED BY MORALLY CORRUPT CORPORATIONS. THINGS ARE BAD AND THEY'RE ONLY GETTING WORSE.
WHAT'S FUNNY?
YOU ARE SO BEHIND THE TIMES.

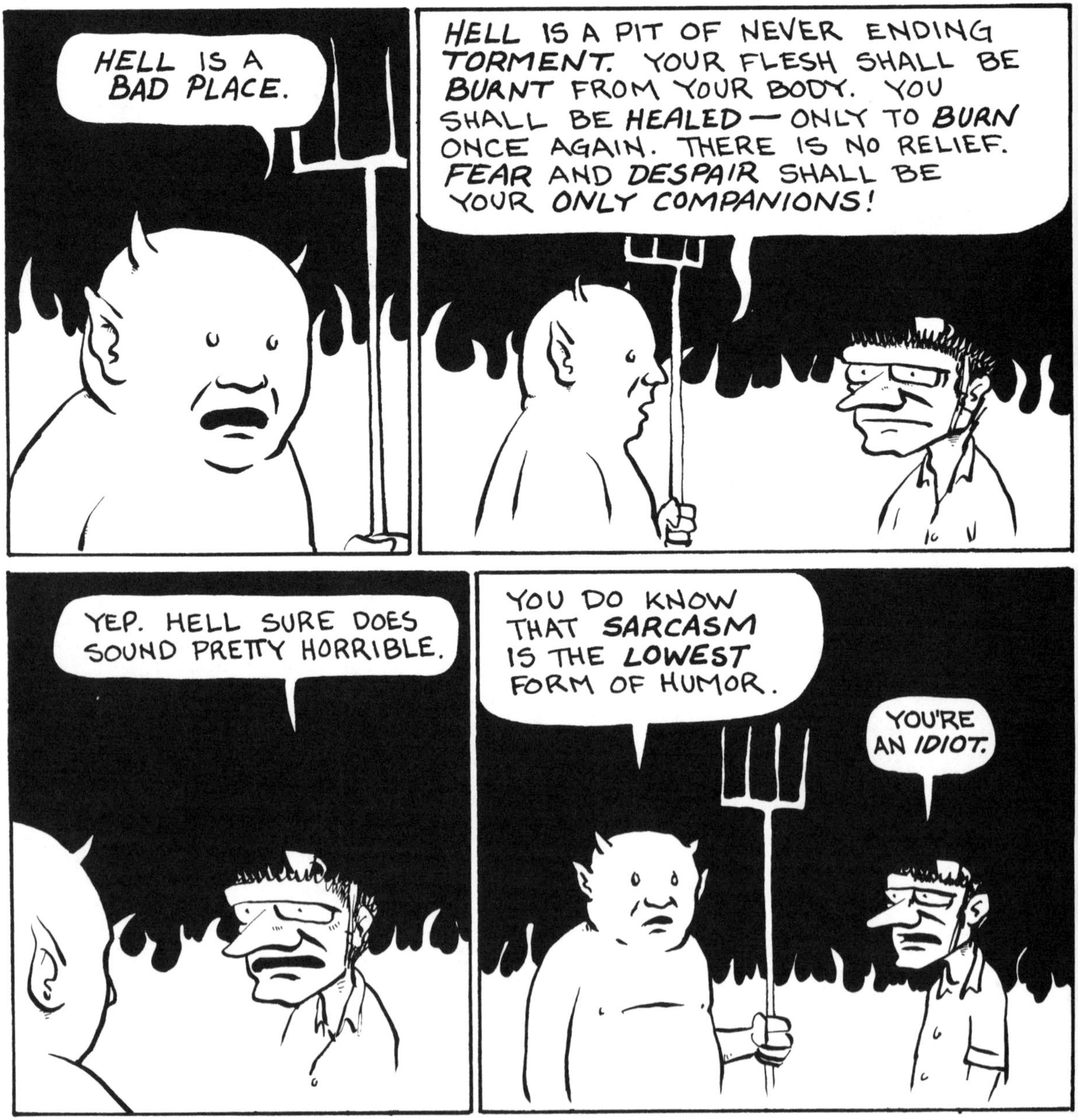
HELL IS A BAD PLACE.
HELL IS A PIT OF NEVER ENDING TORMENT. YOUR FLESH SHALL BE BURNT FROM YOUR BODY. YOU SHALL BE HEALED — ONLY TO BURN ONCE AGAIN. THERE IS NO RELIEF. FEAR AND DESPAIR SHALL BE YOUR ONLY COMPANIONS!
YEP. HELL SURE DOES SOUND PRETTY HORRIBLE.
YOU DO KNOW THAT SARCASM IS THE LOWEST FORM OF HUMOR.
YOU'RE AN IDIOT.

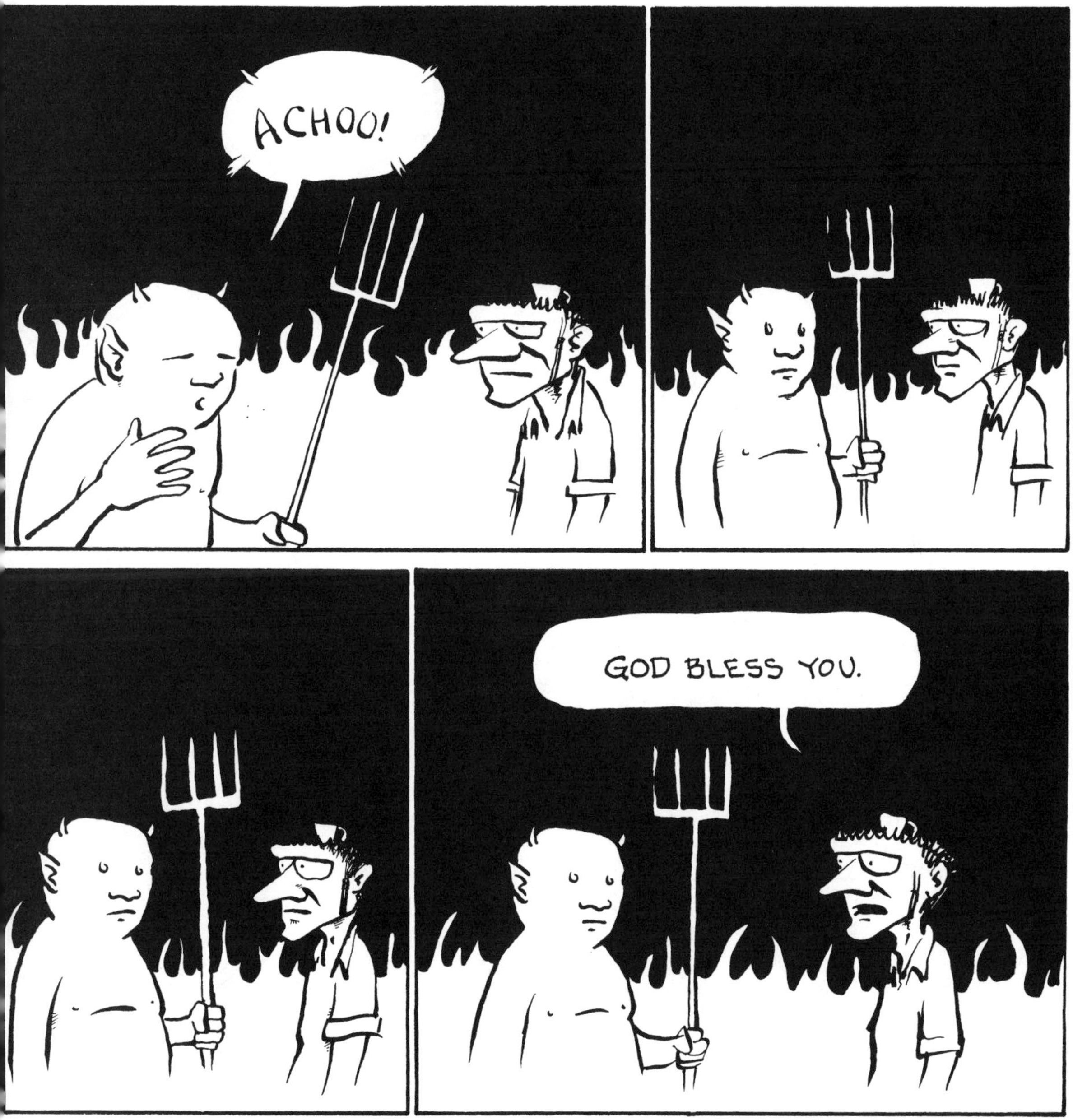
ACHOO!
GOD BLESS YOU.

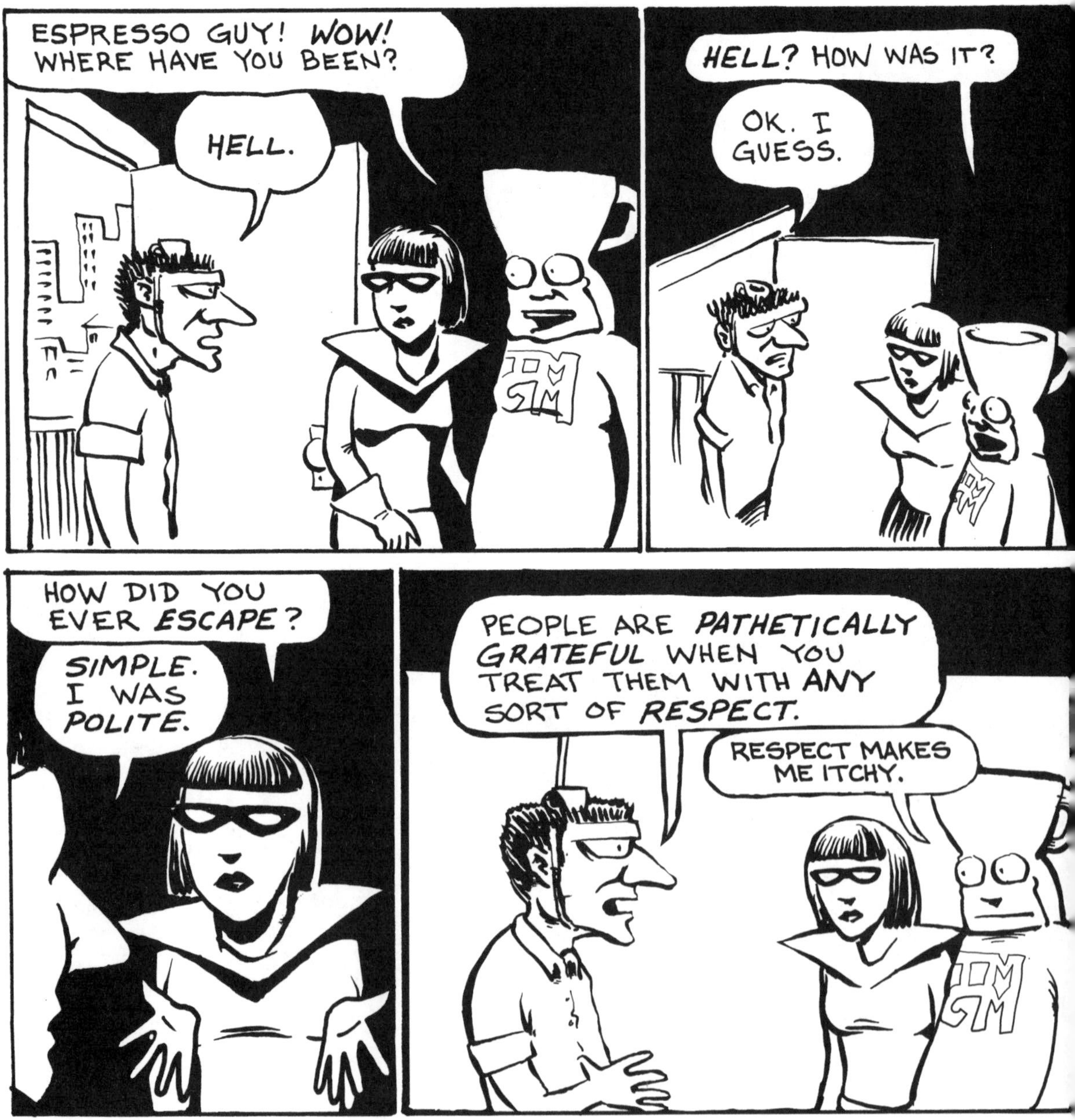
ESPRESSO GUY! WOW! WHERE HAVE YOU BEEN?
HELL.
HELL? HOW WAS IT?
OK. I GUESS.
HOW DID YOU EVER ESCAPE?
SIMPLE. I WAS POLITE.
PEOPLE ARE PATHETICALLY GRATEFUL WHEN YOU TREAT THEM WITH ANY SORT OF RESPECT.
RESPECT MAKES ME ITCHY.

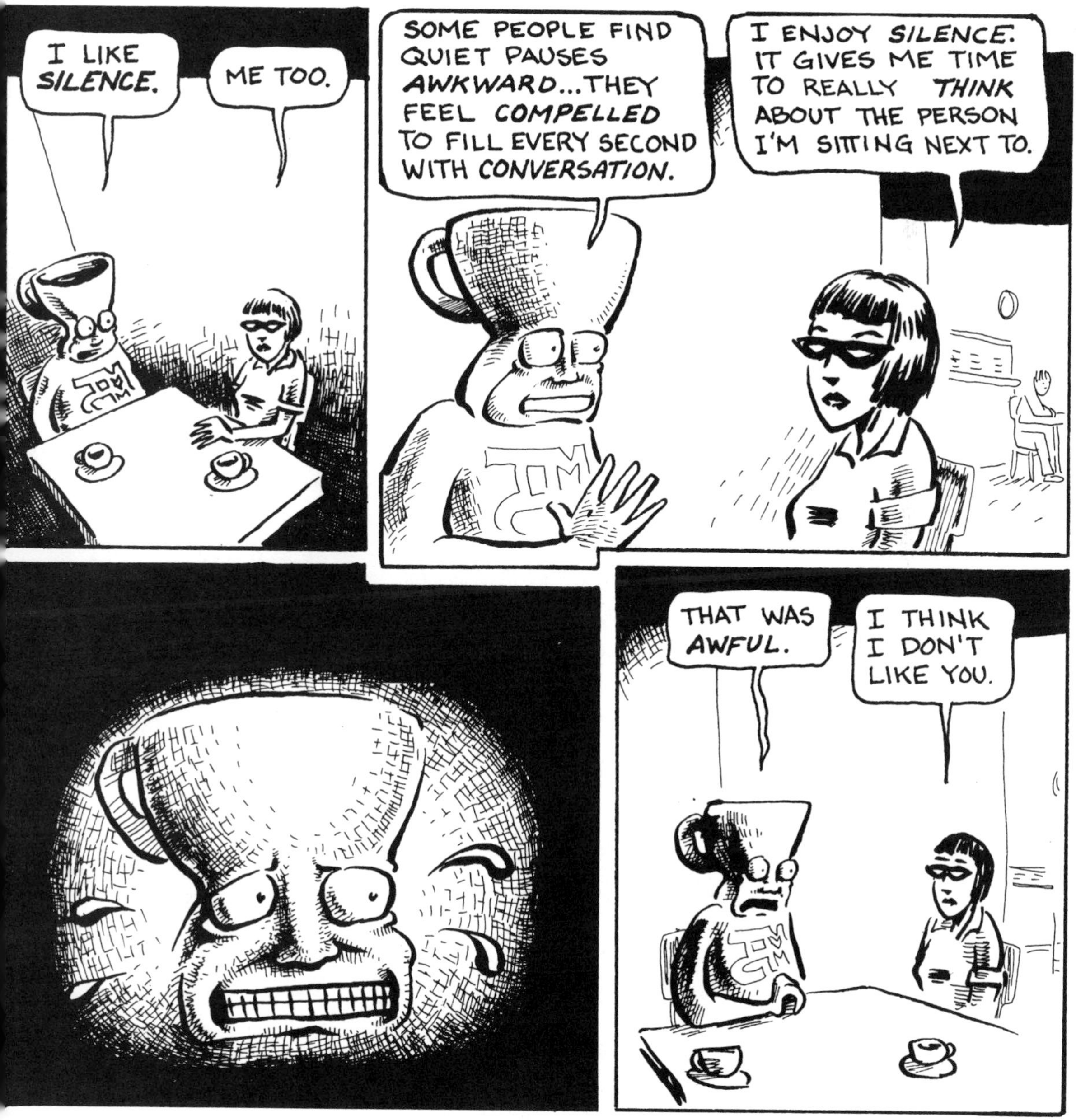
I LIKE SILENCE.
ME TOO.
SOME PEOPLE FIND QUIET PAUSES AWKWARD...THEY FEEL COMPELLED TO FILL EVERY SECOND WITH CONVERSATION.
I ENJOY SILENCE. IT GIVES ME TIME TO REALLY THINK ABOUT THE PERSON I'M SITTING NEXT TO.
THAT WAS AWFUL.
I THINK I DON'T LIKE YOU.

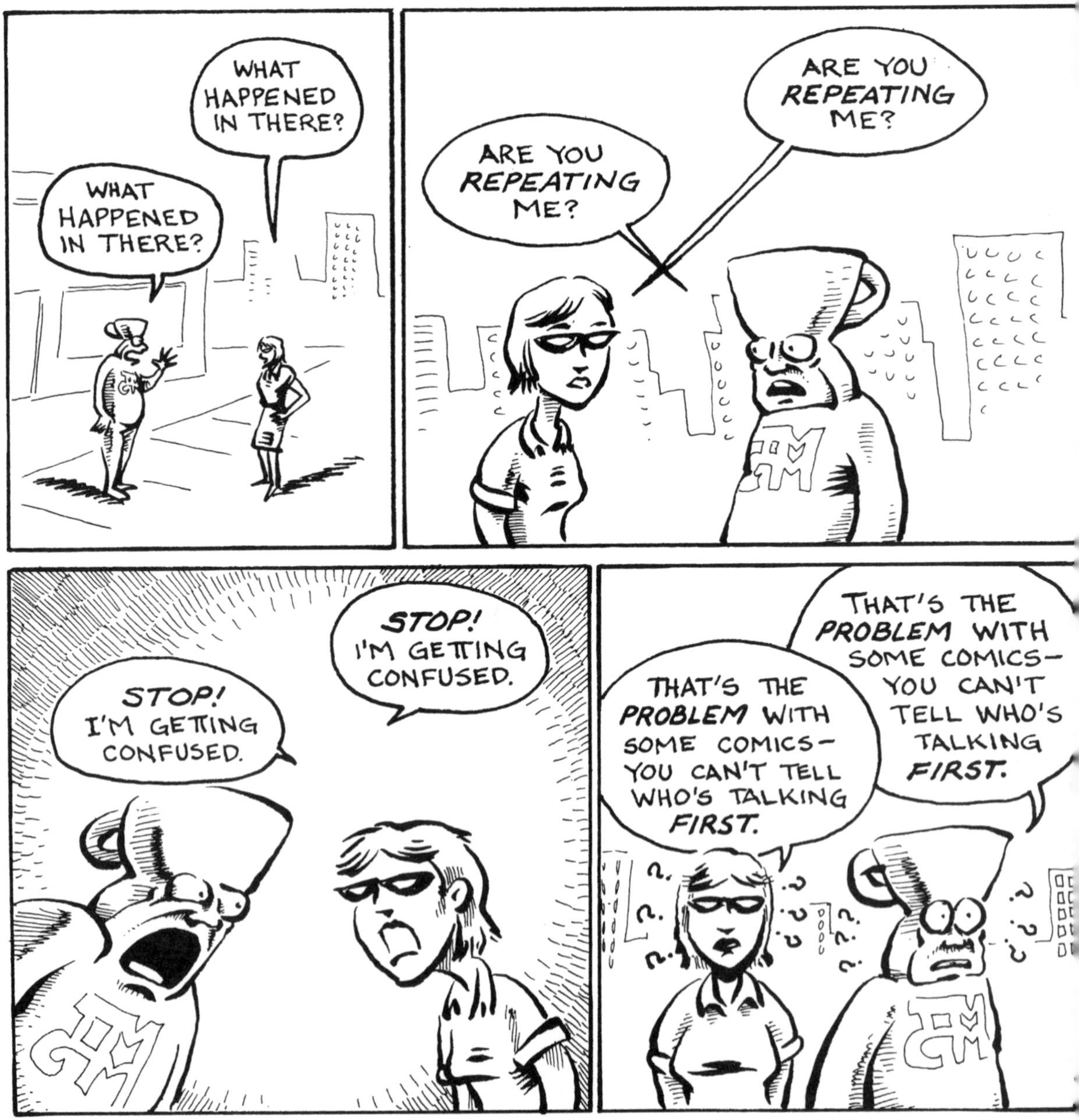
WHAT HAPPENED IN THERE?
WHAT HAPPENED IN THERE?
ARE YOU REPEATING ME?
ARE YOU REPEATING ME?
STOP! I'M GETTING CONFUSED.
STOP! I'M GETTING CONFUSED.
THAT'S THE PROBLEM WITH SOME COMICS- YOU CAN'T TELL WHO'S TALKING FIRST.
THAT'S THE PROBLEM WITH SOME COMICS- YOU CAN'T TELL WHO'S TALKING FIRST.

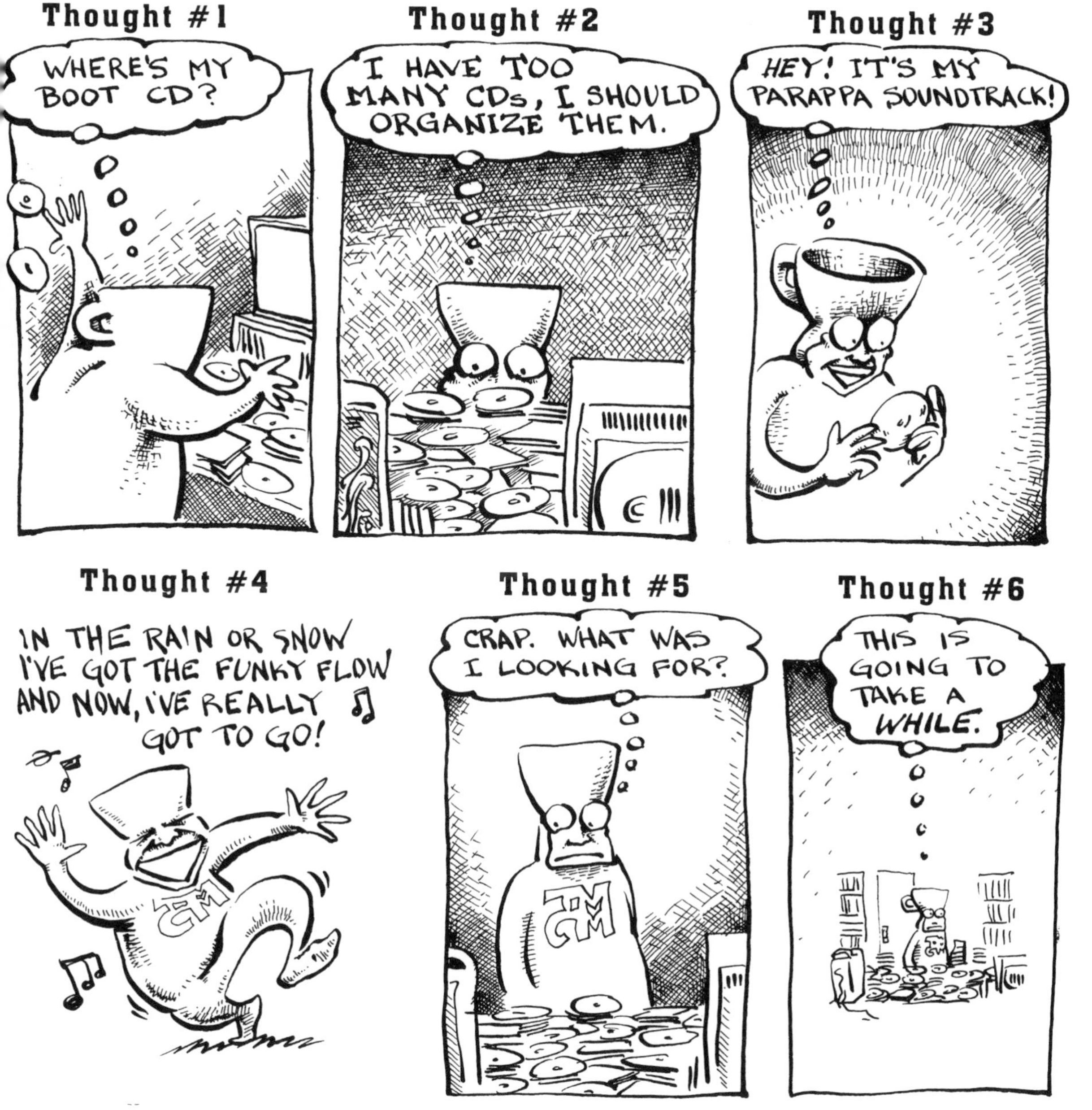
Thought #1
WHERE'S MY BOOT CD?
Thought #2
I HAVE TOO MANY CDs, I SHOULD ORGANIZE THEM.
Thought #3
HEY! IT'S MY PARAPPA SOUNDTRACK!
Thought #4
IN THE RAIN OR SNOW
I'VE GOT THE FUNKY FLOW
AND NOW, I'VE REALLY GOT TO GO!
Thought #5
CRAP. WHAT WAS I LOOKING FOR?
Thought #6
THIS IS GOING TO TAKE A *WHILE*.

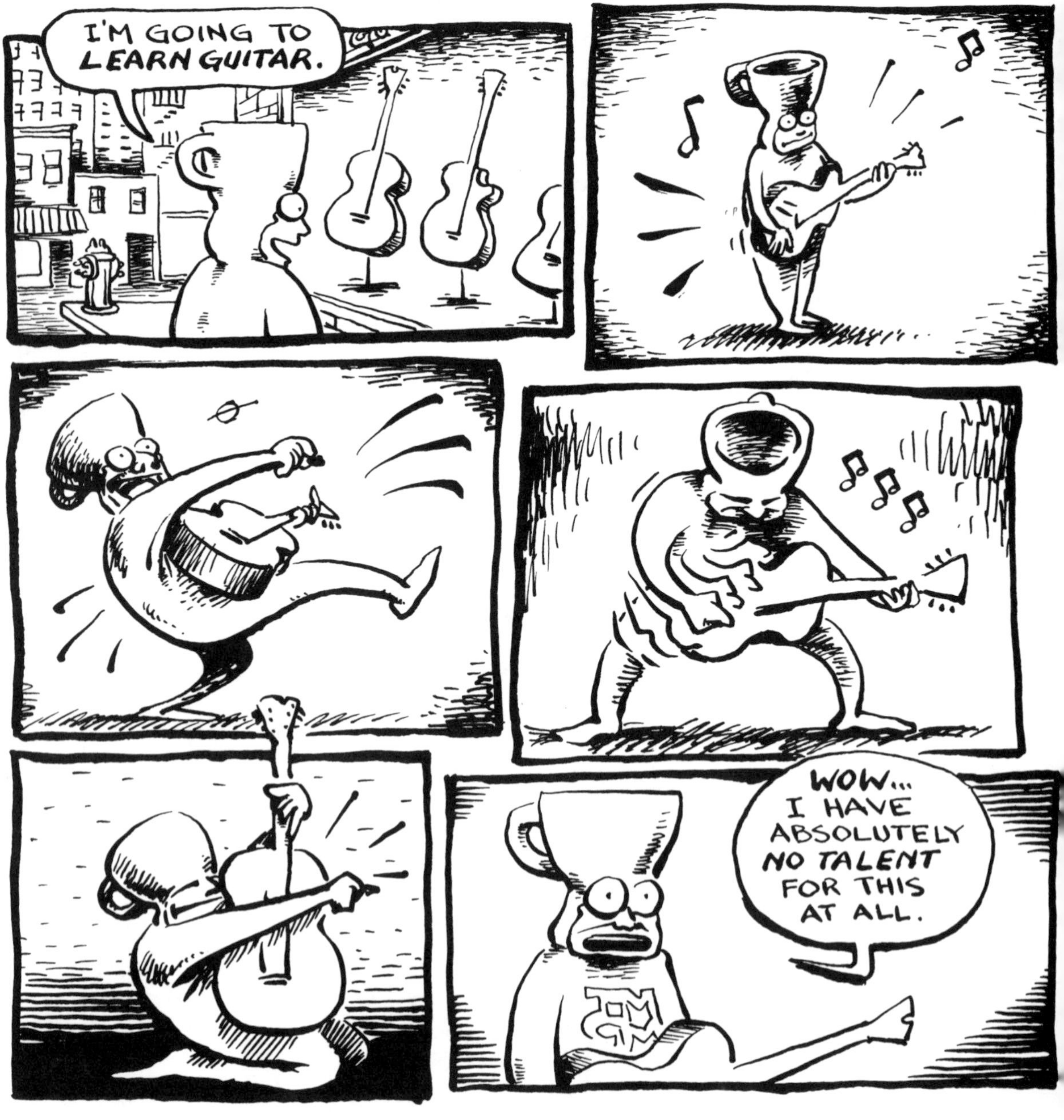
I'M GOING TO LEARN GUITAR.
WOW... I HAVE ABSOLUTELY NO TALENT FOR THIS AT ALL.

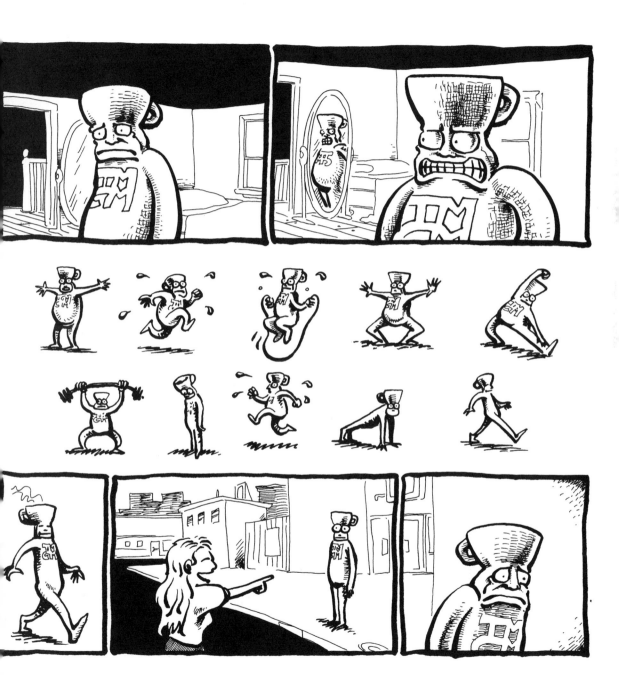

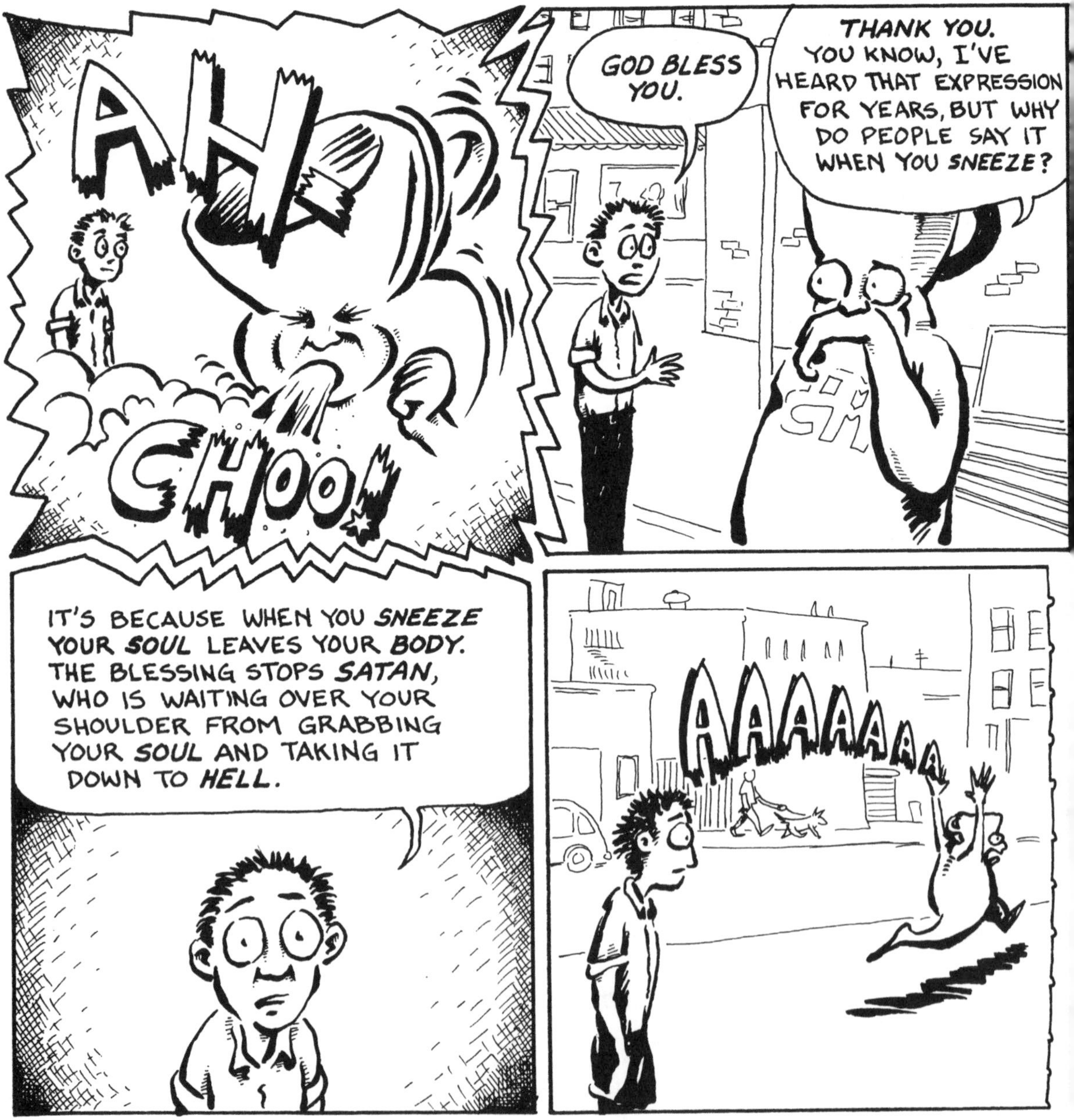
AH-
CHOO!
GOD BLESS YOU.
THANK YOU. YOU KNOW, I'VE HEARD THAT EXPRESSION FOR YEARS, BUT WHY DO PEOPLE SAY IT WHEN YOU SNEEZE?
IT'S BECAUSE WHEN YOU SNEEZE YOUR SOUL LEAVES YOUR BODY. THE BLESSING STOPS SATAN, WHO IS WAITING OVER YOUR SHOULDER FROM GRABBING YOUR SOUL AND TAKING IT DOWN TO HELL.
AAAAAAA

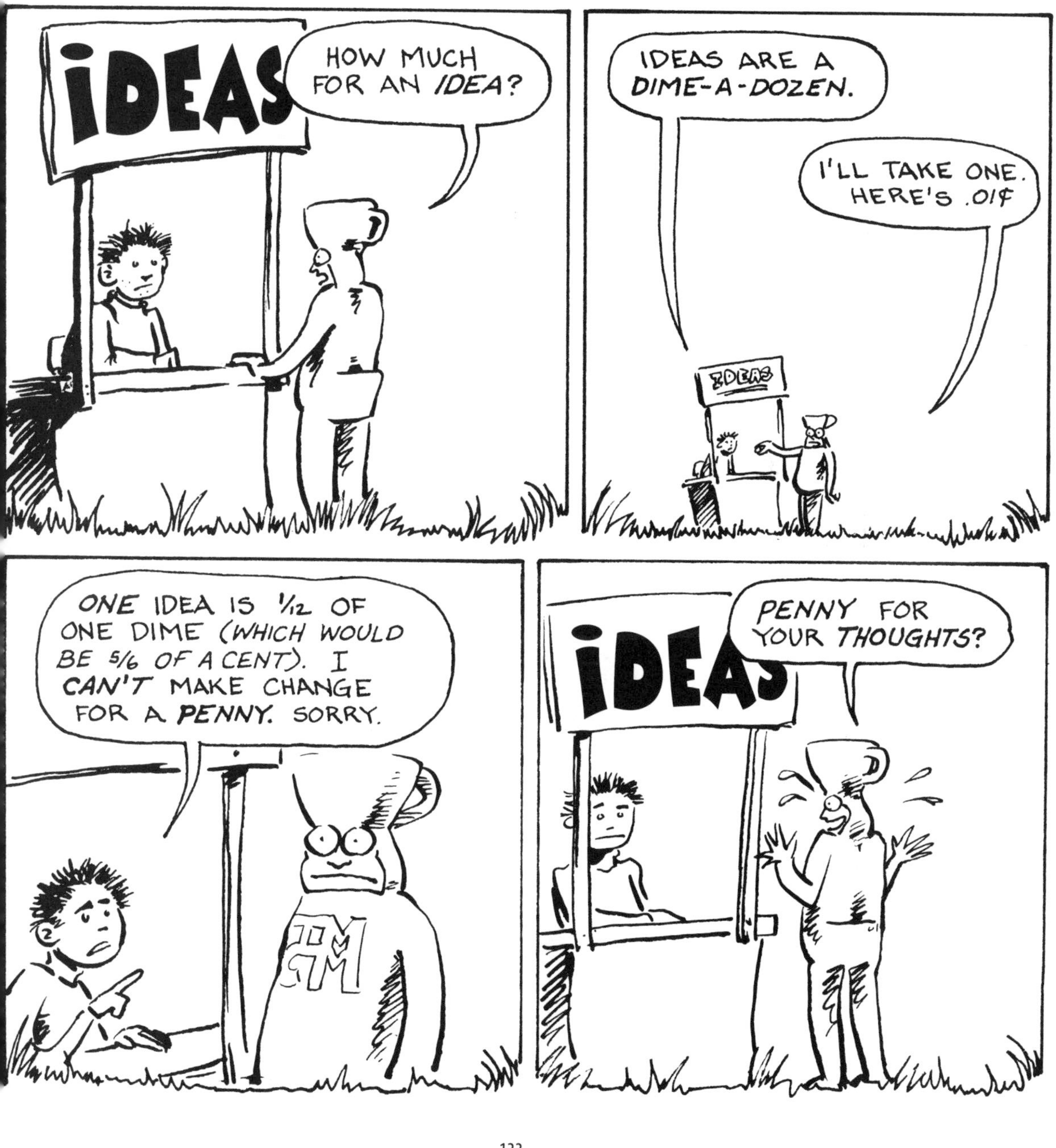
IDEAS
HOW MUCH FOR AN *IDEA*?
IDEAS ARE A *DIME-A-DOZEN*.
IDEAS
I'LL TAKE ONE. HERE'S .01¢
ONE IDEA IS 1/12 OF ONE DIME (*WHICH WOULD BE 5/6 OF A CENT*). I *CAN'T* MAKE CHANGE FOR A *PENNY*. SORRY.
IDEAS
PENNY FOR YOUR *THOUGHTS*?

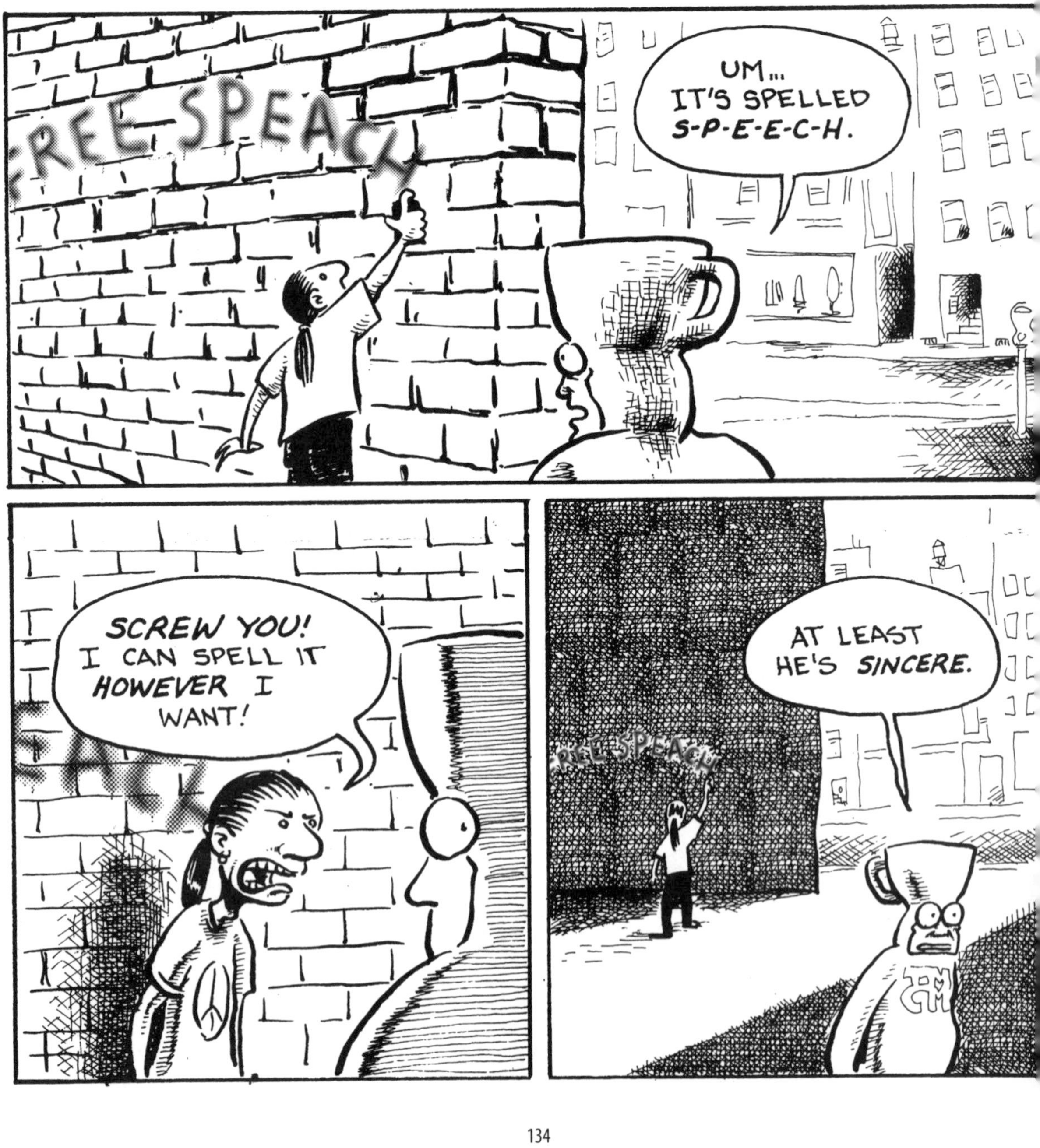
FREE SPEACH
UM... IT'S SPELLED S-P-E-E-C-H.
SCREW YOU! I CAN SPELL IT HOWEVER I WANT!
AT LEAST HE'S SINCERE.

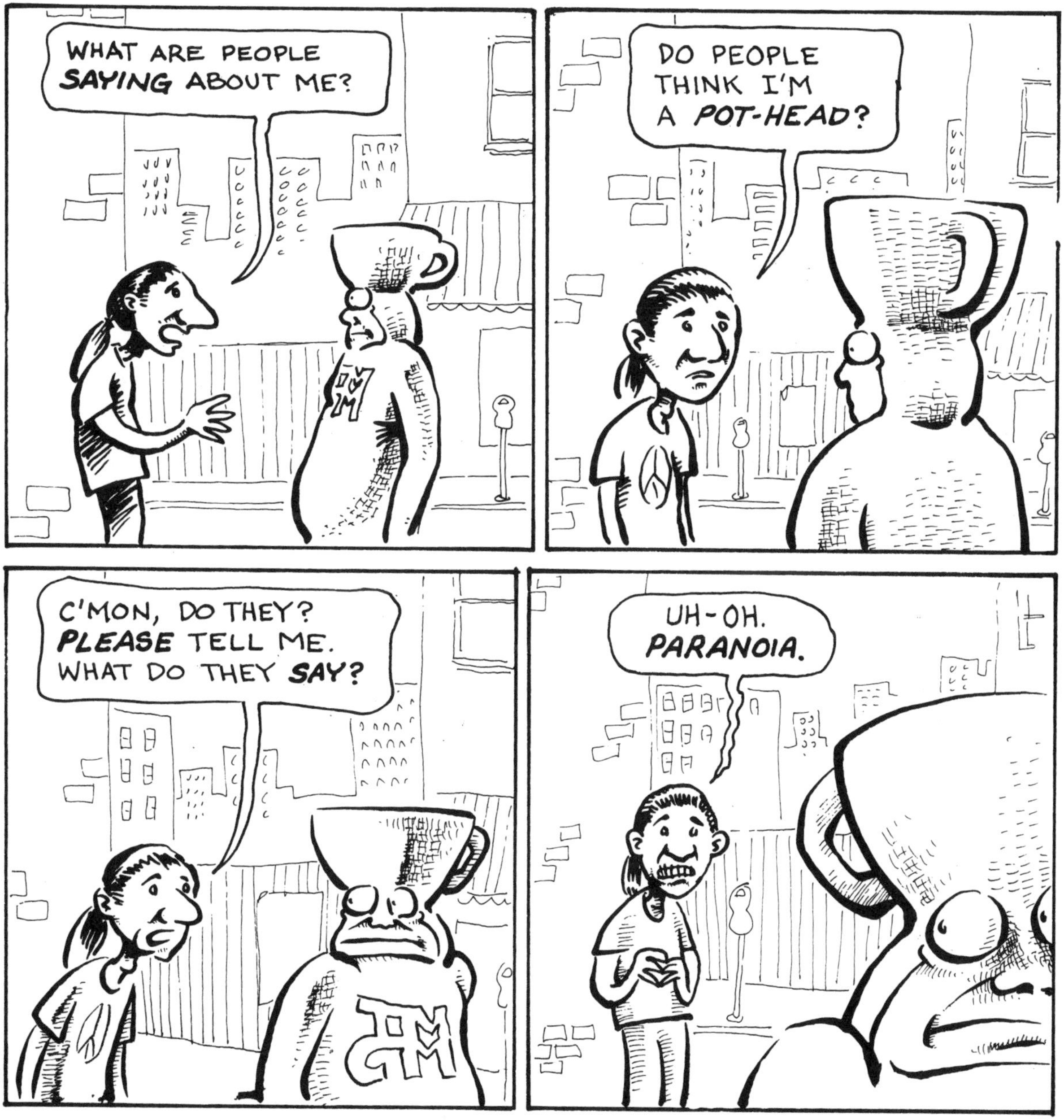
WHAT ARE PEOPLE **SAYING** ABOUT ME?
DO PEOPLE THINK I'M A **POT-HEAD**?
C'MON, DO THEY? **PLEASE** TELL ME. WHAT DO THEY **SAY**?
UH-OH. **PARANOIA.**

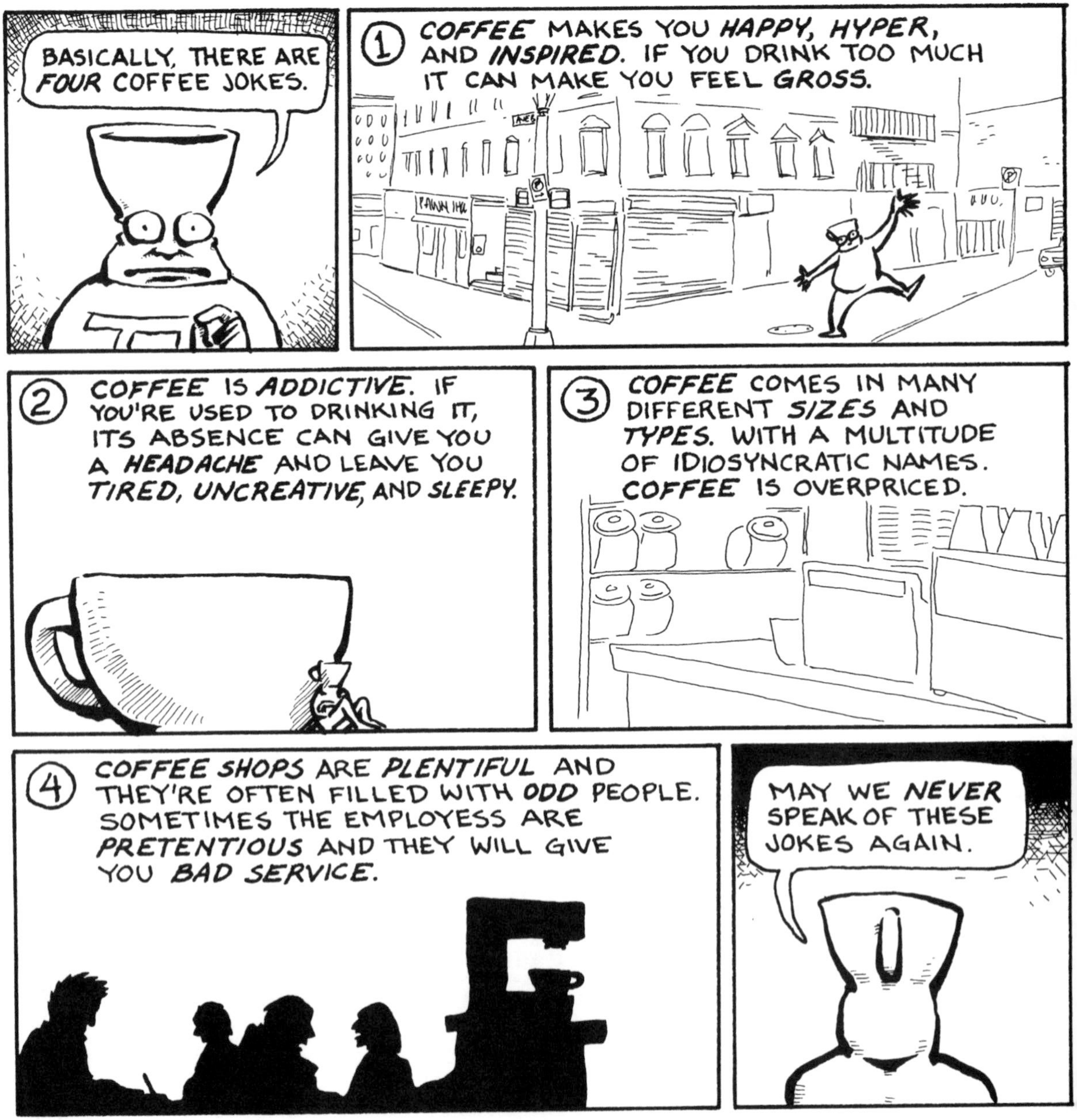
BASICALLY, THERE ARE FOUR COFFEE JOKES.
① COFFEE MAKES YOU HAPPY, HYPER, AND INSPIRED. IF YOU DRINK TOO MUCH IT CAN MAKE YOU FEEL GROSS.
PAWN INC
② COFFEE IS ADDICTIVE. IF YOU'RE USED TO DRINKING IT, ITS ABSENCE CAN GIVE YOU A HEADACHE AND LEAVE YOU TIRED, UNCREATIVE, AND SLEEPY.
③ COFFEE COMES IN MANY DIFFERENT SIZES AND TYPES. WITH A MULTITUDE OF IDIOSYNCRATIC NAMES. COFFEE IS OVERPRICED.
④ COFFEE SHOPS ARE PLENTIFUL AND THEY'RE OFTEN FILLED WITH ODD PEOPLE. SOMETIMES THE EMPLOYESS ARE PRETENTIOUS AND THEY WILL GIVE YOU BAD SERVICE.
MAY WE NEVER SPEAK OF THESE JOKES AGAIN.

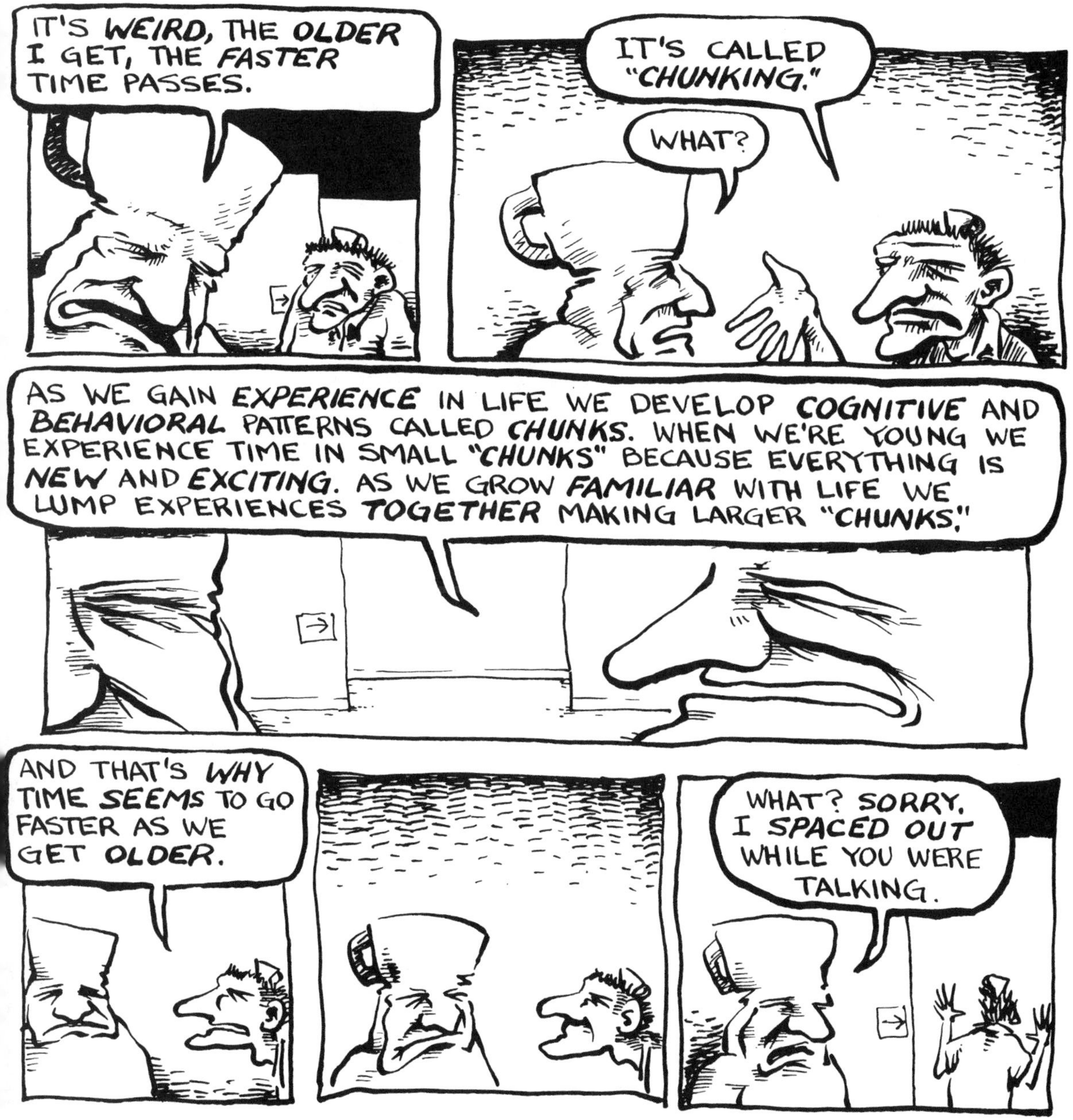
IT'S WEIRD, THE OLDER I GET, THE FASTER TIME PASSES.
IT'S CALLED "CHUNKING."
WHAT?
AS WE GAIN EXPERIENCE IN LIFE WE DEVELOP COGNITIVE AND BEHAVIORAL PATTERNS CALLED CHUNKS. WHEN WE'RE YOUNG WE EXPERIENCE TIME IN SMALL "CHUNKS" BECAUSE EVERYTHING IS NEW AND EXCITING. AS WE GROW FAMILIAR WITH LIFE WE LUMP EXPERIENCES TOGETHER MAKING LARGER "CHUNKS."
AND THAT'S WHY TIME SEEMS TO GO FASTER AS WE GET OLDER.
WHAT? SORRY. I SPACED OUT WHILE YOU WERE TALKING.

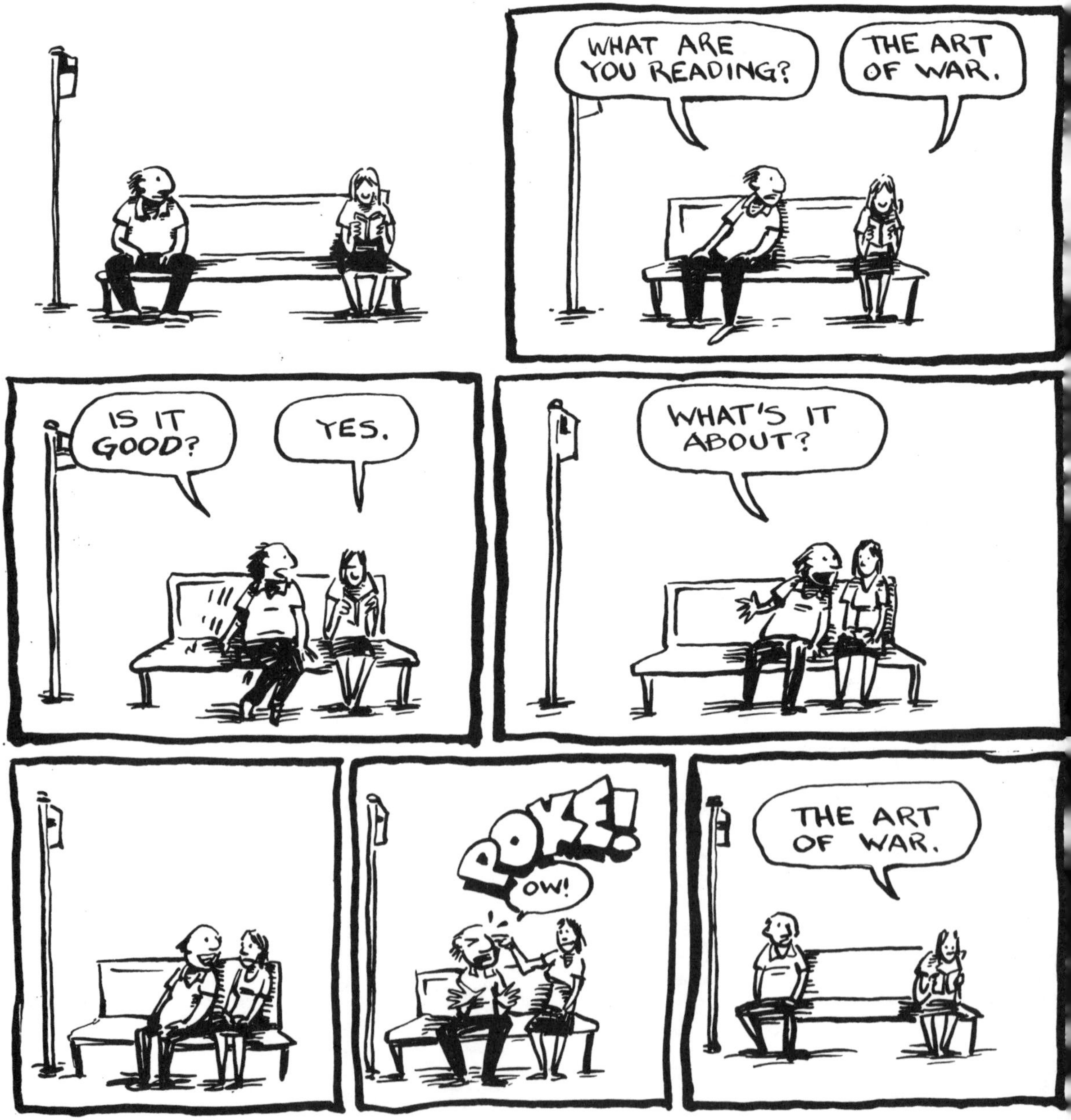
WHAT ARE YOU READING?
THE ART OF WAR.
IS IT GOOD?
YES.
WHAT'S IT ABOUT?
POKE!
OW!
THE ART OF WAR.

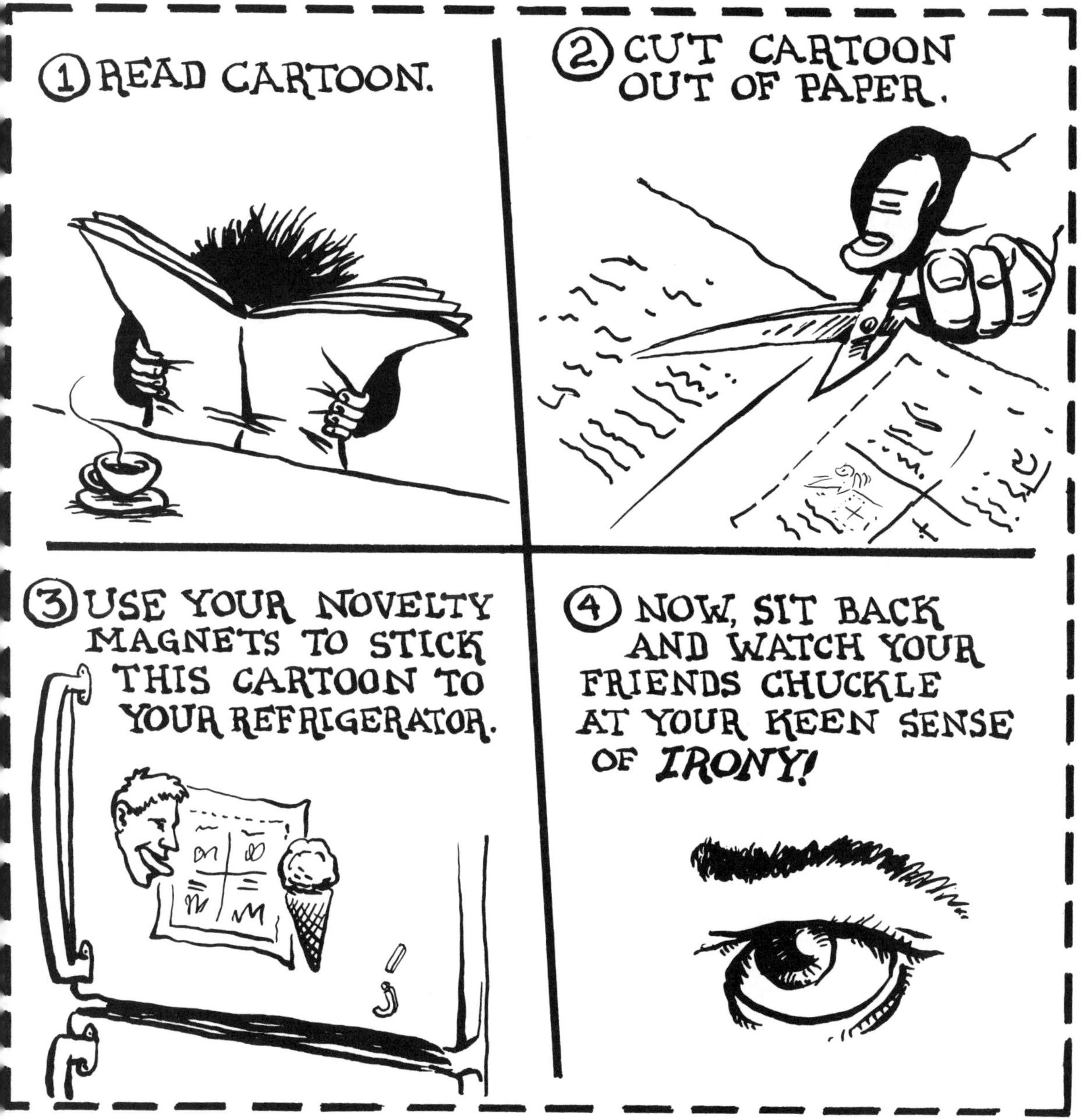

① READ CARTOON.
② CUT CARTOON OUT OF PAPER.
③ USE YOUR NOVELTY MAGNETS TO STICK THIS CARTOON TO YOUR REFRIGERATOR.
④ NOW, SIT BACK AND WATCH YOUR FRIENDS CHUCKLE AT YOUR KEEN SENSE OF IRONY!

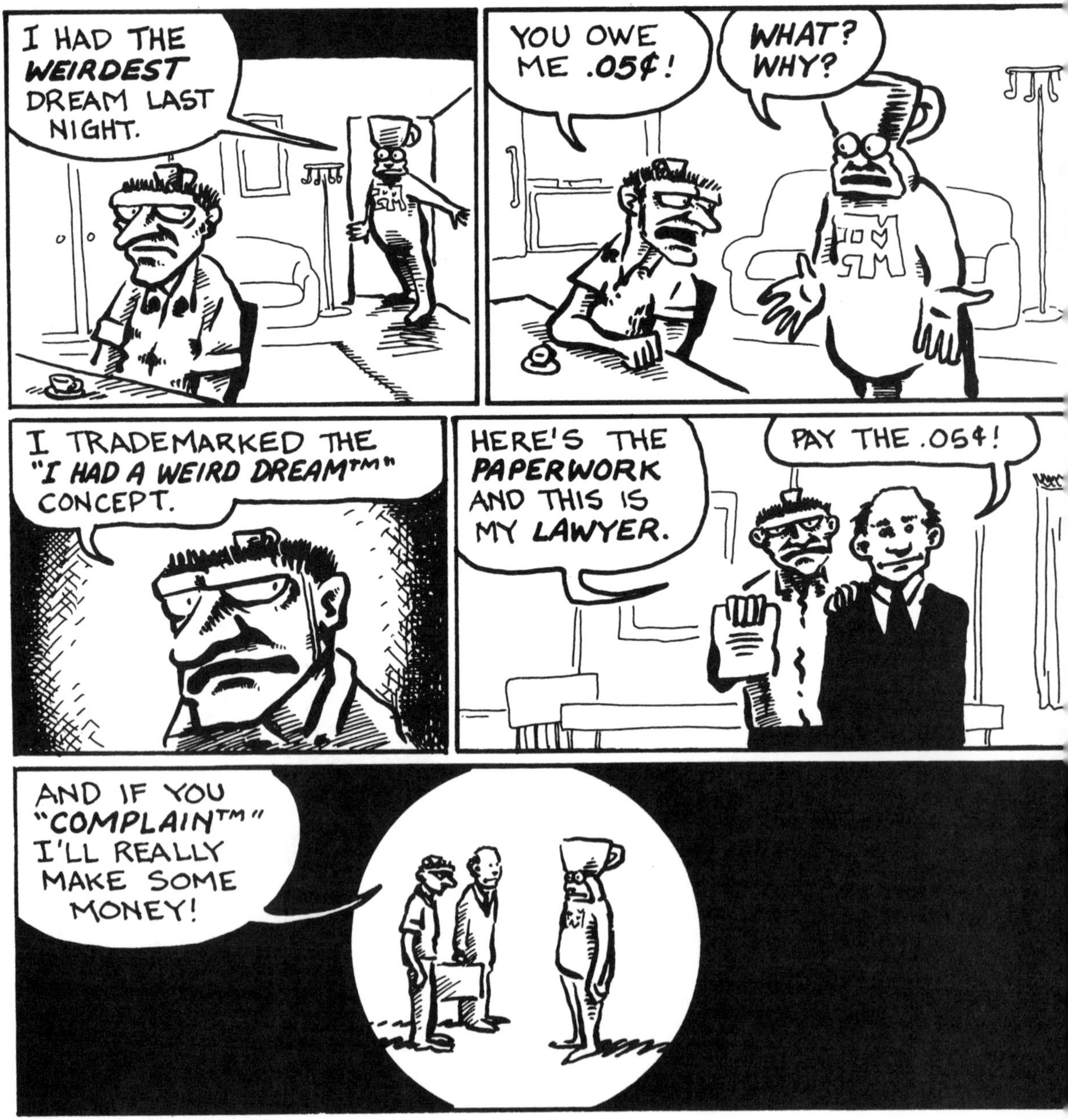
I HAD THE WEIRDEST DREAM LAST NIGHT.
YOU OWE ME .05¢!
WHAT? WHY?
I TRADEMARKED THE "I HAD A WEIRD DREAM™" CONCEPT.
HERE'S THE PAPERWORK AND THIS IS MY LAWYER.
PAY THE .05¢!
AND IF YOU "COMPLAIN™" I'LL REALLY MAKE SOME MONEY!

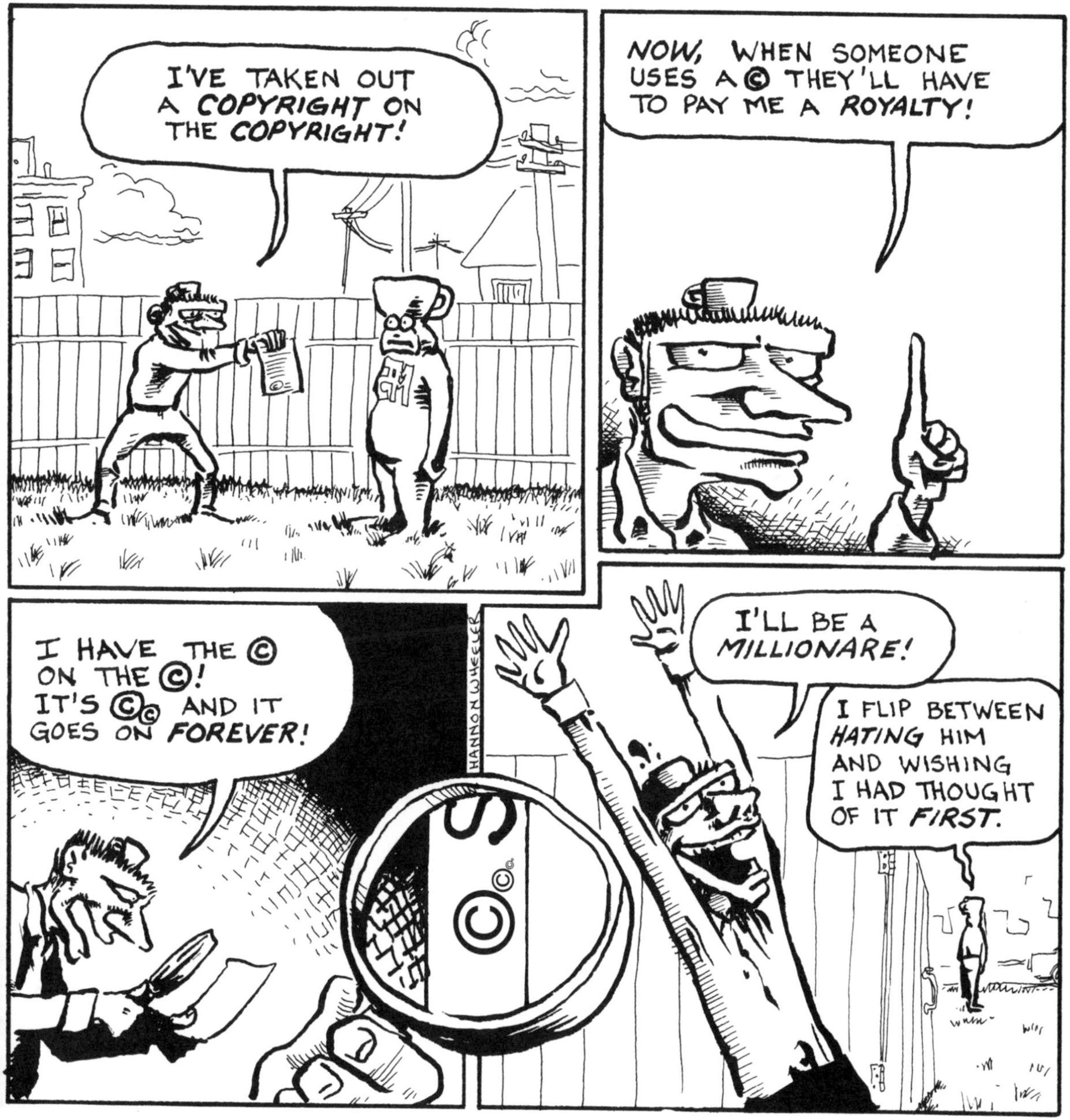
I'VE TAKEN OUT A *COPYRIGHT* ON THE *COPYRIGHT*!
NOW, WHEN SOMEONE USES A © THEY'LL HAVE TO PAY ME A *ROYALTY*!
I HAVE THE © ON THE ©! IT'S ©© AND IT GOES ON *FOREVER*!
HANNON WHEELER
I'LL BE A *MILLIONARE*!
I FLIP BETWEEN *HATING* HIM AND WISHING I HAD THOUGHT OF IT *FIRST*.

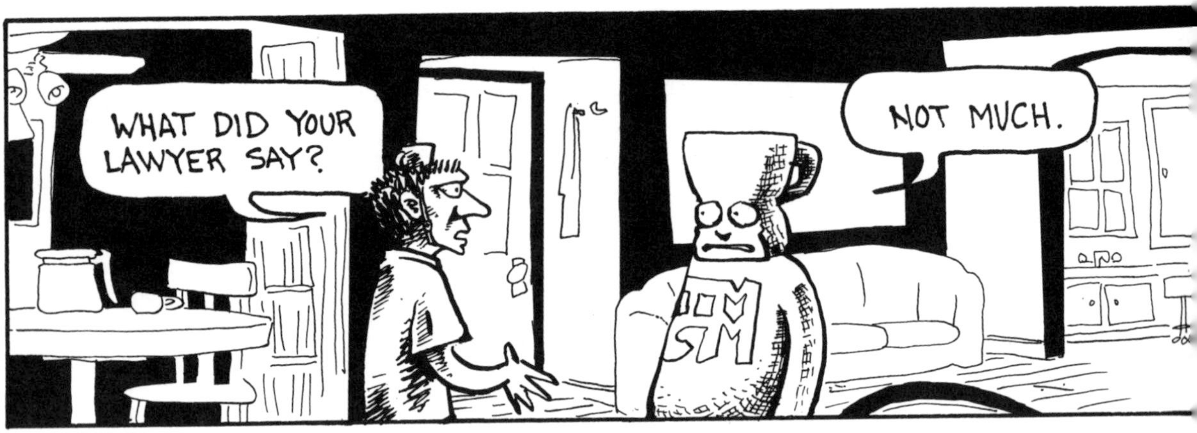
WHAT DID YOUR LAWYER SAY?
NOT MUCH.

This is an agreement between you, hereafter known as the 'reader', and the creator of this cartoon, hereafter known as the 'creato This agreement is binding and non-negotiable except in cases where negotiation has been agreed upon, thereupon new binding an non-negotiable agreements shall replace all previous binding non-negotiable agreements.

This agreement is is a legal document, read it carefully before reading the above cartoon. By reading the cartoon, you are agreein to the terms and conditions of this agreement regardless of whether you read this agreement or not.

The humor of this cartoon, hereafter known as the 'joke' will be gotten and understood by some, but not by others. The scope of th contract shall extend to those who get the joke in addition to those who do not get the joke. The getting of the joke does not in an way affect the influence and acceptance of the contract.

The extent of this contract shall include all media known and unknown. The unknown media is assumed to become known at som time, but may remain unknown. The contract shall include the past, present and future. The present shall heretofore be known a 'now'.

The cartoon may be described to a third party, as long as the complete and unaltered agreement is also described and agreed to The agreement to the contract by a third party, heretofore known as an 'audience' is implicitly agreed to by the description of th cartoon, either in concept, a literal description, or a shared viewing. The contract will be in effect with the audience regardless c whether or not the joke and humor is understood.

This contract constitutes a license and not a sale. The ownership, both in abstract and in realization resides solely with the creato except for agreements whereas future ownerships may constitute a new ownership, thus preceding and superceding any previou ownership and may be regarded as ownership.

You must comply with all applicable laws regarding the reading of this cartoon. LImitation of liability is notwithstanding an damages that might incur for any reason whatsoever including, without limitation, all damages, explicit or implicit. There is no warranty given, or implied, by this cartoon, or the concept, idea, or joke of this cartoon.

This license is effective until terminated.